Parasuicide

Parasuicide

Edited by

Norman Kreitman

*Medical Research Council Unit
for Epidemiological Studies
in Psychiatry
Royal Edinburgh Hospital, Edinburgh*

JOHN WILEY & SONS

London : New York : Sydney : Toronto

Library of Congress Cataloging in Publication Data:
Main entry under title:

Parasuicide.

   Bibliography: p.
   Includes index.
   1. Suicide. 2. Suicide — Prevention. I. Kreitman, Norman.
RC569.P37   616.8'5844   76-30355

ISBN 0 471 99472 3

Typeset in IBM Journal by Preface Ltd, Salisbury, Wilts
and printed by Unwin Brothers Limited, Old Woking, Surrey

CONTRIBUTORS

DOROTHY BUGLASS,
    B.A., M.Phil.
MRC Unit for Epidemiological Studies in Psychiatry, Edinburgh

TREVOR HOLDING,
    M.A., D.M., F.R.C.Psych.
MRC Unit for Epidemiological Studies in Psychiatry, Edinburgh

PETER F. KENNEDY,
    M.D., M.R.C.Psych.
Senior Lecturer, Department of Psychiatry, University of Edinburgh, Royal Edinburgh Hospital

NORMAN KREITMAN,
    M.D., M.R C.P., F.R.C.Psych.
MRC Unit for Epidemiological Studies in Psychiatry, Edinburgh

ALISTAIR E. PHILIP,
    M.A., Ph.D., Dip. Clin.Psychol.
Principal Clinical Psychologist, Bangour Village Hospital, by Broxburn, West Lothian

CONTENTS

PREFACE

This book describes a series of empirical studies carried out by a research unit interested in that form of aberrant behaviour loosely, and we think erroneously, known as attempted suicide. Such an account can only make sense if set against the state of knowledge which obtained at the time each particular project was initiated; accordingly it has been necessary to devote a considerable amount of space to reviews of the existing literature (up to about 1973). The result is inevitably a hybrid between a research treatise and a textbook which, although it cannot possibly be comprehensive, will, we hope, be of interest to a variety of readers concerned with the contemporary problems of self-poisoning and self-injury.

Virtually all the work reported in this volume has been published in various journals, but in bringing it together extensive modifications and interleaving has been required. Generally speaking, the text presented here is rather less detailed than the corresponding versions which have appeared in journals, but the reader interested in pursuing the finer points will find ample references to guide his quest.

It may not be superfluous to mention that the order in which the various projects are presented here is not necessarily the one in which the work was done. As anyone familiar with the activities of research units will recognize, much of the scientific cohesion of a body of work is gained in retrospect.

The preliminary pages show five contributing authors; their contributions are so fused that no attempt has been made to identify the authorship of particular chapters or even sections. Had accidents of geography and time permitted, at least four additional individuals might well have been involved, and it will rapidly be appreciated that we have freely drawn on the work of colleagues such as Wallace McCulloch, Robert Hicks, John Duffy, Irene Ovenstone, and Nilima Chowdhury. Such merit as the volume possesses must be equally shared with them.

Of the many individuals to whom the authors are indebted, two must have special mention. One is Dr Henry Matthew, the first Physician-in-Charge of the Regional Poisoning Treatment Centre at the Royal Infirmary, Edinburgh. He set a model of what collaborative work between physicians, clinical psychiatrists, and research workers in a general hospital should be, and we are vastly indebted for his sympathetic co-operation over many years. The other is Professor Neil Kessel who, as Assistant Director of the research unit, was the first to appreciate the research potential of the Regional Poisoning Treatment Centre, and whose Milroy Lectures in 1965 opened up the field and indicated many of the lines of enquiry which have subsequently been pursued.

In addition, we are obliged for the collaboration not only of all our consultant colleagues, notably Doctors I. Oswald, A. Proudfoot, and L. Prescott, but also to a large body of registrars and other junior staff whose continuing efforts in collecting basic data on admissions to the Regional Poisoning Treatment Centre over many years provided an essential background for our work. We are similarly indebted to Miss E. Burns, Mrs A. Low, Mrs J. Foster, and Mrs V. Bagshaw for their help in data processing and for their assistance in many other ways.

ACKNOWLEDGEMENTS

Some of the work described in this book has appeared in journals, though the presentation and analysis adopted here does not always correspond closely to previous publications. Acknowledgements of copyright and thanks for permission to cite are made to the following:

Applied Social Studies for
  Chowdhury, N., and Kreitman, N. (1971), 'A comparison of parasuicides ("attempted suicide") and the clients of the Telephone Samaritan Service', **3**, 51–57.

British Journal of Psychiatry for
  Buglass, D., and Horton, J. (1974), 'A scale for predicting subsequent suicidal behaviour', **124**, 573–578.
  Buglass, D., and Horton, J. (1974), 'The repetition of parasuicide: a comparison of three cohorts', **125**, 168–174.
  Buglass, D., and McCulloch, J. W. (1970), 'Further suicidal behaviour: the development and validation of predictive scales', **116**, 483–491.
  Holding, T. (1974), 'The B.B.C. "Befrienders" series and its effects', **124**, 470–472.
  Kennedy, P. F., and Kreitman, N. (1973), 'An epidemiological survey of parasuicide ("attempted suicide") in general practice', **123**, 23–34.
  Kennedy, P. F., Kreitman, N., and Ovenstone, I. M. K. (1974), 'The prevalence of suicide and parasuicide ("attempted suicide") in Edinburgh', **124**, 36–41.
  Kreitman, N., and Chowdhury, N. (1973), 'Distress behaviour: a Study of selected Samaritan clients and parasuicides ("attempted suicide" patients). Part I: General aspects, **123**, 1–8. Part II: Attitudes and choice of action, **123**, 9–14.
  Kreitman, N., Smith, P., and Tan, E. (1970), 'Attempted suicide as language: an empirical study', **116**, 465–473.
  Ovenstone, I. M. K., and Kreitman, N. (1974), 'Two syndromes of suicide', **124**, 336–345.

British Journal of Preventive and Social Medicine for
  Buglass, D., Dugard, P., and Kreitman, N. (1970), 'Multiple standardisation of parasuicide ("attempted suicide") rates in Edinburgh', **24**, 182–186.
  Kreitman, N., Smith, P., and Tan, E. (1969), 'Attempted suicide in social networks', **23**, 116–123.
  Philip, A. E., and McCulloch, J. W. (1966), 'Use of social indices in psychiatric epidemiology', **20**, 3, 122–126.

Her Majesty's Stationery Office for
    Ebie, J. C., Hicks, R. C., Lythe, G. J., and Short, R. (1970), 'An integrated approach to a community's health and social problems', *Health Bulletin*, **XXVIII**, no. 2, 35—41.

Psychological Medicine for
    Kreitman, N. (1976), 'Age and parasuicide ("attempted suicide")', 6, 113—121.

Social Psychiatry for
    Chowdhury, N., Hicks, R. C., and Kreitman, N. (1973), 'Evaluation of an after-care service for parasuicide ("attempted suicide") patients', **8**, 67—81.
    Ebie, J. C. (1971), 'Features of psychiatric relevance at an experimental multi-disciplinary social casework centre in Edinburgh', 6, 3, 122—128,

1

INTRODUCTION

1.1 THE CONCEPT OF PARASUICIDE

A clear terminology is a minimum requirement of an adequate theory, and although discussions about terminology are always at risk of degenerating into semantic quibbling, there are conceptual issues which arise at the very beginning of any study of suicidal behaviour and which must be clarified if any progress is to be made. Even a term like 'suicide' is by no means free of ambiguity; the position is far worse with that form of behaviour which is still widely, loosely and regrettably designated as 'attempted suicide'. As is so often the case, the best approach to elucidation of the problem may be an historical one, although a major review of the literature will not be attempted.

Prior to 1958 only a few authors had expressed any misgivings about the concept of attempted suicide: it was seen as a simple failure to complete a suicidal act for whatever reason. Even today this viewpoint has not entirely disappeared, although it is sometimes disguised as a special preoccupation with the so-called 'lethality' of suicide attempts. However, even prior to 1958 attention had been drawn to the differing demographic characteristics of individuals 'attempting suicide' as compared to those who killed themselves (e.g. Dahlgren 1945; Schmidt and van Arsol 1955). These early studies were invariably conducted on highly specialized samples. They also yielded a distorted picture of the frequency with which 'attempted suicide' and completed suicide occurred in the general population, it being generally considered that the 'attempts' were less common than suicidal deaths.

In 1958 Stengel and Cook published their classic monograph *Attempted Suicide*, which expanded and updated an earlier communication by Stengel in 1952. This work presents a succinct summary of the state of research at that time. These authors appear to have been the first to appreciate that 'attempted suicide' may represent from the psychological viewpoint something other than incomplete suicide and their monograph was devoted largely to documenting the differences between the two groups and to opening up for enquiry a number of facets of 'attempted suicide' which had not previously been given due weight. In particular their stress on the social and communicational aspects of 'attempted suicide' has proved immensely valuable.

For their definition of attempted suicide, Stengel and Cook used a formulation which with hindsight they would probably not have chosen as the starting point of their enquiry. 'Every act of self-injury consciously aiming at self-destruction' was regarded as a suicidal attempt. They regarded their definition as somewhat arbitrary but believed that it relied upon observed behaviour and its effects, and also on statements regarding conscious motivation. Patients uttering purely verbal threats which did not lead to acts of self-damage were excluded, as were those whose self-destructive intention had to be inferred. On the other hand triviality of physical self-harm did not exclude that patient from the group, provided that the intent criterion was met.

A key phrase in their definition is 'consciously aiming at self-destruction'. Despite their interest in components of the act which were not death-directed — particularly the ambivalence between the wish to live and the wish to die, and the use of self-aggression as a cry for help — it seems that they were still tending to regard the consciously intended outcome of the self-damage in the 'attempted suicide' group to be suicide. Indeed, in several sections of their monograph they appear to revert to the older view as when, for example, discussing data from suicide studies in such a way as to illuminate, rather than contrast with, the psychological or social mechanisms involved in attempted suicide.

The reliance on the conscious intent of the individual at the time of the act, with the stipulation that his motivation must be to kill himself, poses a serious constraint on research enquiries. There is firstly the problem that conscious motivation may be extremely difficult to define, since many patients are unable to give any clear account of their intentions at the time of their self-damaging behaviour. Inferential judgements are uncertain, though recent work of Beck and his colleagues (1974) may enable more reliable assessments to be made in future. Secondly, even for those able to describe the intention of their actions, individuals who wished to damage themselves, but not to die, would presumably have to be excluded. The ommission of such cases might be legitimate for certain purposes, but their loss would grossly distort any understanding of the great majority of patients that the psychiatrist is called upon to see, or whose behaviour the social scientist might wish to explain. In practice it seems that Stengel and Cook circumvented these problems by postulating an ambivalence between the wish to live and the wish to die. The 'intent' criterion ceased to be based on the patient's own statement, so that the operational definition became instead a question of inference.

It was for these reasons that in 1965 Kessel proposed that the term 'attempted suicide' should be replaced by 'deliberate self-poisoning' and 'deliberate self-injury'. His views were emphatic:

> for four-fifths of the patients the concept of attempting suicide is wide of the mark. [The patients] performed their acts in the belief that they were comparatively safe — aware, even in the heat of the moment, that they would survive their overdosage and be able to disclose what they had done in good time to ensure their rescue. What they were attempting was not suicide.

He also writes, 'If the term "attempted suicide" were just meaningless, it could be tolerated, but it is positively wrong and should be discarded.'

It seems in retrospect that Kessel's invaluable contribution was to establish two important points. Whereas Stengel wrote of 'consciously aiming at self-destruction' Kessel implicitly recognizes that the phrase 'consciously aiming' in fact embraces two quite distinct intentions. There is firstly the intention to *initiate* an act of self-damage, and it is on this point that accidental poisoning or injury can be differentiated from 'attempted suicide'. Secondly, there is the *ultimate* objectives, if any, which the patient may have set himself. The behaviour to be considered is defined by the first intention, quite independently of the likelihood of the act being suicidal in its final purpose.

The proposal to abandon the term 'attempted suicide' led to considerable opposition, though by the late 1960s it was widely accepted in Britain that suicidal intent was no longer to be taken as the hallmark; Stengel himself appears to have accepted this latter contention (Stengel, 1970). The concept governing the studies to be described in this volume were broadly in agreement with Kessel's, though differing on certain minor points. For example, it appeared that Kessel considered he had eliminated the problem of motivation from the definition but, as suggested above, this is not quite so. The motivational issue has been divided into two parts, and while it is indubitably much easier to assess the deliberations of initiating an act than its postulated consequences, nevertheless some inference is still necessary: genuine doubt may arise with some patients. Secondly, the term 'deliberate self-poisoning' in itself carried some ambiguities. To be poisoned means to be suffering from the undesired physical effects of a substance which has been ingested or inhaled; it is a physiological or pharmacological concept, yet a patient who has taken a quantity of Vitamin C tablets deliberately and in the expectation of harming himself would not show any toxic effects. Nevertheless, since patients are not pharmacists an individual of the kind just cited should not be excluded from the group. Conversely a patient may suffer serious toxic effects to the point of death from an excess of alcohol, yet no investigator has chosen to include uncomplicated intoxications of this sort in his series. Physical evidence of toxicity is not an appropriate criterion.

It may be expecting too much of any word or phrase that it should embrace the numerous problems that arise along with margins of the concept it represents, but experience with the old term 'attempted suicide' has made painfully obvious the importance of terminology, especially for the non-specialist. (Thus patients who had deliberately poisoned themselves were sometimes given slight attention by general practitioners because they were not judged to be 'attempting suicide'.) Moreover, although the separation of self-poisoning from the rubric of suicide was in general desirable, the omission of all lexical reference to suicide neglected the very real association that exists between deliberate self-poisoning and completed suicide at a later date. A terminological rather than a major conceptual innovation was introduced by the term 'parasuicide' (Kreitman et al., 1969) in an attempt to supply a word which would indicate a *behavioural analogue* of suicide, but without considering a psychological orientation towards death being in any way essential to the definition.

A formal definition of parasuicide might therefore run as follows:

Parasuicide is a non-fatal act in which an individual deliberately causes self-injury or ingests a substance in excess of any prescribed or generally recognized therapeutic dosage.

In practice this definition has been proved to be relatively straightforward to operate, but three details require to be explained.

Firstly, the decision as to whether an act was accidental or not, though usually straightforward, has sometimes posed problems. The patients used in the following studies have been selected so that the accidental cases and the possibly accidental ones have been excluded.

Secondly, patients with alcohol intoxication alone have similarly been omitted from the study. There is no generally recognized 'dose' of alcohol, and their omission is also in line with convention. Patients taking a substance that was never meant for consumption, such as weed killer, have of course been included; the 'therapeutic dose' of such preparations is nil.

Finally, there is the question of experimental drug use and toxic reactions occurring in drug addicts. Both fall within the definition of parasuicide since the initiation of self-damage is deliberate and the drugs are employed in quantities outside a therapeutic range (as well as outside a therapeutic context). The purpose of the act is not relevant. However, these groups have been separately identified wherever possible for purposes of special study. They are not numerous (see chapter 2 for details).

1.2 EDINBURGH CITY

All the original work to be described in this book is based on the city of Edinburgh and its surrounding area. The city is located on an estuary known as the Firth of Forth and comprises a population of a little over 450,000, compactly contained within an area of slightly more than 50 square miles. It is the capital of Scotland and the legal and adminstrative centre. Finance, banking, and insurance interests are heavily represented but industries are relatively few, and of these printing, publishing, brewing, light engineering, and biscuit and cake manufacture are perhaps the most prominent. There is also a small seaport (Leith) within the city boundary. There are two universities, one of which, the University of Edinburgh, is the second largest in the United Kingdom.

Compared to other cities of similar size, Edinburgh has a distinctly middle-class bias which owes much to the long-established professions of law and finance, and its university connections. The air of general stability is reflected in the architecture of the city, much of it of great antiquity and beauty. Nevertheless, it is essential to recognize that certain areas enjoy relatively little in the way of amenities and these are frequently referred to by various contributors discussing variations in the rates

TABLE 1.1   Edinburgh city population 1961—71

1961—%				1971—%		
	Male	Female			Male	Female
−15	11.66	11.08		−15	11.36	10.81
−25	6.55	7.28		−25	8.17	8.32
−35	6.08	6.28		−35	5.53	5.67
−45	6.00	6.63		−45	5.29	5.75
−55	6.48	7.62		−55	5.64	6.39
−65	5.27	6.93		−65	5.62	7.04
−75	2.89	4.94		−75	3.57	5.76
75+	1.37	2.94		75+	1.44	3.66
All ages	46.30	53.70		All ages	46.62	53.40
	100%				100%	
	$n = 468,361$				$n = 453,585$	

TABLE 1.2   Scotland total population 1961—71

1961—%	Male	Female		1971—%	Male	Female
−15	13.23	12.62		−15	13.29	12.62
−25	6.69	6.96		−25	7.57	7.39
−35	6.25	6.48		−35	5.86	5.94
−45	6.25	6.64		−45	5.71	5.99
−55	6.34	6.89		−55	5.67	6.16
−65	5.03	6.02		−65	5.30	6.17
−75	2.77	4.15		−75	3.34	4.82
75+	1.37	2.31		75+	1.34	2.82
All ages	47.93	52.07		All ages	48.08	51.91
	100%				99.99%	
	n = 5,179,344				n = 5,228,963	

of parasuicide for different city wards. The central area in particular contains a number of slum districts now undergoing a process of urban clearance and development. Two city wards on the periphery are generally regarded as problem areas, both largely representing housing developments of the pre-war and immediately post-war period to accommodate families displaced from the city centre. The zone around the docks is also slowly deteriorating. Characteristics of these special areas will be described in more detail in chapter 2.

Demographically, the city shows considerable stability. Between 1961 and 1971 its population fell from 468,000 to 454,000 a decline of only 0.03 per cent per annum. Tables 1.1 and 1.2 illustrate that the main age-sex subgroups have remained reasonably constant in their representation among the total population. In

TABLE 1.3   Duration at current address on census days 1961 and 1971, for Edinburgh and all Scotland: percentages of persons

	Duration of residence			
	Less than 1 year		Less than 5 years	
	M	F	M	F
1961				
Edinburgh	11.3	11.1	35.4	34.3
All Scotland	10.5	10.3	34.9	34.4
1971				
Edinburgh	12.6 (8.5)	12.0 (8.1)	33.2 (23.0)	32.4 (22.3)
All Scotland	12.1 (7.0)	11.5 (6.8)	35.4 (21.3)	34.7 (21.1)

The figures in brackets, derived from the 1971 Census 10% sample, indicate the percentages of persons who had previously had an address within the *same* local authority area.

comparison with the rest of Scotland, Edinburgh has relatively fewer children and rather more 15—24-year-olds, though the discrepancies·are not large. Table 1.3 shows that population mobility is no greater for Edinburgh than for other parts of Scotland.

1.3 TOWARDS AN EPIDEMIOLOGY OF PARASUICIDE

It is probably still true to say that the majority of studies of parasuicide in the literature are based upon patients admitted to psychiatric hospitals. Such patients are undoubtedly convenient to study since they can be examined at leisure, their families and other informants interviewed over a period of time, and their subsequent progress charted fairly readily. The great disadvantage from the epidemiological viewpoint is that patients admitted to psychiatric hospitals form only a minority of those who come to medical attention following parasuicide, and they differ in a number of conspicuous respects from those not admitted to psychiatric services (Buglass, 1976).

Other studies are based on admissions to a general hospital, usually for treatment of the sequelae of self-injury or self-poisoning. Studies at this level avoid the heavy filtration effect just mentioned, but it is not always clear in the various accounts whether investigators have considered not simply those actually admitted, but all those referred to accident and emergency departments of the general hospital.

However, in recent years studies have begun to appear which have reported comprehensively on referrals to general hospital, irrespective of their subsequent disposal (e.g. Greer and Lee, 1967; Greer and Bagley, 1971; Morgan et al., 1975). Such studies are not easy to execute unless the investigator is either prepared to spend virtually all his time in the emergency departments in order to avoid missing patients, or to rely on routine documentation, often of the briefest kind. A further problem is that accident services and treatment facilities for the self-poisoned are rarely withheld from a patient who walks into a hospital (and the majority of self-poisonings are ambulant), without much reference to his official 'catchment area'. Consequently it is often difficult to specify with precision the size of a population served by a given hospital, or even to identify all the hospitals serving a given area.

These problems are largely obviated by having a designated treatment centre which is officially recognized as the receiving point for all self—poisonings in a defined area. Such a focus is represented by the Regional Poisoning Treatment Centre (RPTC) at the Royal Infirmary, Edinburgh. Patients *referred* to any hospital of the city are officially deflected to the RPTC which itself operates a 100 per cent admission policy; every patient seen in the accident or emergency service with self-poisoning, no matter how trivial, is according to hospital policy admitted to inpatient care. A fuller description of the RPTC is given below, but here it may be mentioned that repeated checks on the operation of its activities have shown that the policy it represents has in fact been satisfactorily implemented over the years since it was formally created in 1962.

Most of the studies described in this book are based upon patients admitted to the RPTC, but it has always been evident that hospital—treated patients must represent only a proportion of all those known to extramural medical services. Consequently, a substantial survey was undertaken in 1970 of parasuicide as seen at the general practice level. This work is presented in the next chapter.

Clearly, the story does not stop there. There may well be a substantial number of episodes of self-poisoning and self-injury which never receive any kind of medical attention. It appears that only one study is reported in the literature which has attempted a general population survey of this kind, but it acheived little or no success. Such surveys do not seem feasible at present.

The 'filtration' process as outlined above essentially refers to factors affecting the numbers of patients counted, numbers which are frequently employed as numerators in calculating rates. Equally important is the designation of the population studied, which comprises the denominator. Patients are also admitted to the RPTC from surrounding areas and data from them have sometimes been used, but as it is not possible to be confident that complete coverage is obtained outside the city perimeter, such patients have been excluded from all calculations of rates. Wherever rates are quoted in this book they refer to the population of Edinburgh city aged 15 years or over.

The effects of population migration have not been specially considered in the presentation of basic epidemiological data (as in chapter 2 and the appendix to that chapter). However, when special issues had arisen, such as the interpretation of the differences in rates for city wards or the concentration of parasuicide in socially connected groups (chapter 4), attempts have been made to determine the possible contribution migration might make to the findings.

1.4 THE ORGANIZATION OF THE REGIONAL POISONING TREATMENT CENTRE (RPTC)

Two wards at the Royal Infirmary, Edinburgh, have traditionally always been set aside for the treatment of delirious patients. They formed a natural locus for the establishment of a centre set up in 1962 in accordance with the findings of the Atkins Committee (1962) which recommended the creation nation-wide of special units for the treatment of acute poisoning, a policy reiterated by the Hill Committee (1968). Such centres were to provide a service staffed by specially interested physicians for all poisonings within a demarcated population and also acting as a regional dissemination point for information by telephone on the recognition and management of poisoining on a 24—hour basis. It was strongly recommended that all cases of self-poisoning should be psychiatrically assessed as soon after the event as possible.

These then are the main features of the RPTC. Physically it comprises two wards with a bed complement which has varied between 18 and 22: no patient has ever been refused admission through lack of a bed. A team of physicians with a special interest in toxicology and fully supplied with facilities for resuscitation laboratory services take charge of the patient when he is first admitted. A wide range of severity of poisonings is seen, from the majority whose degree of physical damage is so slight as to require little or no specific therapy, to the profoundly comatose patient for whom heroic procedures are required. The centre has also acted as a major teaching and research establishment for toxicological studies.

Once the patient is deemed by the physicians to be fit enough he is then seen by one of the psychiatric team, though occasionally a patient is missed owing to premature self-discharge. The psychiatric staff typically comprise two psychiatric registrars who are trainees in their second year of instruction, a senior registrar or university lecturer available for advice or assistance at times of heavy patient flow, and a consultant psychiatrist who conducts ward rounds twice a week and is available at all other times as required. A social worker completes the team but it is a weakness of the system that there has not always been a fully trained worker in the post. Finally, research staff of the Medical Research Council Unit for Epidemiological Studies in Psychiatry have assisted from time to time primarily in a research context but often contributing substantially to the service demands.

The nursing staff does not include specially trained psychiatric personnel but the senior nurses have become experienced in the psychological management of patients and their families. Administrative responsibility for the ward remains with the physicians throughout.

With a small number of beds and a very large number of admissions the average duration of stay is necessarily limited and for the years under review the modal value was approximately 2 days. Needless to say a system of this kind depends upon harmonious working relationships between the physicians and the psychiatrists. This has always been successfully achieved, and over the course of years both sides have come to have considerable understanding and appreciation of the problems being dealt with by the other. A joint ward round is held weekly to discuss particular difficulties relating to patient care, but informal contact is maintained continuously.

Despite its label, the centre also receives cases of self-injury presenting at the Royal Infirmary. Undoubtedly some of these patients, particularly those in need of major sugical intervention, are directed to other sections of the hospital, and liaison with the psychiatric team may not always ensue. Similarly there is no regional policy in operation whereby the hospital is recognized as the official receiving centre for such patients. Self-injuries represent only about 5 per cent of all admissions to the RPTC and there is little doubt that self-injury is under-represented. However, as the next chapter indicates, even at the general practice level self-injury represents only 10 per cent of parasuicidal acts so that the effect of a reduction at the RPTC level is relatively slight so far as the general epidemiological pattern is concerned.

The other group of individuals who are not seen are children. Since special provision for them is made at another hospital patients under the age of 15 are admitted infrequently. They are usually omitted from the statistical tabulations presented in the rest of this book.

It cannot be assumed that the official policy is always followed to the letter, and a number of studies have been carried out to determine the extent to which it is in fact implemented. Shortly after the centre opened in 1962 Kessel et al. (1964) found that approximately 95 per cent of all patients presenting at the Royal Infirmary were admitted to the RPTC as the policy stipulated. On the other hand they found that about 10 per cent of parasuicides presented to all the general hospitals throughout the city were being seen initially at centres other than the Royal Infirmary, and of these only approximately 40 per cent were then transferred to the RPTC. Overall, about 9 per cent of all Edinburgh hospital-contact parasuicides were not being admitted to the RPTC.

Over the years a number of more limited checks on the functioning of the official policy have been carried out. In 1967 it was established that of all parasuicides aged 15 and over admitted to any hospital in the Edinburgh region for self-poisoning, 95 per cent were received as admissions to the RPTC. In 1969 a similar exercise showed that the figure had risen to 98 per cent. Kennedy's study in

1970 (see chapter 2) indicated that virtually all parasuicides known to their general practitioners who were referred to a hospital were admitted to the same centre. Spot checks based on sample months in 1973, 1974, and 1975, showed that over 95 per cent of patients presenting at the accident and emergency department of the Royal Infirmary were continuing to be admitted in line with the official rulings, and these percentages include self-injuries as well as self-poisonings.

Thus admissions to the RPTC represent a sufficiently high proportion of all hospital-contact cases for epidemiological studies of parasuicide in Edinburgh to be worthwhile.

1.5 COMPARABILITY WITH OTHER AREAS

The epidemiological method is essentially a comparative one, and depends upon contrasting two populations with specified characteristics in terms of rates for a given phenomenon. The term 'population' is of course employed in a mathematical sense simply to indicate collections of individuals, who may well be subgroups of a given geographically-defined community. The relationship between the rates is more important than the absolute numerical values attached to the groups being compared. Indeed, the quest for absolute values is largely misconceived since any particular figure will be critically affected by the definition of what constitutes a case and by the intensity of case-finding techniques, as well as the frequency of the behaviour in the group being studied. Of these factors the first is usually a matter of choice, with the 'correct' definition only very rarely being self-evident, while the second tends to be a matter of resources.

Nevertheless, it must also be accepted that the relationships between contrasting groups, or subgroups or a single community, may be unusual if the overall situation is highly atypical of that which might be supposed to prevail in other communities. Questions of this kind have sometimes been raised in connection with the Edinburgh data on parasuicide, since the city is the only one which at the time of writing has a formally established Regional Poisoning Treatment Centre. It is at least arguable that the existence of a well-established facility of this kind might influence not only the numbers of patients being seen at hospital but might also have a differential effect on referrals from various subgroups of the city. It is therefore appropriate to compare parasuicide as seen in Edinburgh with reports from other centres, especially in the United Kingdom. Comparisons will be attempted in terms of parasuicide rates, age-sex specific rates (or curves), secular trends, and qualitative characteristics of patient samples.

Parasuicide rates

Many British studies unfortunately either do not quote rates at all or do so on the basis of figures which are acknowledged to be incomplete. Recently, however, data has become available from Bristol (Morgan *et al.*, 1975) and Oxford (Bancroft *et al.*, 1974). Both studies used a definition approximately comparable with our own and instituted special enquiries to ensure complete collection of information as far as was humanly possible on all hospital referred cases in their areas. The Bristol study reported a patient rate, i.e. an annual person rate per 100,000 of those aged 15+, which, averaged for 1972 and 1973, was 157 for men and 307 for women. During the same period and similarly averaged the Edinburgh values were 212 and

340 for men and women respectively. Thus the Edinburgh figures are relatively high, the discrepancy being proportionally greater for men. On the other hand the Oxford study reported rates for mid—1972 to mid—1973 for the city of Oxford as 245 and 472 for males and females, which are slightly higher than the corresponding Edinburgh figures of 219 and 354. (The Oxford rates may in fact be underestimating the situation according to Edinburgh criteria since cases of coal—gas poisoning and those due to drug experimentation appear to have been excluded.)

Further afield Henderson *et al.* (1972) reported from Tasmania, Australia, that there were no significant differences between Hobart and Edinburgh in either person or admission rates for the years 1968 and 1969. They too used a very similar definition of parasuicide with an analogous case-finding technique.

From these reasonably comparable studies there emerges no reason to suppose that the existence of a Regional Poisoning Treatment Centre in Edinburgh produces an inflated number of hospital-referred parasuicides. For an international review of prevalence rates, the reader is referred to Weissman (1974).

Age-sex specific rates

The difficulties which attend the establishment of a total prevalence rate are even more cogent when age-specific rates come to be considered. The Oxford and Bristol studies previously mentioned are at one with the Edinburgh data in showing that the rate among young women is conspicuously higher than in young men or in those of either sex over the age of 40. (See chapter 2.) Indeed this find has been almost universally reported in every series of parasuicides: even when the calculation of rates is not possible, authors have commonly compared the percentage distribution of their patients in terms of age and sex *vis-à-vis* that of the surrounding population and have consistently reported the over-representation of the young, especially young women.

Thus again it appears that the Edinburgh situation is in no way unique.

Secular trends

A series of investigations have examined the changes in parasuicide at various periods in the last decade (Evans, 1967; Graham and Hitchins, 1967; Alderson, 1974; Bancroft *et al.*, 1974). All agree that there has been a marked increase of approximately 10 per cent per annum, though the estimates range somewhat and Bancroft *et al.* (op. cit.) consider the increase even more dramatic. The Edinburgh trends receive detailed consideration in chapter 2, section II, but again there is no reason to suppose that the city is atypical.

Qualitative characteristics of patient samples

The literature is now replete with clinical descriptions of hospital-admitted parasuicides. Some of the major British studies, apart from those already cited, include Sclare and Hamilton (1963), Bridges and Koller (1966), Whitlock and Schapiro (1967), Stanley (1969), Smith and Davison (1971), Lyons and Sharma (1972), Lukianowicz (1972), and Smith (1972). Though each of these has one or two distinguishing points, the general impression to be gained from these reports is their marked similarity, despite variations in case definition, admission policies, and the like. Close scrutiny does not suggest that there is any salient aspect in which the Edinburgh patients are consistently different from those of other areas.

Thus, of all four grounds it is reasonable to infer that the size and the nature of the problem of parasuicide in Edinburgh are analogous to those of other large urban populations in Britain. It is not, however, permissible to assume that the management of parasuicide in Edinburgh is typical, particularly with regard to the proportion of cases receiving inpatient care in a general hospital.

2

THE EPIDEMIOLOGY OF PARASUICIDE

The interpretation of hospital-based data must take account of any selective factors which might distort the pattern of parasuicide occurring in the community. Section I describes an attempt to consider parasuicide as it is seen at the level of general practice and to compare the emergent picture with that obtained from hospital data alone.

SECTION I

2.1. EARLIER STUDIES

General practice surveys stand between hospital-based studies and field surveys in which everyone in a random sample of the population is screened. Theoretically, simultaneous case-detection at all three levels is the ideal. Yet when Mintz (1970) attempted a field survey by questionnaire in Los Angeles, only 65 per cent responded and the rates of 'attempted suicide' obtained were unbelievably low. Denial at the time of a parasuicidal episode when the patient is being treated for poisoning is common enough: it is much more likely at a later date, particularly if the episode was not reported to a doctor in the first place. Nothing is known about persons who may have resorted to parasuicide without the knowledge of their general practitioner.

Schneider (1954) tried to estimate the frequency of parasuicide in the Canton of Vaud, by circulating questionaires to all general practitioners. Only 27 out of 2,000 returned his questionnaire. Farberow and Shneidman (1961) were somewhat more successful in Los Angeles, obtaining a 70 per cent response to their questionnaire which was sent to all physicians and osteopaths working in the area. Twice as many cases were reported as were detected in available hospital records. However, the doctors provided further information on only one-third of cases they reported, reducing the effective response rate to less than 25 per cent. Parkin and Stengel (1965) and Hershon (1968) sent questionnaires to all general practitioners in Sheffield and Shrewsbury respectively, obtaining response rates of between 60 and 70 per cent. The proportion of cases not admitted to hospital was estimated at about 20 per cent in both studies, but in neither was it considered possible to obtain any further information about the non-admitted patients.

These studies confirmed expectations that large numbers of cases are not admitted to hospital. However, since they were retrospective and the response rates were so low, the results were open to the possibility of large and unknown errors. Few doctors would even attempt to provide detailed information about cases they had seen in the past year. In addition, the operational definitions of 'attempted suicide' were unlikely to have been applied consistently by busy doctors with varied interests and experience. For instance, Stengel's definition, which was used in both British studies, included 'any non-fatal act of self-damage inflicted with self-destructive intent, however vague and ambiguous'. Such assessments are unlikely to have been reliable.

Although it is probably true to say that complete samples of parasuicides are unobtainable, it was necessary to strive as far as possible towards this objective in Edinburgh. Because of expense, ethical considerations and the sensitivity of the general public, a field survey was not considered feasible. A prospective survey was planned in general practice to determine whether aetiological theory and expensive endeavours in prevention were being misled by hospital statistics contaminated by factors influencing referral. The primary methodological considerations were: the need to obtain good co-operation from a representative sample of doctors whose practice populations could be considered representative of the area and the need to derive simple, reliable and valid case criteria for use by busy general practitioners.

2.2 THE EDINBURGH GENERAL PRACTICE STUDY

Outline of the project

Doctors in a random sample of 32 Edinburgh practices were asked to report cases during 1970 while hospitals in the area were being simultaneously screened for admissions from their practices. The unit of sampling had to be the practice rather than the individual doctor because doctors in partnership frequently see each other's patients and it can be impossible to determine the population at risk for cases reported by one practice member. Co-operation of the doctors was solicited by personal visits from the investigator, who emphasized that demands on their time would be minimal and that they would not be expected to record the data themselves. A 24-hour telephone answering service was to be used to avoid any inconvenience in reporting. As soon as possible after a case occurred the investigator would visit the practitioner to record the data himself in a brief standardized interview.

48 doctors (94 per cent) in 30 (94 per cent) complete practices agreed to collaborate. By chance, the random sample had not included any of the twelve practices situated in the two city wards with the highest rates of hospital-treated parasuicide. At the expense of complete randomness, but to ensure that adequate data would be obtained to allow full evaluation of variation in rates across city wards, one other practice was selected whose premises were situated in the middle of a peak rate area. When approached the practitioners agreed to collaborate, making a final sample of 52 doctors in 31 practices, with a population at risk of 106,261, including children. The promised co-operation of 52 out of 55 doctors approached, a response rate of 95 per cent, was very encouraging.

To avoid confusion surrounding the term 'attempted suicide', and because the differential diagnosis of deliberate and accidental poisoning is sometimes difficult, the following strategy was adopted: (1) The doctors were asked to report all cases of poisoning, that is, gassing, ingestion of non-ingestants, and where a drug had been taken in excess of the therapeutic dose irrespective of motive or the toxic consequences, if any, as well as known or suspected cases of deliberate self-injury, in persons aged 15 years and older. (2) The decision as to whether a case was one of parasuicide was made uniformly by the investigator on the basis of all the information available, using the definition of parasuicide discussed in chapter 1.

The size and composition of the population at risk in the 31 practices was estimated from Edinburgh Local Executive Council records: (1) The population base was calculated as the computed average of five quarterly total counts provided by the Executive Council on these practices during 1970. (2) Age-sex composition was estimated by a 25 per cent analysis of Executive Council records, which give sex and date of birth of each registered patient. (3) A more economical approach for determining the distribution of the at-risk population by area of residence was used since classifying patients by city ward from their addresses in the Executive Council records proved too laborious. A random subsample of ten practices was drawn from the 31 practices taking part in the study. The study of variations in rates by area of residence was confined to these ten practices for which a 25 per cent analysis of addresses in the Executive Council records was carried out. The city was divided into three 'areas' by ranking the 23 city wards according to the 1969 hospital-based parasuicide rates and then clustering them into three composite areas; Area I had person rates greater than 350 per 100,000 Area II had between 130 and 350 per 100,000 and Area III less than 130 per 100,000.

The method has been described in detail elsewhere (Kennedy and Kreitman, 1973).

Main findings

Classification of cases

Out of 295 detected episodes of poisoning and deliberate self-injury, eight resulted in death, six were considered accidental poisonings, and three involved persons who were not registered in the practices, leaving a total of 278 parasuicidal episodes involving 201 persons.

Proportions not admitted

30 per cent of the 278 parasuicidal *episodes* were not treated in the RPTC. 21 per cent of the 201 *persons* involved were never admitted to the RPTC at any time in 1970. These proportions were certainly large enough to represent potentially serious sources of bias in the hospital sample.

Repetition frequencies

Repetition of parasuicide was more common than was apparent at the RPTC. 19.6 per cent persons identified in general practice repeated at least once within the year of study, but only 15.1 per cent of admitted patients were identified as 'repeaters' in the RPTC by being admitted more than once during the same period. Episode/person ratios for all detected cases and for admitted cases only were 1.38 and 1.22 respectively.

Variations in rates

Figure 2.1 shows that sex did not influence referral to the RPTC and the findings in

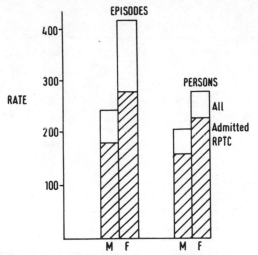

FIGURE 2.1. Sex-specific rates per 100,000 age 15+. Critical ratios: Male *v.* female (episodes) = 4.48; $p \leqslant .001$. Male *v.* female (persons) = 2.31; $p \leqslant .05$

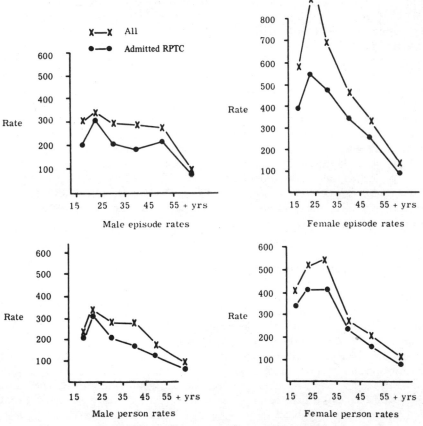

FIGURE 2.2. Age-sex specific rates per 100,000

16

TABLE 2.1   Area of residence differences in rates

Standardized (age and sex) Morbidity Ratios (SMR) for city areas

	Episodes		Persons	
Area	All cases	RPTC only	All cases	RPTC only
I	145	142	160	165
II	144	144	130	140
III	64	54	63	58

general practice confirm that rates of parasuicide for women are significantly higher than for men.

Figure 2.2 clearly shows that the curves for age-sex specific rates for all cases detected in general practice and for admitted cases only are very similar. Comparisons of the proportions admitted and not admitted in each age-sex group showed no statistically significant differences. The results confirm relatively high rates in teenagers, reaching a peak in young adults, then declining with advancing age. The age variations are particularly marked in females.

Major area differences in rates were found. Lest these area differences in rates were contaminated by age and sex differences in the area populations sampled, the rates were standardized for age and sex and the results expressed as Standardized Morbidity Ratios. Table 2.1 shows that the area differences in parasuicide found in studies based on admissions to the RPTC are confirmed in general practice, especially for person rates.

The high-rate areas (Area I) were the working-class districts with overcrowded, substandard tenement housing and poor social amenities. The low-rate areas (Area III) were the more affluent middle-class suburbs. No statistically significant differences were found in the proportions of admitted and non-admitted cases from these different areas. General practitioners in the respectable middle-class areas were not protecting their patients from the stigma of admission to the 'poisons ward'; the rates were really lower.

Comparison of admitted and non-admitted parasuicides on other variables

Parasuicides admitted and not admitted to the RPTC were compared on the medical, psychiatric, and social variables which previous hospital studies in Edinburgh had suggested may be important in explaining parasuicide. No significant differences were found on civil state, the presence of physical illness or disability, previous inpatient psychiatric treatment, alcohol or drug misuse, unemployment, overcrowding, dislocation from family, a history of crime, a history of violence towards or from a family member, or being currently in financial debt. The positive results, variables on which admitted and non-admitted cases were significantly different, are shown in Table 2.2

TABLE 2.2   Factors affecting selection for admission to RPTC

	Episodes			Persons		
	No. in group	No. (%) admitted RPTC	P	No. in group	No. (%) admitted RPTC	P
Method						
Barbiturates and salicylates	83	70 (84)				
Other drugs (mainly psychotropic)	146	111 (76)				
Coal gas and non-ingestants	19	11 (57)	< .001			
Self-injury	26	0 (0)				
N.k. method	4					
Social Class						
I and II	45	21 (47)		24	18 (75)	
III	100	72 (72)		77	60 (78)	
IV	59	45 (76)	< .01	47	40 (85)	n.s.
V	51	38 (74)		34	26 (76)	
No usual occupation	12			10		
N.k.	11			9		
Previous parasuicide						
Yes	148	95 (64)		73	53 (72)	
No	124	94 (76)	< .05	122	101 (83)	n.s.
N.k.	6			6		
Previous outpatient psychiatric treatment						
Yes	142	79 (56)		75	54 (72)	
No	139	109 (78)	< .001	119	99 (83)	n.s.
N.k.	7			7		
Family history psychiatric treatment						
Yes	86	47 (55)		47	29 (62)	
No	141	108 (77)	< .001	112	94 (84)	< .01
N.k.	51			42		

Episodes and persons

The only factor which affected referral of episodes *and* persons to the RPTC was a family history of treated psychiatric disorder. Persons with a positive family history were under-represented in the hospital, which is to say that findings in general practice indicate more, not less, pathology in the families of parasuicides. In all other aspects admitted and non-admitted patients were very similar.

Episodes only

Individual episodes of parasuicide involving upper social class persons, those with a history of outpatient psychiatric care, or previous parasuicide, were significantly *less* often referred to the RPTC.

The method of parasuicide was also an important factor affecting selection for referral to the centre. Episodes involving overdosage with barbiturates or salicylates were significantly more likely to be referred and admitted than when the method involved less toxic psychotropic drugs or self-injury. 20 out of the 35 non-admitted cases in the 'other drugs' category had taken benz-diazepines which are regarded as relatively safe in overdose. Although gassing can be very dangerous, among those who used this method and were not admitted it was relatively harmless because very little was inhaled, consciousness was never lost, and recovery was immediate.

Reliability of the results

Before drawing any conclusions from these results it is necessary to consider several sources of error.

(1) Although the study aimed to obtain as complete a picture as possible of parasuicide occurring in the community, it could not of course encompass patients whose parasuicides were not disclosed to general practitioners. This possible source of bias cannot be estimated. Neither was any account taken of Edinburgh citizens who were not registered with a general practitioner. Gray and Cartwright (1953) found that only 2.3 per cent of adults were not registered. Though there are reasons for suspecting that unregistered persons are a high-risk group for parasuicide they form such a small fraction of the population that the effects of any bias cannot be great. Another possible source of bias results from the imperfections of the method of population sampling by the random sampling of general practices. The 95 per cent response rate from doctors was remarkably high but those few who declined could have biased the results.

(2) All calculated prevalences must be considered underestimates proportionate to the inflation error in Executive Council lists. Inevitably this record system is somewhat out of date and cards are held for persons who have left the area and are no longer at risk (within the terms of reference of the study). The inflation error was estimated at between 8 and 12 per cent so that the rates shown might be considered underestimates by approximately 10 per cent. The inflation error is proportionate to migration rates and these were highest in the younger age groups and among residents of the areas designated Area 1. It is worth emphasizing on account of this, that age and area differences in rates of parasuicide are likely to have been even greater than results indicate.

(3) It can be assumed that case criteria were used consistently because they were applied by the investigator alone in all cases of poisoning, and since there is ample avidence that accidental poisoning in adults is rare, there was little room for

TABLE 2.3   Non-admitted case reported in each annual quarter as proportions of all detected cases

	January–March	April–June	July–September	October–December	All
Admitted	43 (74%)	54 (71%)	59 (75%)	62 (76%)	218 (74%)
Non-admitted	15 (26%)	22 (29%)	20 (25%)	20 (24%)	77 (26%)
All cases	58 (100%)	76 (100%)	79 (100%)	82 (100%)	295 (100%)

TABLE 2.4   Reliability checks: agreements between information obtained from the GP
and the patients
(Persons admitted to the RPTC, n = 159)

Information from the GP	Information from the patient			Percentage agreement
	Yes	No		
Chronic alcohol misuse				
Yes	26	14	40	$\dfrac{96 + 26}{139} \times 100 = 88\%$
No	3	96	99	
	29	110	139	
Previous parasuicide treated in RPTC				
Yes	27	7	34	$\dfrac{103 + 27}{144} \times 100 = 90\%$
No	7	103	110	
	34	110	144	
Previous inpatient psychiatric treatment				
Yes	41	7	48	$\dfrac{91 + 41}{140} \times 100 = 94\%$
No	1	91	92	
	42	98	140	
Previous outpatient psychiatric treatment				
Yes	30	20	50	$\dfrac{79 + 30}{141} \times 100 = 77\%$
No	12	79	91	
	42	99	141	

The totals appearing in the four sections of the table are not constant owing to variations in
the completeness of the data.

error. The crucial questions are whether the doctors were efficient in reporting
known non—admitted cases and whether the detailed information on their cases
was reliable. Table 2.3 shows that the numbers and proportions of non-admitted
cases reported remained constant throughout the year, which at least suggests that
difficulties in remembering reporting procedures at the beginning of the study,
summer holidays when reporting depended on locums, or waning enthusiasm
towards the end of the study, did not impair the efficiency of case detection.
Table 2.4 shows that the information supplied by the doctors on patients admitted
to the RPTC agreed well with that obtained from patients themselves when seen by
the ward psychiatrist (who also recorded these items on the standard ward
proforma).

Overall the study was reasonably successful and, taking account of these errors,
some important conclusions can be drawn from the results.

Conclusions

RPTC statistics underestimate the rates of parasuicidal *episodes* by at least 30 per
cent in Edinburgh, even though the admission policy is more liberal than elsewhere.

20 per cent of *persons* involved in parasuicide were not admitted for any episode but they were found to be very similar to those who were, which means that studies of hospital samples have not been misleading in respect of patient characteristics.

Marked variations in rates with sex, age, and area of residence were confirmed in general practice. Hospital studies had shown that civil state, social class, overcrowding, unemployment, and family dislocation also influenced the rates of parasuicide. Since non-admitted cases closely resembled admitted cases in all these respects it seems reasonable to conclude that the effects of these factors on the rates are real, not artefacts of hospital sampling. Histories of crime, debt, domestic violence, previous parasuicide, and psychiatric treatment were equally common in admitted and non-admitted patients. The study, therefore, confirms that those involved in parasuicidal acts have experienced a great deal of social pathology, and that chronic interpersonal and financial stresses often formed the background to the crisis in which parasuicide occurred.

The overall frequency of repeated parasuicide was seen to be underestimated in the RPTC, but more important for the prediction of repetition (see chapter 6) is the finding that the detection of 'repeaters' in the hospital was somewhat biased. Because individual episodes of parasuicide in upper social class persons, those with a history of previous parasuicide and those who had had outpatient psychiatric treatment, were less often referred to the RPTC, repetition among such persons was underestimated in the hospital to a relatively greater extent. The association between low social class and repetition found in the hospital is weaker than it seems and conversely the associations between previous parasuicide and outpatient psychiatric treatment are even stronger.

A major factor influencing referral of parasuicides to the RPTC was the medical seriousness of the episode, and it is appropriate to end the discussion of the study on this important clinical finding. From the medical point of view it is appropriate that those who had taken the more toxic drugs were the more often referred. However, the medical seriousness of an episode is not related to the need for psychiatric treatment, the risk of repetition or of subsequent suicide (Kessel, McCulloch and Simpson, 1963; Kessel and McCulloch, 1966; also see chapter 6). Although, as will be documented in subsequent chapters, the risk of suicide is greater in males, the older age group, among alcoholics and parasuicide repeaters, and, although the risk of further episodes of parasuicide is also higher for persons with the latter two characteristics as well as a history of psychiatric treatment, none of these factors increased the likelihood of referral to the RPTC where expert psychiatric assessment is the rule. Indeed, previous parasuicide and outpatient psychiatric treatment meant referral was less likely. From the psychiatric point of view, therefore, the criteria used by general practitioners in selecting cases for referral to the RPTC are not ideal. Since admission the RPTC does seem to reduce the risk of repetition general practitioners might be advised to change their referral habits. A third of the patients not admitted to the RPTC were subsequently referred by their general practitioners to outpatient psychiatric clinics. Unfortunately it seems that this was often too late to be effective, for nearly 40 per cent of such patients repeated in the course of the year — a much higher proportion than for the sample as a whole. The matter of the effectiveness of the RPTC in the prevention of further episodes of parasuicide, with data from both the general practice survey and other sources, is taken up again in chapter 7.

One can only speculate about the reasons why general practitioners were less likely to refer patients to the RPTC if they had a previous history of parasuicide, or a history of psychiatric treatment. It is possible that when the doctor has already received a psychiatric assessment of the patient at an earlier time he feels confident to deal with the crisis unaided. Therapeutic pessimism about those with recurrent psychiatric problems is a second possibility, even though many forms of psychiatric disorder are relapsing conditions, including the most treatable. Whatever the reasons, current patterns of management appear to be less than ideal.

SECTION II

This section concerns Edinburgh city parasuicides admitted to the RPTC from 1962 to 1974. It pays special attention to trends but also presents some descriptive data for the period 1968—74. From mid—1962 to mid—1963 a study of RPTC parasuicides was conducted by Kessel and McCulloch (Kessel, 1965a and b; McCulloch, 1965): routine data collection began in 1967 and a comparison of the 1962—3 and 1967 series has already been reported (Aitken *et al.*, 1969). Since 1968 data on all referrals have been coded in a more standardized form and stored by year of admission on magnetic disk. Information has been gathered for variables on which census figures are available, namely, sex, age group, civil state, social class, area of residence, and density of occupation in private households. Selected social and clinical data have also been recorded.

Data spanning the period 1962—74 will be presented first; data confined to the 7-year period 1968—74 will be presented second, and a discussion of these findings and of the significance of repeat episodes will be presented third. Since the primary data, the rates, are bulky but may be of value to other workers, a selection is given in the appendix to this chapter; the figures presented in the text are intended only to be illustrative.

For most years referrals are divided into three categories: 'first evers', or *persons* who have no previous history of parasuicide; 'patients', referring to the first episode by an individual within a calendar year, so that 'patient' rates provide an unduplicated account of all the *persons* seen during the period; and 'admissions', which are all *episodes* within a calendar year.

The rates refer to the population of Edinburgh aged 15 years and older (350,620 — 1971 census). A total of 8,628 episodes have been analysed; a further 5 per cent of episodes were not included since the patient could not be interviewed, mostly because of premature self-discharge.

2.3 PARASUICIDE RATES 1962—74
(Table 2.5, Appendix Table I. Figure 2.3)

The number of admissions, and the admission rate, have increased 2½-fold from 1962 to 1974 for both sexes, but whereas from 1962 to 1968 the proportional increase in the admission rate for men was almost twice that for women, from 1968—74 the rate for women accelerated twice as fast as that for men (Table 2.5).

For women the steep rise in admissions up to 1972 has been followed by a levelling off, whereas for men there was a steep rise in 1971 followed by a slight fall. The rates for women are consistently higher than those for men and the annual

TABLE 2.5   Men and women admissions 1962/3, 1968, 1974

	Number (rate per 100,000)			Annual percentage change in rates		
	1962/3	1968	1974	1962/3—8	1968—74	1962/3—74
Men	176 (109)	310 (193)	423 (265)	12.8	6.2	11.9
Women	332 (166)	462 (236)	815 (428)	7.0	13.6	13.2

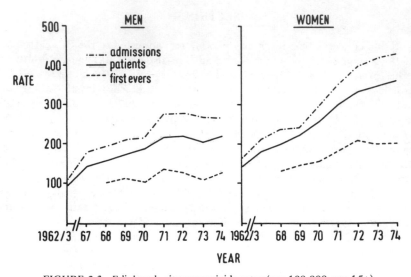

FIGURE 2.3. Edinburgh city parasuicide rates (per 100,000, age 15+)

female to male ratio of these rates has increased in recent years, that is to say, the sex gap has widened (Figure 2.3, Appendix Table I).

Age-sex specific rates

Men (Appendix Table I, Figure 2.4)

For men admissions the trend in the rates is upward, with the most dramatic increase in the 15—19-year-olds. For first evers under 35 years there was an increase up to 1971 but no change since, and for those aged 35—54 years the first-ever rates have changed little since 1968. All the rates for men aged 55 years and older have changed little and have been consistently the lowest. (That the oldest group has the lowest first-ever rate might be expected as increasing age implies a greater time at risk.)

Women (Appendix Tables II, Figure 2.5)

For women under 35 years the rates have fluctuated, but since 1970 it is the youngest who have had the highest rates (of each kind) and who have shown the

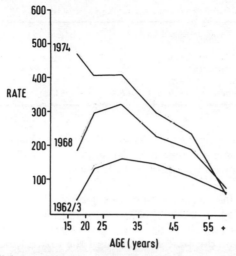

FIGURE 2.4. Age-specific rates (per 100,000), men admissions

greatest increase. Admission rates for the 35—44-year-olds have consistently been greater than those for the 45—54-year-olds and for both age groups have roughly trebled between 1962 and 1974. Those aged 55 years and older have the lowest rates and these have changed little over the years.

Civil state (Table 2.6 Appendix Table III).

Because the numbers of divorced and widowed are small, the rates quoted refer to ages of 15 and over. The single and married have been divided into those aged 15—34 years and those 35 years and older, since civil state and age are related.

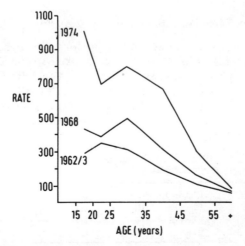

FIGURE 2.5. Age-specific rates (per 100,000), women admissions

TABLE 2.6   Civil state rates per 100,000 — 1972

	Aged 15—34		Aged 35+	
	Single	Married	Single	Married
Men	428	428	252	147
Women	819	666	131	225

For both men and women the rates (of each kind) are highest amongst the divorced. The rates for divorced men declined from 1962 to 1973 but those for divorced women showed no such trend. The widowed have low rates and show a small increase.

For the married and single the findings can be briefly illustrated by reference to 1972 (Table 2.6). Single women aged 15—34 years have rates almost twice that for single men of the same age, but single men aged 35 years and older have higher rates than single women of the same age. Amongst the married, both men and women aged 15—34 years have rates three times higher than those for older married men and women. Whilst for men aged 35 years and older it is the single who have higher rates than the married, for women of the same age the married have higher rates than the single.

Over the years the proportional increase has been greatest for single women, as Figure 2.5 illustrates. Within civil state categories age effects are clear for women and for married men, the young having the highest rates, but single men do not consistently illustrate the decline with age (Appendix Table III).

To correspond with census publications, rates for the married include those for the separated. This masks the finding that two-fifths of married men and women referrals were currently separated at the time of admission due to disharmony or desertion (see below).

2.4 PARASUICIDE RATES 1968—74

Social class (Appendix Table IV, Table 2.7, Figure 2.6)

Census figures for social class are available only for Edinburgh men. Parasuicide rates are consistently higher in Class IV (partly skilled) and Class V (unskilled occupations) than in upper social classes. There is a 14-fold difference between the mean 7—year admission rates for Classes I and II and Class V, and differences of eleven— and eight—fold for patient and first-ever rates respectively. The admission rates for Classes I, II, and III have remained constant over the years, but in Class IV

TABLE 2.7   Admission:patient ratio* by Social Class for men

Classes I and II		1.06.
Class	III	1.15
Class	IV	1.20
Class	V	1.40

*Calculated from mean 7—year rates.

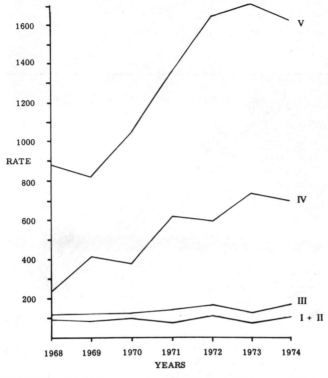

FIGURE 2.6. Social class rates (per 100,000, age 15+), men admissions

the rate has nearly trebled and in Class V it has nearly doubled (Appendix Table IV, Figure 2.6). Similar findings have been recorded for patients and first evers. If the admission:patient ratio is taken as a rough index of repetition within a calendar year, then repetition steadily increases with lower social class (Table 2.7).

Area of residence (Table 2.8, Map 2.1)

Edinburgh is divided into 23 municipal wards which show large and consistent difference in rates of parasuicide. The mean 7– year ward rate for men and women

TABLE 2.8   Kendall's coefficient of concordance (*W*)
for city ward rates 1968—74

	Men	Women	Men and women
First evers	0.52	0.53	0.63
Patients	0.72	0.70	0.79
Admissions	0.75	0.69	0.81

Approximate 5% and 1% significance values for *W*
(with $k = 7$, $n = 23$) are 0.22 and 0.26.

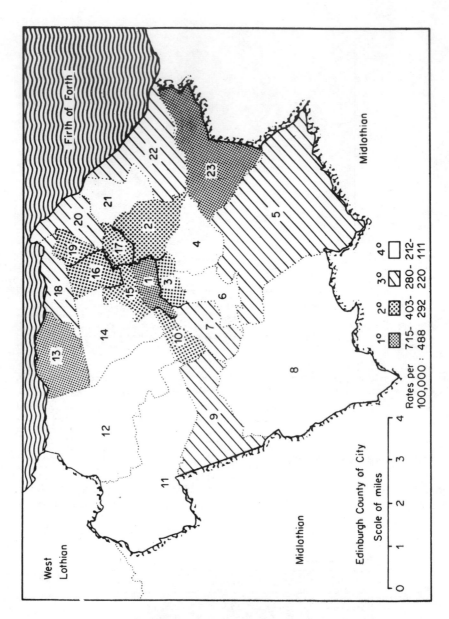

West
Lothian

Firth of Forth

Midlothian

Midlothian

Edinburgh County of City

Scale of miles

0 1 2 3 4

Rates per
100,000 :

1°	2°	3°	4°
715-	403-	280-	212-
488	292	220	111

MAP 2.1. 7-year mean admission rates — ward quartiles

admissions shows a six-fold difference between the highest and lowest ranking ward (from 715 to 111 per 100,000). The rank order of ward rates is relatively stable over the years, more so for admissions and patients than for first evers which are based on smaller numbers. The increase in parasuicide cannot therefore be attributed to dramatic changes only in certain wards (Table 2.8). Wards are similar in their rank order for men and for women separately: the correlation coefficient for the mean 7-year rank order of ward rates by sex was 0.92 and 0.83 for admissions and patients respectively.

The geographical distribution of ward rates has been summarized by dividing the wards into quartiles so that each has contributed approximately the same number of episodes over the 7 years (Map 2.1). Ward 1 which has the highest rate is a central area containing hostel and night shelter accommodation for the destitute homeless, in contrast to the predominantly middle-class owner-occupier suburbs which have the lowest rates. The distribution does not correspond exactly with that reported from Bristol (Morgan *et al.*, 1975), with high rates in central and low rates in peripheral areas, but this comparison probably reflects geographical rather than ecological differences between the cities.

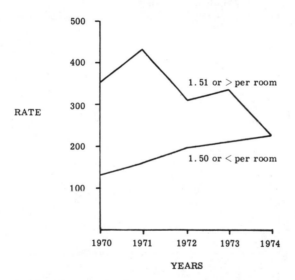

FIGURE 2.7. Density of occupation in private households: admissions (rate per 100,000, age 15+)

Density of occupation in private households (Appendix Table V, Figure 2.7)

Data are available since 1970 for overcrowding in private households, defined as 1.51 or more persons per room. The rate of parasuicide amongst the overcrowded has fallen whilst the rate amonst those not overcrowded has risen and in 1974 the rates were the same. Figure 2.5 illustrates the trend for admission rates.

2.5 CLINICAL FINDINGS

Method of parasuicide (Figure 2.8)

There has been a marked fall in poisoning by barbiturates and domestic gas, no change in poisoning by salicylates, but a roughly three-fold increase in poisoning by other drugs, which are largely psychotropic drugs (Figure 2.8). Since 1971 a more detailed breakdown of poisoning by 'other drugs' has been recorded and the percentage of admissions from 1971—4 taking overdoses of these was: minor tranquillizers 18, non-barbiturate hypnotics 13, anti-depressants 10, and pheno-thiazines and butyrophenones 2. The ingestion of multiple agents has increased during the last 2 years and now accounts for 12 per cent of episodes. It seems likely that changes in the drugs used reflects changing prescribing habits and, in the case of domestic gas, decreased toxicity. Since 1972 the source of the drug taken has been recorded. The pooled data for 1972 to 1974 show that 56 per cent took drugs prescribed for themselves and 15 per cent took drugs prescribed for others, usually another family member. Of the remainder, 19 per cent were poisoned by freely purchased drugs and 10 per cent were obtained illegally. That there had been *no* change in the proportion of poisonings by prescribed as compared to non-prescribed drugs since 1962 militates against the often-cited opinion that the increase in parasuicide is largely the consequence of more liberal prescribing by doctors.

In 1962 self-injuries accounted for 11 per cent of episodes but since 1967 the proportion has been less than 5 per cent.

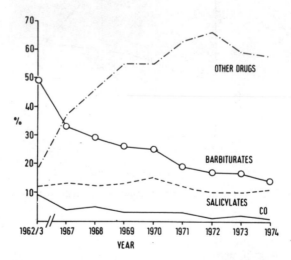

FIGURE 2.8. Method of parasuicide, Edinburgh patients

Alcohol taken before the parasuicidal act (Appendix Table VI)

The proportion of men who had consumed alcohol shortly before the parasuicidal act has remained constant over the years and comprised two-thirds of the admissions; half of those men who had consumed alcohol were judged to have been drunk at the time of the act. In contrast to the men, the proportion of women admissions who had consumed alcohol has increased, from 25 per cent to 45 per cent, and approximately one-third of these were drunk, The increase in alcohol use at the time of the episode amongst women has been most marked in the 15—24-year-olds: the proportion has more than doubled from 16 per cent of admissions in 1968 to 40 per cent in 1974. For both men and women, however, the 25—44-year-olds have the highest proportions who have been drinking. The findings for first evers and patients are closely similar to those for admissions and the results for 1974 are presented in the appendix to this chapter (Table VI). The increase in alcohol use may reflect a change in drinking behaviour in the general population but, if this is so, it is surprising both that such a large change has occurred over so short a period of time and that it is demonstrable only for women. Data on alcohol dependence and alcoholism, as distinct from acute intoxication, are presented below.

Psychiatric assesment (Table 2.9)

Psychiatric assessment refers to the diagnosis both of mental illness and of abnormal personality, which are separately assessed amd recorded. Alcohol and drug misuse, past history of psychiatric care, and agreed psychiatric and social work management following discharge from the RPTC have also been systematically noted. The data are summarized in Table 2.9.

Whilst possible changing diagnostic fashions amongst the psychiatric staff at the RPTC are acknowledged, consistent diagnostic findings have been recorded nevertheless. Women were diagnosed as suffering from mental illness more often than men, and for both sexes the most common diagnostic category was depression (which includes neurotic depression) which was diagnosed in 40 per cent of women and 28 per cent of men.

TABLE 2.9   Clinical findings — 7-year percentages (admissions)

	Men	Women
Mental illness	37.0	46.3
Personality disorder	53.0	50.0
Problem with alcohol	48.1	16.3
Habitual misuse of drugs	23.4	12.5
*Admitted because of habitual misuse of drugs/experimentation	18.5	4.4
Past psychiatric care		
Inpatient	41.1	34.4
Outpatient	41.3	39.1
Management		
Inpatient psychiatric care	14.2	19.9
Outpatient psychiatric care	30.0	31.9
Social work care	19.4	25.4

*4-year percentage.

A diagnosis of abnormal personality was more common for men than women and for admissions than first evers of both sexes. More men than women have a problem with alcohol but the proportion of problem drinkers among both men and women admissions has remained fairly constant over time. Of men admissions 6 per cent were chronic alcoholics with physical damage from alcohol, 14 per cent were alcohol dependent without physical damage, and 28 per cent were judged to be excessive drinkers. The corresponding proportions for women were 1 per cent, 3 per cent, and 12 per cent.

The operational definition of parasuicide includes episodes in which drugs are taken experimentally for 'kicks' with inadvertant consequences and overdoses resulting from the habitual misuse of drugs. In addition data have been collected concerning a history of habitual misuse of drugs, whether or not the admission follows drug misuse. Referral following drug misuse is four times more common in men than in women, representing 18 per cent of men compared to 4 per cent of women admissions. Roughly one-half of all admissions following drug misuse occur in men aged 15—24 years, and one-third of admissions in men of this age group follow drug misuse. The proportion of persons with a history of habitual misuse of drugs has *fallen* since 1972.

High proportions of both men and women referrals, about 40 per cent have a past history of psychiatric care, and it is to be expected that more patients and admissions than first evers should have had a previous psychiatric contact as a consequence of their earlier parasuicidal episode. More men than women had a previous psychiatric contact, perhaps a reflection of their being older. Proportionately more women than men were referred for psychiatric and social care following discharge from the RPTC.

Social problems (Table 2.10)

For most of the 7 years data have been recorded on certain social problems: criminal record, current police proceedings, debt, unemployment, and marital separation: the results are summarized in Table 2.10. For each of these variables a higher proportion of men than women reported problems, and for both sexes proportionately more admissions than patients and more patients than first evers had social difficulties. None of the variables shows a trend over the years.

TABLE 2.10   Social problems — percentages (admissions)

	Men	Women
*Criminal record	48.4	11.3
*Previous imprisonment	21.3	2.2
*Current police proceedings	12.9	2.8
*Debts	25.4	17.8
†Unemployment	49.1	20.7
‡Current marital separation	40.0	38.1

*6-year percentage.
†7-year percentage.
‡4-year percentage.

Nearly one-half of men admissions reported one or more convictions in a court of law, more than one-fifth reported previous imprisonment, and more than one in ten were currently in trouble with the law. The proportion of women reporting past or current offences was much smaller. Most persons with current debts had arrears of payment without threatened legal action but 4 per cent of men and 2 per cent of women had debts currently involving court action.

It is to be expected that more men than women were currently unemployed as many women were housewives, but for both sexes the proportions of unemployed are high (approximately 50 per cent and 20 per cent respectively). It was considered possible that the peak in men referrals in 1971 could reflect high unemployment in Edinburgh at that time. The 3-monthly proportion of un-employed men referrals to the RPTC were therefore compared with the published 3-monthly proportion of unemployed men aged 18 and over in Edinburgh. No correspondence was found. Unemployment in the community continued to rise in 1972 associated with a *fall* in unemployment amongst parasuicide referrals.

Permanent childhood separation (Table 2.11)

More persons had experienced childhood loss of a father, through death, desertion, or divorce, than of a mother, and more women than men had lost a father. The percentage of first evers who reported a loss was only marginally less than that for patients and admissions.

TABLE 2.11   Permanent childhood separation from parents — 7—year percentages (admissions)

Age at separation	Maternal separation		Paternal separation	
	Men	Women	Men	Women
< 10 years	9.0	9.5	13.7	16.1
10—15 years	4.1	4.3	5.8	6.3
	13.1	13.8	19.5	22.4

Repetition (Table 2.12)

The admission:patient ratio can be taken as a rough index of repetition within a calendar year, although it fails to distinguish between a high rate of repetition by a small number of individuals and a lower rate of repetition by a larger subgroup. For the years 1970, 1973, and 1974 the frequency distribution of episodes within the same calendar year by persons has been derived by manual case linkage (Table 2.12).

Repetition was slightly more frequent for men than women. Most persons who repeat within a calendar year have a second episode only, multiple repetition being relatively uncommon. There is no evidence of an increased tendency to repetition over the years, a point of some importance when considering the possible reasons for the rising admission rate. Studies specifically directed to the problem of repetition are reviewed in chapter 4.

TABLE 2.12   Distribution of parasuicide episodes for persons by sex – 1970, 1973, and 1974

	Men			Women		
	1970	1973	1974	1970	1973	1974
Number of episodes per person within calendar year						
1	268	286	331	447	623	623
2	26	41	22	40	49	54
3	3	12	9	6	13	15
4 or >	2	8	7	3	7	5
Total number of persons X	299	347	369	496	692	697
Total number of episodes Y	341	453	434	560	799	801
Admission ratio Y/X	1.14	1.31	1.18	1.13	1.15	1.15

2.6 DISCUSSION

The data presented in this section, although by no means exhausting all the material available, are nevertheless voluminous. Their discussion and interpretation may be facilitated by considering the findings from three aspects, namely (a) those features which appear to have remained constant over time, (b) those which have showed reasonably continuous and consistent changes, and (c) by offering some spec-ulations on the nature of the dramatic increase in some of the rates.

It is important to recall that in many respects the characteristics of parasuicide in recent years are much the same as they have always been. Women have always had higher rates (however defined) than men, while despite the marked acceleration in the rates among adolescents it has always been true that the risk of parasuicide was appreciably higher in the first half of life than in the second. Similarly there is a rather striking consistency in the rank order of the rates across the 23 city wards of Edinburgh. There has been no change in the proportion of patients with psychiatric morbidity nor in the diagnostic distribution among them, either for psychiatric illness or for personality disorder. The proportions of patients reporting a criminal record, current policy proceedings, debt, marital separation, and unemployment has also remained more or less consistent over the years. The unemployment aspect is interesting as the Edinburgh data do not reflect the increasing role of unemploy-ment as reported from other cities (Smith and Davison, 1971). It may be recalled that at least one-third of male admissions have experienced prolonged periods of unemployment which appear to be unrelated to their work capacity or the labour market, a group for whom 'unemployment' can be seen as 'a way of life' (McCulloch and Philip, 1972).

In other respects the picture of parasuicide has been changing markedly, most evidently with respect to the 2½–fold increase in the admission rates between 1962 and 1974. This general trend in admission rates will be considered in more detail below. Of the various age-sex subgroups the increase has been most dramatic among the young, especially among young women.[1] Analysis by civil state has consistently shown that the divorced carry a particularly high risk, yet, intriguingly, the rate for divorced men has fallen while that for divorced women has markedly increased. The explanation is by no means obvious. It would appear that as divorce has become more frequent, it may represent a less deviant state than hitherto. In consequence the male rate might reflect an easing of the marginal status of divorced males, but no explanation is then available for the trend in divorced women. There may be new stresses accruing to divorced women in recent years which are not yet understood.

Social class rates (of all three types) show a sharp increase for men in IV and V in contrast to the stable rates of other social groups. No definitive explanation can be offered. It may be relevant that the first—ever rate (which it will later be argued is the most important type of rate to consider in interpreting temporal changes) has risen in the lower social classes because the number of individuals in those groups among the city population declined between the two censuses of 1966 and 1971, while the numerator has remained constant; in other social classes the population size has varied very little. This suggests at least the possibility that the shrinkage, especially of Social Class V, may be due to the upward mobility of the more able members, leaving a residual group that is more parasuicide-prone. Additional though unsupported hypotheses might include an increasing level of stress in members of the lower social class, or a change in the social meaning of being a member of that class.

Another trend which was quite unexpected until the analysis was completed was the changing relationship of overcrowding to parasuicide. A marked difference in rates between the overcrowded and the non-overcrowded was a salient feature of early years; subsequently it has entirely disappeared. The decline in the over-crowded rate is particularly surprising in view of the increasing rates in Social Class V and in the young, since both these variables have traditionally tended to be associated with overcrowding. The fall in rate is the product of a constant number of cases in relation to an increasing denominator. Again, no definitive explanation can be offered, especially in the absence of census data in sufficient detail to make more refined analysis possible, but it may be that the housing shortage of recent years has affected so many sections of the community that to be overcrowded is less of an indicator than formally of personal maladjustment or a pathological family situation.

Alcohol consumption in Scotland causes concern in conncection with a wide range of problems. There has been a doubling of the proportion of women who have consumed alcohol shortly before their parasuicide over the years in question. Increasingly widespread use of alcohol by women may thus be contributing to the increase in the female rates to some degree. On the other hand the data for men show relatively little change, and similarly the proportion of patients of both sexes who have been recognized as having a long-standing alcohol problem has not changed markedly over the period 1968—74. In respect of drug misuse there was evidence of a fall both in the proportions admitted because of drug induced experiments which had led the patient into difficulty, and in the proportion with a history of drug abuse, since about 1972. Finally there remains the vexed issue of why the rates have been increasing, and even though a definitive explanation may not be available, some comments are clearly called for.

Perhaps the simplest explanation for a climbing rate is of the kind which implicates an increase in the prevalence of some characteristic in the population known to be associated with the disorder in question, but for which detailed population data are not available. If, for example, it were the case (which it is probably not) that manic-depressive psychosis has become much commoner in recent years, then, given no change in the proportion of manic-depressives who become parasuicides, an increasing rate of parasuicide would be expected within the community. Of course if adequate population data were available on the numbers of individuals with manic-depressive psychosis in each year, and if similar data had been ascertained concerning the patients, then the *rate* for manic-depressive parasuicide could be shown to be constant. Population data of this kind is hardly ever available, however, and it is possible that in some subtle way the general population of Edinburgh has become more sensitized to the factors which conduce to parasuicide.

An explanation of this kind holds little attraction. It would logically imply some *proportional* change in the characteristics of the patient samples; thus in the fictitious instance quoted it would be expected that the proportion of manic-depressives among all parasuicides would increase. The findings, on the other hand, are more impressive as regards the similarity of successive patient cohorts than any differences; an exception may be the increasing use of alcohol by young women. The main trends have been in variables which are capable of being characterized as rates — such as social class and age — and here the changes in the base population are of course automatically allowed for.

A second possibility which is worth more serious consideration as a partial explanation of the trend, specifically of the admission rate increase, concerns the differential likelihood to repetition. If it were the case that successive cohorts are more prone to repeat their parasuicide, then to that degree the climbing numbers of admissions would be attributable to such a change. This argument is not tenable in its more simple forms. It has been shown that the likelihood of short-term repetition (i.e. within the same calendar year as the individual's key admission) was much the same in 1970, 1973, and 1974, even when the sexes were separately considered. Further evidence against a changing frequency of repetition is provided by the demonstration that all seven cohorts of patients studied between 1968 and 1974 were largely similar on those variables which have been shown to predict repetition, at least over a medium time span (Buglass and Horton, 1974b; Holding *et al.* (in press)).

Nevertheless, the role of repetition in explaining the trend in admission rates may be of critical importance. After his first parasuicide an individual's risk of a further episode is very much higher than for an otherwise similar individual drawn at random from the general population. Consequently a *constant* first—ever rate would be expected to lead to an *increasing* admission rate as illustrated in the hypothetical data set out in Table 2.13.

The 'model' displayed postulates a constant total population and a fixed first—ever rate. The first—ever cases and those individuals with a previous history of parasuicide have different likelihoods of repetition, but these risks also remain constant. First-ever cases (individuals) enter the pool of potential repeaters the following year. It can be seen that over the 5 years, during which the first-ever rate remains the same, the patient rate (i.e. that based on an unduplicated count of individuals) increased by 120, or 24 per cent above the base line, and the admission rate increased by 162, or 28 per cent.

In reality the first-ever rate for men is not stable but increasing very slightly, while that for 'non first-ever men' is increasing rather more rapidly. For women both types of rate have increased. The striking increase in the admission rate is in part at least attributable to the augmenting or 'gearing' effect produced by the enhanced likelihood to further episodes already mentioned.

In other words, given the propensity to repetition, the epidemic of parasuicide over recent years, while undoubtedly posing a real burden for the National Health Service, is less dramatic in terms of individuals than it at first appears. The precise relationship between the three types of rate presented in Figure 2.1 have been further analysed by considering the frequency distribution of repeat episodes per patient in a number of cohorts, each subdivided by sex and whether or not the parasuicide was the first ever in the patient's life. It emerges that the best distribution which characterizes repetition frequency for all groups is the log series distribution, although this finding in turn raises certain mathematical problems.

TABLE 2.13   An arithmetical model of trends in parasuicide rates

Year	No. of first-ever patients	No. of admissions generated by (c)	Size of pool of potential repeaters	No. of repeater patients	No. of admissions generated by (d)	Total no. of patients (a) and (d)	Total no. of admissions (b) and (e)
	(a)	(b)	(c)	(d)	(e)	(f)	(g)
1	300	318	2,000	200	270	500	588
2	300	318	2,300	230	311	530	629
3	300	318	2,600	260	351	560	669
4	300	318	2,900	290	392	590	710
5	300	318	3,200	320	432	620	750

The model assumes a constant population size which produces 300 first-ever parasuicides (patients) per year, and that each of these individuals generate 1.05 admissions (events) within the same year. The pool of potential repeaters, i.e. individuals with at least one previous episode is initially taken to be 2,000 and thereafter to grow by the addition of the first-ever cases from the previous year. 10 per cent of the 'potential repeater pool' become patients, and each such patient generates 1.35 admissions in the same year.

In such a situation the first-ever patient rate remains constant, the patient rate increases, and the admission rate increases even faster.

Moreover it has been shown that the admission rate for a given year can be reasonably accurately predicted given the sex and first-ever/other composition of the cohort. The interested reader is referred to Duffy (1977).

This analysis suggests that the admission rates for parasuicide will not stabilize until the first-ever rates have actually begun to fall. Moreover it helps to redefine the research problem by indicating that it is the increase in the first-ever rate which requires primary attention. That increase is relatively modest, which is not to deny that the causes still remain to be elucidated.

NOTE

1 When considering which age-sex subgroup has increased its rates most markedly, it should be borne in mind that there are two quite different ways of describing such an increase, namely as absolute or proportional. The reader interested in comparing these different methods will find the data to hand in the appendix to this chapter.

APPENDIX

TABLE I   Sex ratio of rates per 100,000 aged 15+ woman: men

	1962/3	1967	1968	1969	1970	1971	1972	1973	1974
Admissions	1.52	1.17	1.22	1.15	1.37	1.27	1.42	1.56	1.62
Patients	1.51	1.26	1.25	1.28	1.37	1.38	1.51	1.70	1.63
First evers	–	–	1.30	1.32	1.53	1.32	1.65	1.80	1.59

TABLE II   Age-sex specific rates per 100,000

Men admissions

Age	1962/3	1967	1968	1969	1970	1971	1972	1973	1974
15–19	39	168	183	295	266	442	433	375	471
20–24	132	315	295	278	331	573	431	411	405
25–34	162	287	320	291	285	339	433	424	407
35–44	146	245	228	321	236	238	343	375	295
45–54	112	133	188	178	260	235	217	198	236
55+	65	48	77	71	77	93	77	74	62
15+	109	179	193	210	215	275	278	268	265

Women admissions

Age	1962/3	1967	1968	1969	1970	1971	1972	1973	1974
15–19	288	304	429	413	564	770	1018	1097	1006
20–24	345	393	386	449	497	743	652	801	693
25–34	309	396	491	520	511	611	713	719	797
35–44	187	232	309	262	378	426	508	526	670
45–54	104	174	154	153	241	238	271	255	293
55+	55	79	62	76	94	70	87	80	78
15+	166	210	236	242	295	349	396	417	428

Men patients

Age	1962/3	1967	1968	1969	1970	1971	1972	1973	1974
15–19	39	139	172	255	254	371	373	283	358
20–24	112	289	254	222	299	418	346	329	315
25–34	155	212	238	212	273	291	349	323	338
35–44	121	199	185	269	207	192	210	251	250
45–54	99	102	150	147	175	164	177	159	208
55+	54	48	67	67	69	83	72	62	60
15+	94	142	158	173	187	218	220	204	219

Women patients

Age	1962/3	1967	1968	1969	1970	1971	1972	1973	1974
15–19	247	261	397	375	503	644	840	945	861
20–24	310	363	347	406	405	595	553	601	588
25–34	241	300	378	459	446	529	564	595	619
35–44	164	200	242	241	321	391	418	457	545
45–54	93	152	121	146	217	204	253	208	241
55+	49	71	60	73	82	67	81	76	78
15+	142	179	198	221	256	300	333	347	357

TABLE II (contd.)   Age-sex specific rates* per 100,000

Men first evers

Age	1968	1969	1970	1971	1972	1973	1974
15−19	150	227	133	248	271	172	245
20−24	142	144	184	284	194	149	181
25−34	70	90	170	147	177	178	171
35−44	104	158	93	88	111	106	145
45−54	84	89	85	106	91	91	108
55+	46	54	35	62	43	47	37
15+	100	111	102	135	126	110	126

Women first evers

	1968	1969	1970	1971	1972	1973	1974
15−19	307	315	374	454	568	640	560
20−24	229	294	231	379	373	355	307
25−34	236	284	219	292	288	272	332
35−44	146	117	179	188	256	251	266
45−54	78	97	132	128	158	108	121
55+	37	47	62	36	55	48	42
15+	130	146	156	178	208	198	200

*First-ever rates for 1962/3 and 1967 not available.

TABLE III   Civil state. Admission rates per 100,000

Men aged 15−34

	1962/3	1967	1968	1969	1970	1971	1972	1973	1974
Single	120	281	260	336	284	496	428	401	412
Married	213	210	274	190	288	361	428	369	346

aged 35+

Single	104	237	284	276	370	279	252	235	198
Married	90	87	114	129	116	130	147	149	128

aged 15+

Widowed	84	138	98	186	176	209	152	125	143
Divorced	2077	1170	1337	1326	1129	855	470	482	804

Women aged 15−34

Single	321	361	406	417	560	696	819	893	807
Married	285	347	444	489	452	632	666	707	692

aged 35+

Single	76	59	87	102	70	85	131	111	72
Married	111	151	162	144	223	213	225	244	269

aged 15+

Widowed	74	121	94	101	141	131	168	104	172
Divorced	571	715	706	598	596	981	988	995	1027

TABLE III (contd.)   Civil state. Patient rates per 100,000

Men aged 15−34

	1962/3	1967	1968	1969	1970	1971	1972	1973	1974
Single	103	205	221	250	265	384	352	309	334
Married	88	202	212	178	272	309	357	303	281

aged 35+

	1962/3	1967	1968	1969	1970	1971	1972	1973	1974
Single	99	155	192	230	231	121	112	169	160
Married	70	82	97	112	98	117	117	118	115

aged 15+

	1962/3	1967	1968	1969	1970	1971	1972	1973	1974
Widowed	84	110	84	186	161	209	152	109	143
Divorced	1662	990	1179	907	1129	513	470	337	760

Women aged 15−34

	1962/3	1967	1968	1969	1970	1971	1972	1973	1974
Single	253	286	343	370	466	563	648	711	663
Married	251	304	385	449	406	545	576	607	622

aged 35+

	1962/3	1967	1968	1969	1970	1971	1972	1973	1974
Single	73	59	75	102	58	77	108	100	65
Married	98	134	135	136	196	191	204	212	225

aged 15+

	1962/3	1967	1968	1969	1970	1971	1972	1973	1974
Widowed	67	111	77	91	121	125	148	98	151
Divorced	429	527	459	465	502	862	791	726	847

TABLE III (contd.)   Civil state. First-ever rates* per 100,000

Men aged 15−34

	1968	1969	1970	1971	1972	1973	1974
Single	148	189	138	233	213	160	197
Married	143	85	200	198	200	167	173

aged 35+

	1968	1969	1970	1971	1972	1973	1974
Single	92	166	83	65	47	75	104
Married	61	74	55	74	65	66	66

aged 15+

	1968	1969	1970	1971	1972	1973	1974
Widowed	42	86	73	134	122	109	96
Divorced	629	419	314	285	209	193	402

Women aged 15−34

	1968	1969	1970	1971	1972	1973	1974
Single	240	263	280	361	391	431	384
Married	268	319	250	353	375	342	367

TABLE III (contd.)   Civil state. First-ever rates* per 100,000

aged 35+

Single	39	78	43	35	54	58	34
Married	85	78	119	106	130	112	122

aged 15+

Widowed	47	47	77	74	94	67	87
Divorced	176	233	282	238	452	376	359

*First-ever rates for 1962/3 and 1967 not available.

TABLE IV   Social Class rates for men — per 100,000 aged 15+

Admissions

Class	1968	1969	1970	1971	1972	1973	1974	Mean
I and II	91	81	94	71	109	73	105	89
III	117	121	123	139	167	128	174	139
IV	239	411	376	611	589	731	695	522
V	878	818	1043	1351	1645	1709	1626	1296

Patients

I and II	88	71	94	68	96	67	101	84
III	101	103	111	116	150	104	164	121
IV	177	374	333	500	493	564	612	436
V	666	609	856	967	1117	1192	1096	929

First evers

I and II	65	45	52	51	51	35	76	54
III	73	76	78	85	108	64	110	85
IV	111	263	159	283	271	340	342	253
V	345	325	410	517	486	472	530	441

TABLE V   Density of occupation of private households. Rates per 100,000

1.50 or less persons per room

	1970	1971	1972	1973	1974
First evers	77	93	110	104	115
Patients	118	140	172	176	192
Admissions	133	160	195	208	222

1.51 or more persons per room

First evers	189	232	144	143	116
Patients	320	380	225	276	191
Admissions	353	432	308	336	224

TABLE VI   Alcohol known to have been consumed before the parasuicidal act –
1974, percentages

Age group	Men			Women		
	First evers	Patients	Admissions	First evers	Patients	Admissions
15–24	60	59	61	38	39	40
25–44	70	75	75	49	56	55
45+	64	65	69	36	40	41
All ages 15+	64	66	68	40	45	45

3

CLINICAL DIFFERENCES IN SUBGROUPS OF PARASUICIDES

3.1 INTRODUCTION

Much research on parasuicide is handicapped by including under a single term a great range of psychological syndromes and social reactions. Yet within this diversity certain regularities can be observed, suggesting the possibility, as well as the desirability, of subclassification within the broad group.

Delineation of the various subgroups might be attempted in a number of ways, of which the most obvious is that of orthodox psychiatric diagnosis. Unfortunately with so large a proportion of patients in the categories of deviant personality and neurosis, clinical diagnosis lacks precision and reliability. Another approach is through psychological studies such as those described in chapter 5. Other possibilities might be based on an analysis of the social processes leading to parasuicide, or from a more general theoretical concept of the varieties of parasuicide. At present such ventures would have to rely heavily on assumptions, and there is no immediate prospect of theories both powerful enough to elicit widespread assent and applicable to everyday clinical and research problems. This is not to deny the great need for imaginative studies, but investigators and clinicians meanwhile require an empirical basis for their work.

The aim of the study to be reported here is to determine whether *age* alone is a variable which can provide a useful classification: clinical experience certainly suggests that it might do so. It has the additional advantage of simplicity and objectivity, and can readily be employed epidemiologically, thus facilitating collation with knowledge of other pertinent groups, such as completed suicides. A secondary aim is to draw attention to certain age-related characteristics of parasuicide which do not seem to be widely appreciated, especially regarding eventual death by suicide.

3.2 METHOD

The data to be considered comprise two 1—year cohorts of patients (persons) admitted to the RPTC in 1968 and 1969. They were divided into three age groups, age 15 to 34, 35 to 54, and over 55. This produces an older age group whose lower boundary is a little too low for easy comparison with other investigations, but the point of division was influenced by the need to have available an adequate number of cases.

It seemed that the question which could most usefully be put was how the patients in the middle age group differed from the younger ones, who being commoner and more familiar clinically form a convenient base line, and how in turn those in the oldest group differed from those of the middle age bracket. Comparisons have therefore been made between adjacent age groups, and not by testing whether a given variable distinguishes between all three groups considered simultaneously.

The 1968 patients were analysed first. If a comparison on a particular variable between two adjacent age groups was found to be statistically significant, the same comparison was then made using the 1969 cohort. Only if a significant result was again found, using two-tailed tests, is the difference reported. Although 14 per cent of the men and 9 per cent of the women in the 1969 cohort had also been admitted in 1968, this overlap was considered small enough to regard the cohorts as sufficiently independent for validation purposes. Probability values will not be quoted as they were often different for the 2 years but all reported differences are statistically significant beyond the 5 per cent level.

Results are given for men and women separately only when a sex-linked difference exists, i.e. when a difference between men and women *within* a group was found in the 1968 cohort and confirmed in the 1969 data: otherwise it may be taken that no consistent and statistically significant sex differences have been detected.

Except where otherwise stated, the data refer to persons, not admissions: if an individual came into the ward more than once during a calendar year the information collected at the first admission has been used. Occasional variations in method will be described as they arise.

3.3 RESULTS

The number of patients in each group in 1968 and 1969 is shown in Table 3.1.

TABLE 3.1   Composition of 1968 and 1969 patient cohort by sex and age-group

	Age		
	15—34	35—54	55+
1968 Males	176 (37%)	112 (45%)	42 (42%)
Females	300 (63%)	139 (55%)	59 (58%)
	476 (100%)	251 (100%)	101 (100%)
1969 Males	187 (35%)	132 (48%)	41 (36%)
Females	339 (65%)	141 (52%)	72 (64%)
	526 (100%)	273 (100%)	113 (100%)

Comparison of middle and younger age groups

Table 3.2 summarizes the findings regarding demographic and social data. Males represent a larger proportion of the middle-aged. The remaining differences can probably be understood in terms of age and the associated changes in civil status. Many of the younger patients (of any marital state) were living with their parents or

TABLE 3.2   Comparison of middle and younger age groups:
demographic and social data

Variable	In comparison with younger group, the middle group has
Sex	More men
Marital status	
men	More married, divorced; fewer single
women	More married, divorced; fewer single
Duration at present address	Longer duration
No. of changes of dwelling in past 5 years	Fewer changes
Overcrowding (1.5 persons or more per room)	Less overcrowded

There were no differences in nominal religion or in proportions
living with close family (parents or spouse).

in-laws in overcrowded conditions, while the middle-aged group were more often
settled in their own premises, were less often overcrowded, and had had less
occasion to change their address in the preceding 5 years.

Diagnostic finesse was necessarily limited by the emergency conditions under
which the service operates, but as described in the last chapter an attempt was made
to classify patients regarding both their formal psychiatric 'illness', if any, and by
personality deviance. More of the middle age group were considered to have a
depressive illness (including reactive depression): in both cohorts approximately
half the patients in this age bracket were so diagnosed. Correspondingly, fewer were
classed as 'no formal disorder'. The men in the middle group also contained a higher
proportion of problem drinkers, and fewer labelled as sociopaths without alcoholic
problems, or as minor character disorders, than in the younger group. Women
reflected a similar pattern, though at lower absolute levels.

A separate and rather finer assessment of the patients' use of alcohol showed
that the *majority* of the middle-aged males were judged to drink in excess of local
norms, with addiction to alcohol being more common than non-addictive heavy
drinking. This pattern was significantly different from the younger patients, among
whom addiction was rarely identified though over-indulgence was common. The
differences were found for both sexes, though females again had lower proportions
in these categories than the men. Imbibing alcohol shortly before the act was
significantly commoner among male than female patients in both age groups. When
the sexes were considered separately no significant differences were found (for
either sex) between age groups in this respect, but when combined there was a
highly significant excess of drinking just before the parasuicidal act in the middle
age group, approximately 45 per cent of whom reported this behaviour.

Dependence on drugs, excluding alcohol, was also significantly commoner in the

TABLE 3.3 Comparison of middle and younger age groups: diagnosis, personality and abuse of alcohol and drugs

Variable	In comparison with the younger group, the middle group has
'Illness diagnosis'	More depressive illness; fewer with 'no formal abnormality'
Personality disorder (including alcoholism)	
males	Fewer 'character disorders', fewer sociopaths, more with alcohol abuse
females	Fewer 'character disorders', fewer sociopaths, more with alcohol abuse
Alcohol problems	
males	Fewer with no problem, fewer with excessive but non-addictive drinking, more alcoholics
females	Fewer with no problem, fewer with excessive but non-addictive drinking, more alcoholics
Dependency on drugs	Commoner, especially for barbiturates

middle age group, particularly for sedatives. Physical illness or disability, chiefly chronic, was similarly more frequent. These findings are summarized in Table 3.3.

There were no significant differences between the groups in the proportions reporting previous parasuicide (in 1968, 42 per cent of the middle and 36 per cent of the younger group had a positive history). Among those with a former episode(s) a similar pattern was found in both groups, namely of a recent clustering of acts

TABLE 3.4 Comparison of middle and younger age groups: previous psychiatric history and family history

Variable	In comparison with younger group, the middle group has
Previous inpatient care	Larger proportion
Previous outpatient care	Larger proportion
Previous parasuicide	
Previously treated at RPTC	No difference
Previously treated at hospital elsewhere	No difference
Previously not treated at hospital	No difference
Interval since last parasuicide, if any	No difference
Frequency distribution of number of previous episodes	No difference
1st degree relatives with	
specialist treated mental illness	No difference
history of parasuicide	No difference
history of suicide	No difference

rather than a series spread out over their lifetime: the middle age group, however, had received psychiatric care relatively more frequently, presumably having seen a psychiatrist for some problem which was not directly associated with their parasuicide. Other details are given in Table 3.4.

The drugs used for self-poisoning differed between the groups, with the middle age group showing a relative preference for barbiturates and less use of the newer psychotrophic drugs or salicylates. There were no differences in the (minority) proportions who took active steps to avoid being discovered after their overdose.

After-care and follow-up

More men in the middle age group than in the younger were admitted to a psychiatric hospital after assessment in the centre; correspondingly fewer returned to the sole care of their general practitioner. A similar trend among women was not consistently significant.

Repetition of parasuicide was considered in two ways. The first was by determining the frequency of re-admission to the centre within the same calendar year (actually the proportion of first among all admissions within the year). Secondly, the percentage of individuals re-admitted over the 12 months following their first or key admission was considered. By both methods males (of both age groups) tended to have slightly higher repetition rates than women, and the middle age group as a whole had higher rates than the younger patients. Thus the lowest repetition rate obtained in either cohort by the follow-up method for the younger women (12 per cent) and the highest for middle-aged men (23 per cent). Nevertheless, none of the age group discrepancies, whether for the sexes separately or in combination, were consistently and significantly different.

Subsequent suicide

It was possible to ascertain how many patients had died and had been officially classified as suicides during the calendar year of their admission or in the following 2 years. The figures relate only to deaths occurring within the city, and will therefore be minimal estimates. Since the absolute numbers were small the two cohorts have been combined in order to provide more dependable data. Details are shown in Table 3.5. The subgroup with the highest rate was the middle-aged males, of whom 1 in 25 had died by suicide within the follow-up period. This is over twice as high as the women in the same age group, and ten times higher than in the younger men.

Deaths classified as 'undetermined whether accidentally or purposefully inflicted' (E 980—989) were also considered. None was found for the younger patients but five (all but one in men) were discovered in the middle group. It is likely that these deaths were in most instances suicides. Their inclusion raises the 'suicide' rate to over 6 per cent in the middle-aged males, underlining still further their special vulnerability.

To summarize: the middle age group when compared with the younger patients contained more men; had a higher proportion who were married or divorced, and fewer who were single; was more stable residentially and had fewer who were overcrowded; had more individuals who had received psychiatric care on previous occasions unconnected with an earlier parasuicide; more often suffered from

TABLE 3.5   Suicide in young and middle age groups during 2—3-year follow-up
(undetermined deaths in brackets)

	Young (15—34 years)			Middle (35—54 years)		
	M	F	Total	M	F	Total
Within calendar year of key admission	0	3	3	2	1	3
In following year	1	2	3	2 (2)	0	2 (2)
In final year	0	0	0	3 (2)	2 (1)	5 (3)
Total	1	5	6	7 (4)	3 (1)	10 (5)
No. at risk*	253	480	733	172	200	372
% Suicides	0.40	1.04	0.82	4.07	1.50	2.69
± S.E.	0.40	0.46	0.33	1.51	0.86	0.84
% Suicides and undetermined deaths	0.40	1.04	0.82	6.40	2.00	4.03
± S.E.	0.40	0.46	0.33	1.87	0.99	1.02

Critical ratios	Suicide	Suicide and undetermined death
Young group: male v. female	1.05	1.05
Middle group: male v. female	1.48	2.08†
Males: young v. middle	2.35†	3.14‡
Females: young v. middle	0.47	0.88
Combined: young v. middle	2.07†	2.99‡

†$p < .05$
‡$p < .01$
*Represents all the 1968 cohort plus those 1969 patients not admitted in
1968. All data refer to Edinburgh residents only.

depressive illness; had fewer who were described as sociopaths or character
disorders without alcoholism, but more who were considered to be alcohol addicts.
More of them regular consumers of drugs, especially barbiturates, which were also
more commonly used for self poisoning, with salicylates and psychotropic drugs
figuring less commonly. For men but not women, the middle group were more
often admitted to a psychiatric hospital after the act. Previous and subsequent
parasuicide did not distinguish the groups, but the middle-aged (especially the men)
had a much higher risk of death by suicide on a 2—3—year follow-up.

Comparison of the older and middle age groups

Since the numbers available for analysis in the older age range were relatively small,
statistically significant differences from the comparison group, namely those age 35
to 54, were more difficult to demonstrate. The positive findings have been listed in
a single table (Table 3.6) but some negative findings also warrant comment.

The two groups did not differ in the proportion of the sexes. Marital state
differences might have been expected simply on account of the age discrepancy but
were only statistically significant for women, with a larger proportion of widows in

the older group. Among those ever-married, marital separation was no more frequent in one group than the other.

The effect of religious denomination was reflected in a relative deficit of Roman Catholics among the older patients. (This data was available for 1968 only.) Unfortunately social class was not sufficiently well documented to warrant any firm conclusions.

Residential mobility and living conditions also distinguished the two groups, the older patients having changed their dwelling less frequently in the preceding 5 years and having spent more time at their present address. They also contained fewer individuals living in overcrowded conditions. Perhaps for this reason, as well as by virtue of their age, fewer older patients reported either receiving violence or using it on others over the preceding 5 years. Fewer also reported gross neglect or cruelty in childhood.

In their previous psychiatric histories there was *no* significant difference in the proportions who had received psychiatric care in the past, despite the older group having obviously been at risk for a much longer period, nor among those treated at any time was there any difference in how recently they had had attention. Similarly there were *no* differences in the proportions with a past history of parasuicide, whether hospital-treated or otherwise.

As might have been expected, physical illness and disability, almost invariably chronic, was found to be appreciably more common than in the middle age group, and was noted in approximately half the older sample.

There were no consistent differences in a preferred method of self-poisoning or injury. The illness diagnoses of the patients in the two groups were also similar, but

TABLE 3.6   Comparison of the older and middle age groups

Variable	In comparison with the middle group, the older group has
Marital status	More widows
History of marital separation	No difference
Religion	Fewer Roman Catholics
No. of dwelling changes in past 5 years	Fewer changes
Overcrowding (1.5 or more persons per room)	Fewer overcrowded
Violence	
from others	Less common
to others	Less common
Physical illness	Commoner
Personality diagnosis	
males	Fewer personality disorders
females	Fewer personality disorders
Alcohol (males)	
excess drinking	Fewer
alcohol addiction	Fewer
Alcohol taken prior to parasuicide	Fewer

there were differences in personality type: the older patients, of both sexes, contained more individuals considered to be of normal personality and fewer described as personality deviants of any kind. Significantly fewer of the older men had been classified as addicted to alcohol or as drinking in excess of subcultural norms. Fewer had consumed alcohol in association with the parasuicidal act for which they were admitted.

After-care and follow-up

Significantly more older patients than members of the middle age group were admitted to hospital or to some other provision.

On both the criteria of repetition previously mentioned the older patients had somewhat lower proportions who had a further episode, but the differences were not statistically significant.

Subsequent suicide

Table 3.7 gives the data on completed suicide during the follow-up period. Though the numbers are small (and perhaps for this reason statistically significant

TABLE 3.7   Suicide in middle and older age groups during 2–3-year follow-up (undetermined deaths in brackets)

	Middle (35–54 years)			Older (55+ years)		
	M	F	Total	M	F	Total
Within calendar year of key admission	2	1	3	1	0	1
In following year	2 (2)	0	2 (2)	1	2	3
In final year	3 (2)	2 (1)	5 (3)	3	1 (2)	4 (2)
Total	7 (4)	3 (1)	10 (5)	5	3 (2)	8 (2)
No. at risk*	172	200	372	63	93	156
% Suicides	4.07	1.50	2.69	7.94	3.22	5.13
± S.E.	1.51	0.86	0.84	3.41	1.83	1.77
% Suicides and undetermined deaths	6.40	2.00	4.03	7.94	5.38	6.41
± S.E.	1.87	0.99	1.02	3.41	2.34	1.96

Critical ratios	Suicide	Suicide and undetermined death
Older group: male *v.* female	1.22	0.62
Males: middle *v.* older	1.04	0.40
Females: middle *v.* older	0.85	1.33
Combined: middle *v.* older	1.25	1.08

*Represents all the 1968 cohort plus those 1969 patients not admitted in 1968. All data refer to Edinburgh residents only.

differences could not be demonstrated) they suggest that the rates are higher among the men than the women in the older group, and for both sexes are higher than in the middle group. Inclusion of the undetermined deaths changes the picture somewhat, as there is then no real difference in the rates for males in the middle aged and older categories, although the older women retain their comparatively higher risk.

To summarize: some of the differences shown by the older patients, in comparison with the middle age group, can reasonably be ascribed simply to their greater age. These might include the findings of a higher proportion of widows, less residential mobility, and less overcrowding; less involvement in interpersonal violence; and a higher frequency of chronic physical illness. Differences which are less obviously age-connected include a lower proportion of Roman Catholics; fewer patients with personality disorders, excessive drinking or alcoholism, and fewer whose parasuicide occurred after drinking. There was no difference in 'illness diagnosis'. A previous parasuicide was equally common, as was subsequent parasuicide on follow-up, but during that period suicide, strictly defined, was twice as frequent. The addition of 'undetermined' deaths obliterates the distinction for men though not for women.

3.4 DISCUSSION

The literature is replete with descriptive accounts of series of parasuicides (see chapter 1). Nearly all present a picture which is primarily applicable to patients below the age of 35, these being numerically dominant. Many of the characteristics of such young patients are also applicable to patients in the middle and older age range but a number of specific differences between the age groups have emerged. These have already been summarized and only a few points require further comment.

The middle age group

It is clear that, comparatively speaking, this group is dominated by problems of alcohol. This was particularly true for men, among whom alcoholics were more numerous than uncomplicated heavy drinkers, but also applied in considerable measure to women. Taking alcohol immediately prior to the act is a poor indication of long-standing alcohol problems, but it too differentiated the two groups (although only if the sex distinction was dropped). It is also notable that the middle-aged patients had a relative excess of contacts with psychiatrists for problems other than earlier parasuicidal episodes, and presumably some of these contacts were also related to alcohol problems. The relationship between alcoholism, acute intoxication, depression, parasuicide, and suicide merits more detailed study, as illustrated, for example, by the recent work of Mayfield and Montgomery (1972).

Despite their greater age and hence longer period at risk, the middle group in comparison with the younger did not show a significant excess of previous parasuicide, nor was the likelihood of subsequent repetition significantly different. Age, in this comparison, is not a pointer to persistent parasuicidal behaviour (see Chapter 6). In both age groups the pattern of repeated acts appears to be that of a discreet cluster rather than a series spread out over the life span, as already noted by Kessel and McCulloch (1966).

Interpretation of the comparative repetition rates for parasuicide and, more cogently, of completed suicide over the 2–3-year follow-up, should include some consideration of the effects of population mobility. Although younger people are in general more mobile, the main effect of differential mobility between the groups is probably to reduce slightly the rates obtained for the middle age group. Repetition rates for parasuicides were found to be closely similar and it is unlikely that this pattern would be materially affected by adjustment for mobility, especially as the time interval was fairly short. For completed suicide the middle group had a substantially greater mortality, particularly the men, and the true excess may well be higher than Table 3.5 suggests.

The older group

The older age group are of interest if only because they have been relatively neglected in previous studies. Although both alcoholism and recognizable person-ality disorders were found to be significantly less common among them than in the middle group, they were by no means rare. The design of the study stresses the differences rather than the similarities between groups, but it is worth noting that in 1968, 25 per cent of the older patients were considered to have personality disorders and a further 12 per cent to be alcoholics, or 33 per cent and 26 per cent if only the men were considered. A similar picture was found in 1969. Further, the proportion of divorced persons amongst the older patients (7 per cent in 1968) is almost identical with that for the middle-aged, implying that personal relationships have not always been smooth for them. The older group also provide one of the rare examples of nominal religion having a demonstrable association with 'suicidal behaviour'. Possibly the older Catholic woman takes the doctrines of her church relatively seriously.

The findings as regards specific diagnoses differ from those of other authors. Batchelor and Napier (1953) reported that all of their series of 40 parasuicides, age 60 or more, had a recognizable psychiatric illness and that two-thirds were psychotic; among these depressive illnesses were diagnosed in 80 per cent and an organic syndrome in 10 per cent. O'Neill et al. (1965) reported in their smaller series of 19 patients, also aged 60 years and over, that all their patients too had a specific psychiatric disorder but quoted depression in 47 per cent and organic syndromes in 42 per cent. In neither study was comparative data with other age groups offered. In the present enquiry the proportions for 'illness diagnosis' found in the 1968 and 1969 cohorts respectively were : depressive reaction or psychosis 58 per cent and 62 per cent, organic syndromes 8 per cent and 5 per cent and no formal disorder 27 per cent and 27 per cent. These diagnoses were made under emergency conditions by a number of service psychiatrists, yet their consistency is high. The percentages are almost identical with those found for the middle age group, except for a higher proportion of organic cases. Thus non-psychotic illness, personality disorders and alcoholism emerge in the present series as important even for the older subjects. The discrepancies between the three investigations might in part be due to the 5–year difference in the age limit, but more probably are attributable to sampling differences. Moreover there appear to have been considerable changes in the pattern of parasuicide since these earlier papers appeared (see chapter 2).

Much as was noted in the comparison between the middle and the younger groups, so older and middle groups show a similar proportion of patients with at least one prior parasuicidal episode. The rate of subsequent repetition is lower than that of the middle group (e.g. in 1968, repetition in the ensuing 12 months occurred in 14 per cent of the middle and 7 per cent of the older patients) but the difference is not statistically significant.

Completed suicide shows quite a different pattern. Taking officially defined suicides only, older males have twice the rate of middle-aged men, but it should be recalled that the latter in turn have over ten times the rate of young men. The period of increased risk is better considered to begin in the mid-30s than in the 60s. Adding the 'undetermined' deaths supports this contention; the middle group suicide rate then becomes almost identical with that of the older patients. Among women, however, the findings are different. Their rates increase uniformly with age, using either criterion of suicide; they are never as high as those for men of similar age.

Suicide and parasuicide

The relation of parasuicide to suicide in Edinburgh is explored in chapter 9.

The identification of subgroups of parasuicides

A study by Philip (1970) concluded with comments on the need to divide parasuicides into more homogeneous subgroups, and the case for defining subtypes has again been put forward here. What is required is a way of grouping individuals, as in the taxonomy proposed by Katschnig and Sint (1973), rather than of symptoms or personal characteristics as in the factorial study by Fahy *et al.* (1970). But like all classifications the value of any such scheme can only be assessed against the purpose it is to serve. There are four main uses which might be envisaged.

There is firstly the prediction of further parasuicide. Here the age/sex divisions used in the present investigation have not proved efficient, and certainly give less discrimination than the scales developed by Buglass and Horton (1974a) and reviewed in chapter 6.

Secondly there is the prediction of suicide, especially in the short and medium range. As suggested by Tuckman and Youngman (1963a and b) demographic variables, e.g. age and sex, here provide effective pointers. Even using the very simple divisions employed in the present study the highest risk group emerges as having about 20 times the risk of the lowest group. This is encouraging, but must be considered alongside the fact that the majority of suicides are drawn from the much larger low risk subgroups. Further work may well enable precision to be increased by the inclusion of diagnostic and social variables.

It is already evident that the prediction of suicide and of further parasuicide must be two separate exercises requiring two different sets of variables; thus the present classification distinguishes various risks of suicide but not of repetition of parasuicide, while in the study by Buglass and Horton (1974a) patients who subsequently killed themselves fell in the middle, not at the top, of the range of predictive scores for further parasuicide.

Thirdly, there are the clinical uses to which a subclassification might be put, such as to sensitize the clinician to likely findings and their associated treatment or management implications. Such a purpose is difficult to define and validate directly, but a guide to likely success could be gained from the homegeneity (which can be tested statistically) of the subgroups in the classification. No attempt has been made to do this with the present data.

Finally, there are the purposes of research and theory. In this context it must be granted that age and sex in themselves are scarcely illuminating theoretical concepts, but they gain in richness when used as pointers to the differential prevalence of various psychiatric disorders and of social roles.

4

SOCIO-CULTURAL ASPECTS

The distribution of parasuicide in Edinburgh city has been described in chapter 2. The overall pattern has been stable for at least the last 12 years in that despite changes in absolute level the electoral ward where parasuicide is commonest has a first-ever rate five times, and an admission rate seven times, higher than that of the ward where the rate is lowest.

The variation in area rates is not easily explained. In this chapter the characteristics of areas are related to parasuicide and two types of explanatory approaches are considered.

4.1 ECOLOGICAL STUDIES

The Chicago studies of the 1920s and 1930s showed that the social and economic characteristics of a city followed certain patterns. The exact nature of the pattern has been subject to some controversy. One suggestion was that a city consists of concentric circles, the innermost area comprising the business premises and inhabited only by those who have not the means to live elsewhere (Park and Burgess, 1925). Residential land values increase according to the distance from the centre. Hoyt (1939) thought that sectors starting at the centre and widening towards the periphery provided a more accurate description than the concentric circles pattern. Rental values were either homogeneous within a sector or rose steadily towards the outer rim. These patterns were related to social problems as well as to economic factors. Cavan (1928), for example, showed that rates for completed suicides were highest in areas where divorce and deaths from alcoholism were also unusually common.

The early studies fell into disregard; some said they were too atheoretical; some, that they described the *status quo* without illuminating the social processes involved. Moreover, workers sometimes over-interpreted their results. The principal dangers of ecological analyses are, firstly, that a correlation between two variables may be rashly assumed to mean that there is a causal relationship between the variables; and secondly, that the important difference between individual and ecological correlations may be overlooked. It has been amply demonstrated that there is no necessary correspondence between the two types of correlation. For example Robinson (1950) showed that although in the United States illiteracy is positively correlated at an individual level with foreign birth, there is a negative *ecological* correlation between illiteracy and foreign birth. Nevertheless, ecological correlations may be valuable, provided the focus of interest is the *area* rather than how characteristics are related at an individual level (Beshers, 1960).

Indeed, despite being unfashionable, the method has never been wholly abandoned. Recently it has again come into prominence as an adjunct to local government information services seeking to provide geographical data for the rational planning of services and treatment facilities (see, for example, Flynn *et al.*, 1972, on the Liverpool Social Malaise Study). In effect the ecological method of earlier decades has been recreated by the identification and detailed description of 'problem areas', and studies of the overlap of the geographies of different 'problems' within cities. Similarly ecological studies of parasuicide have described the social characteristics of the areas where parasuicide is most frequent, and have related rates for parasuicide to the rates for other characteristics across the various wards of the city.

Choice of geographical unit

Since ecological studies aim to compare the characteristics of different areas, the areas themselves have to be defined. Ideally the geographical unit studied should be one with natural boundaries, which has some sense of community identity and is reasonably homogeneous. In practice, the unit is almost always administratively defined. The calculation of rates depends on information about the total population in an area being available. The only readily available source of total population figures is the Census, which publishes data for electoral wards of cities. The 23 municipal wards of Edinburgh city have been accepted as the geographical unit of analysis. Many of the wards do form natural social and geographical units, but a few, especially two in the south of the city, are too large and too heterogeneous to make desirable units of analysis.

Sources of data

Once the areas have been defined, the next step is to collect relevant information about them. As well as providing the base population, the Census is also useful in giving a wide range of variables relating to age structure, density of occupation, housing conditions and socio-economic status. Unfortunately census data are only collected every 5 or 10 years and are therefore quickly out of date. Local Authority departments are the source of many 'social problem' variables, but only rarely is this information classified in areas by the departments themselves. Similarly, agencies such as the police and voluntary social work bodies have much valuable information in their files but the labour in extracting it is often considerable.

Analysis of data

Ecological studies often generate a very large amount of information. Some users of the information are likely to be interested in the detail — in the relation between one variable and many variables, or in the rates for a specific area of the city. Others want some kind of summary which will describe the city as a whole, or, for example, identify multi-problem areas. The first step after the calculation of the rates is usually to rank the wards, so that the ward with the highest rate for a particular variable is ranked 1, the second highest rate, 2 and so on. It is then possible to see whether the same wards are ranked high for a large number of variables. A more complete description is provided by calculating the rank order correlations between different variables.

A further reduction of data may be achieved by statistical means. Some of the Edinburgh studies have used a form of cluster analysis (Elementary Linkage Analysis, McQuitty, 1957); other studies have used principal component analysis.

The ecology of parasuicide in Edinburgh

The observation that high parasuicide rates were concentrated in certain areas led to the first investigation of the ecological correlates of parasuicide by Philip and McCulloch (1966). They selected 18 variables, including parasuicide, which could be referred to the electoral wards of the city. These variables were derived from 1961 Census material (overcrowding, owner-occupied houses, council houses, private unfurnished houses, private furnished houses, old age pensioners) and from Local Authority departments (children taken into care, eviction notices, peace warnings, rent arrears, school absences, infant mortality, stillbirths). In addition, three variables — adolescent psychiatric referral, adolescent self-poisoning and self-injury, and 'all ages self-poisoning and self-injury' — were taken from surveys carried out as part of the MRC Unit research programme. Two other items, juvenile delinquency and referrals to the Royal Scottish Society for the Prevention of Cruelty to Children, were obtained by personal contact with the agencies involved.

For each electoral ward the rate of occurrence for every 1,000 units at risk was calculated for each variable and the rates ranked. Spearman rank order correlations were calculated between all variables. Table 4.1 shows the matrix derived from this analysis.

An Elementary Linkage Analysis carried out on the matrix produced four clusters (Figure 4.1).

The first cluster is not unexpected as the three variables reflect three stages in the eviction process. Rent arrears lead to a stern reminder (a peace warning) which, if not heeded, leads to an eviction order. These items are so highly correlated that they could be represented by a single variable in subsequent analyses. Parasuicide occurs in the third cluster in conjunction with child-centred problems. It should be remembered that Elementary Linkage Analysis only uses the highest association between variables. Thus the present cluster ignores the substantial relation between parasuicide and overcrowding shown in Table 4.1.

A study of the distribution of social and medical problems in Edinburgh currently undertaken by the MRC Unit has provided a more recent ecological picture. Table 4.2 shows the principal correlates of the 1973 Edinburgh parasuicide rates. Since a large number of variables were investigated, only those significant at the 1 per cent level are listed. Of 65 items obtained from statutory and voluntary agencies, 16 were significantly related to parasuicide rates. Twelve of the 40 census items were also significant.

These items give a general picture of the areas where parasuicide rates are highest. The cardinal feature appears to be economic deprivation. There is more unemployment and more loss of work through sickness; the rateable value is low, overcrowding is common, and families are more often in receipt of clothing grants and free school meals. As is common in areas associated with poverty, deviance and law-breaking are more frequent. There is a demand for services for the elderly, although there is no excess of elderly persons in these areas. It may be speculated that this demand also has an economic base. Health variables are less closely associated with parasuicide. Of over 30 items referring to public health notifications

TABLE 4.1 Spearman rho correlations between 18 social variables

Social variables	2	3	4	5	6	7	8	9	10	11	12	13	14	15	16	17	18
1 Adolescent psychiatric referral	−405	−366	−471	−071	072	102	115	−471	−337	−261	274	461	−006	−190	005	163	−376
2 Adolescent self-poisoning and self-injury		493	475	282	026	−047	−052	410	530	288	−190	−350	−175	538	277	055	472
3 All ages self-poisoning and self-injury			811	858	−031	−066	−131	770	642	031	−027	−410	−203	582	224	024	874
4 Juvenile delinquency				790	223	183	167	851	758	200	141	−735	185	341	−017	−306	844
5 Children taken into care					260	215	202	703	719	077	071	−470	100	292	054	−253	872
6 Eviction notices						928	957	050	172	226	200	−282	638	−473	−617	−358	089
7 Peace warnings							954	016	091	145	193	−113	537	−338	−611	−304	−001
8 Rent arrears								009	125	127	187	−229	662	−528	−703	−417	002
9 Overcrowding (> 1.5 persons per room)									692	421	165	−753	086	469	−160	−307	774
10 School absences (for reasons other than sickness)										−133	−015	−693	209	146	−177	−479	832
11 Infant mortality											216	−436	242	−034	−348	−172	241
12 Stillbirths												−226	274	−150	−213	−017	089
13 Owner-occupied houses													−537	048	412	663	−631
14 Council houses														−678	−945	−801	124
15 Private unfurnished houses															623	423	292
16 Private furnished houses																796	−039
17 Old age pensioners																	−298
18 RSSPCC referrals																	

Decimal points have been omitted.
Significance levels for $n = 23$ are: 0.05, $p = 0.418$; 0.01, $p = 0.549$; 0.001, $p = 0.702$ (all two-tailed tests).

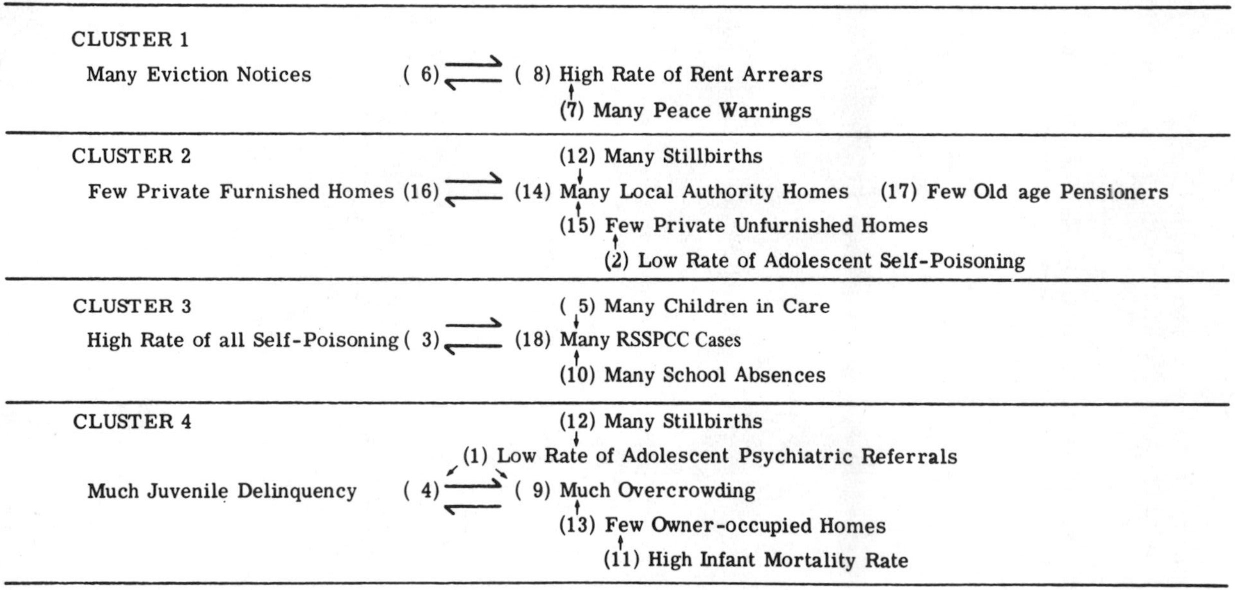

CLUSTER 1

Many Eviction Notices (6) ⇅ (8) High Rate of Rent Arrears

(7) Many Peace Warnings

CLUSTER 2

(12) Many Stillbirths

Few Private Furnished Homes (16) ⇅ (14) Many Local Authority Homes (17) Few Old age Pensioners

(15) Few Private Unfurnished Homes

(2) Low Rate of Adolescent Self-Poisoning

CLUSTER 3

(5) Many Children in Care

High Rate of all Self-Poisoning (3) ⇅ (18) Many RSSPCC Cases

(10) Many School Absences

CLUSTER 4

(12) Many Stillbirths

(1) Low Rate of Adolescent Psychiatric Referrals

Much Juvenile Delinquency (4) ⇅ (9) Much Overcrowding

(13) Few Owner-occupied Homes

(11) High Infant Mortality Rate

⇅ denotes a reciprocal relationship between two variables.

→ denotes that a variable at the tail of the arrow has its highest correlation with the variable at the head of the arrow.

FIGURE 4.1. Linkage analysis of variables

58

and reasons for admissions to hospital, only three are associated with parasuicide above the 1 per cent level. The relation of parasuicide to completed suicide is discussed more fully in chapter 9. In the current analysis parasuicide had an ecological correlation of 0.34 with the rate for completed suicide in Edinburgh, 1971–3.

It is interesting that the spatial distribution reported by Morgan *et al.* (1975) for parasuicide in Bristol is different from that illustrated in Map 2.1 for Edinburgh.

TABLE 4.2   Rank order correlations across city wards (significant at least $p < .01$)

Parasuicide rates (1973) significantly correlated with:

Child-related variables		Crimes and offences	
Illegitimate births	0.83	Crimes against property with violence	0.64
Education Department clothing grants	0.80	Crimes against property without violence	0.68
Free school meals	0.66	Breach of the peace	0.73
Truancy	0.67	Offences under Intoxicating Liquor Laws	0.71
Children taken into care	0.68		
Referrals to the Reporter of Children's Hearings	0.75	Variables related to economic position	
RSSPCC referrals	0.67	*Census 1971*	
		Seeking work — males	0.72
Services for the elderly		Seeking work — females	0.56
		Off work, sick — males	0.75
Persons entering Part IV accommodation	0.59	Off work, sick — females	0.65
		% Owner-occupied households	−0.59
Persons on Part IV waiting list	0.68	% Manual labourers	0.68
Persons receiving meals on wheels	0.63	Household with no car	0.76
Illness variables		*City assessor*	
Admissions to mental hospital for 'other behaviour and personality disorders'	0.55	Rateable value of property	−0.66
Admissions to hospital for peptic ulcer	0.67	Other census variables	
Admissions to hospital for diseases of pregnancy and childbirth	0.68	Divorced males	0.68
		Divorced females	0.79
Debt		Migration within local authority area — males	0.74
Non-payment of electricity bills	0.82	Overcrowding	0.77
		Lone parent families	0.63

High-rate wards are concentrated in the centre in Bristol but not in Edinburgh: the social context of poor housing and economic deprivation is nevertheless very similar.

It must be stressed that none of these associations should be considered causative. This type of description does, however, highlight the social context in which parasuicide occurs, and this context is one of economic stress and conflict with authority.

4.2 MULTIPLE STANDARDIZATION OF PARASUICIDE RATES

It has been shown (chapter 2) that certain demographic and social variables are related to parasuicidal rates. The young, the divorced, the lower social classes, and (until 1974) the overcrowded were at greater risk of parasuicide than other groups. The explanation of high rates in certain districts might be that these areas contained a higher proportion of people at risk, for example the young or the lower social classes. The question arises whether, if the population in all areas (electoral wards) of the city had a similar distribution for *each* of several such key variables, the parasuicide rate would then be the same in all areas. If the answer is affirmative, then the excess of parasuicide in certain areas is explained in terms of the variables considered. If the answer is negative and area differences still persist when their populations are simultaneously standardized on several variables of known relevance, it has been demonstrated that these areas must be distinguished by other, as yet unknown, factors to which further investigation may be directed. A study carried out on 1968 data (Buglass *et al.*, 1970) was designed to discover whether the standardization of parasuicide rates on several variables simultaneously would indeed remove the differences in ward parasuicide rates.

Choice of variables

The variables selected had to satisfy the following criteria:
    (1) They were known to be related to parasuicide.
    (2) Information on the variable had to be available both for the parasuicide group and for the population of the city, i.e. from census data.
    The six items which satisfied these criteria and on which the population was standardized were: sex, age, marital status, social class, overcrowding, and unemployment.

Collection of data

Parasuicides   The parasuicide group consisted of parasuicides admitted to the RPTC from an Edinburgh address between 1 January and 31 December 1968; those admitted more than once within this period were included for their first admission only. Any patient whose address, sex, age, or marital status was unknown was excluded (3 per cent). The number of patients remaining for study was 642.

General population   Information on the general population was obtained from the Sample Census, 1966. So that a sufficiently detailed analysis could be carried out, the General Register Office kindly provided data in the form of specially prepared abstracts from the census punched cards. These abstract cards, covering a 10 per cent sample of the city's population, effectively recorded only the six selected variables plus a coding for the city ward (the ward populations ranged from about 10,000 to about 36,000). They thus gave no data which might have identified a particular individual. Table 4.3 shows the categories used for each of the six variables in the analysis.

    Because of the small numbers of patients from Classes I and II, these were grouped in all analyses. As employment is less easy to define for women, this variable was used only for men. 'Unemployed' was interpreted as not in employment on census day or (for the patients) without a job at the time of admission. Those who were retired, students or 'others economically inactive' were classed as 'not applicable'.

Method of analysis

The Edinburgh city parasuicide rate was used to produce standardized rates for each ward. The procedure was as follows:

(1) The parasuicides for the whole city were tabulated by the six variables subdivided as described in Table 4.3. This tabulation thus comprises 2,880 cells. (An example of a single cell would be: males aged 25—34, single, Social Class IV, overcrowded, and employed.)

(2) A similar tabulation was made for the general population of Edinburgh city and the parasuicide rate was calculated for each of the 2,880 cells.

(3) The population of each city ward was then tabulated in the same way.

(4) The expected number of parasuicides in a given ward was calculated by multiplying the number of persons in each of the cells by the city rate for the corresponding cell, and totalling the results for that ward.

Certain adjustments were made to take account of missing information. About one-third of all parasuicides had information missing on one or more of the variables, social class, overcrowding, and unemployment. If only one of the three items was missing the expected numbers were calculated on the basis of the known information (i.e. instead of standardizing on six items for men and five for women, the available five for men and four for women were used). This was done for 170 patients. The expected numbers for the remaining 55 patients on whom more than one item was missing were calculated by standardizing for age, sex, and marital status only.

A goodness of fit test (χ^2) was applied first to the observed and expected numbers based only on those patients for whom records were complete. The observed and expected numbers were then supplemented by those based on incomplete records and the test was repeated.

The ratios of the numbers observed to those expected after standardization (Standardized Morbidity Ratios or SMRs) for each ward were calculated. For

TABLE 4.3   The subdivision of variables

1	Sex:	Male, female
2	Age (years)	Under 15 35—44
		15—19 45—54
		20—24 55—64
		25—34 65 and over
3	Marital status:	Single, married, widowed, divorced
4	Social Class:	I and II; III; IV; V; not known or not applicable
5	Overcrowding:	Less than 1.5 persons per room; 1.5 persons per room and over; Not known or not applicable
6	Employment (males only):	Employed, unemployed, not known or not applicable

comparison, crude morbidity ratios — which are simply the ward rates expressed as a percentage of the whole city rate — and SMRs derived after standardizing on age and sex only, were also calculated.

In short, these ratios provide a means of comparing the number of parasuicides from each ward with the number to be expected if the inhabitants of that ward behaved like matched individuals drawn from the city as a whole. The nearer the ratio is to 100, the nearer the ward is to the overall city figures.

Results

The results of standardization, firstly by age and sex, and secondly by all six variables, are presented pictorially in Figure 4.2. It is clear that standardization on age and sex scarcely changed the pattern of the crude morbidity ratios at all. Simultaneous standardization on all six variables, however, reduced the spread appreciably, though differences still remained.

Table 4.4 permits a more detailed comparison of the number of parasuicides in each ward with the number expected after standardization on all six variables. If these variables accounted for the differences between wards the observed and expected figures should resemble each other and there should be no significant difference between the two sets of figures. This possibility was assessed by calculating a goodness of fit test on the total numbers observed and expected. The result was highly significant ($p < .001$). A further goodness of fit test was calculated for only the 417 patients on whom complete information was available for all items. This too was significant at the 1 per cent level ($\chi^2_{22} = 45.90$).

It was concluded, therefore, that although standardization had reduced the variation between wards, a significant overall difference remained. Certain wards still had ratios markedly different from 100; in particular, the values for three wards were more than 150 whilst one had an SMR of below 40.

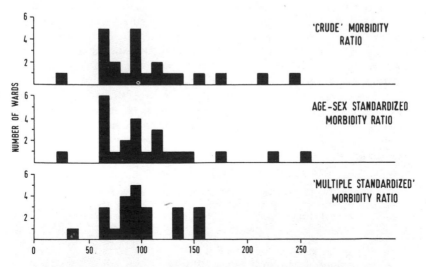

FIGURE 4.2. Effects of standardization on 'crude' morbidity ratio

62

TABLE 4.4   Comparison of observed numbers with
numbers expected after standardization on six variables
(all patients)

Electoral ward	Observed	Expected
1	49	31.62
2	13	18.44
3	27	17.32
4	24	26.74
5	34	50.57
6	25	18.09
7	23	16.78
8	27	29.78
9	30	27.89
10	31	29.87
11	9	23.56
12	27	27.10
13	54	49.49
14	23	33.70
15	14	16.56
16	22	22.95
17	35	25.54
18	14	20.43
19	27	32.44
20	24	26.20
21	25	27.20
22	29	32.65
23	56	37.09
Total	642	642.01

$\chi^2 = 57.78$ df = 22 $p < 0.001$.

To make some (though approximate) estimate of how much of the variation had been accounted for by the standardization exercise, the variance was calculated for each of the three sets of morbidity ratios shown in Figure 4.2. Standardization for age and sex alone does not reduce the variance at all; the inclusion of all six variables reduces the variance by about two-thirds, but as noted above still leaves a three-fold discrepancy between the highest and lowest wards (Table 4.5).

Population migration was also considered as a possible explanation of the differences in area rates. Examination of census figures of migration within the city boundary and of movement into the city from other parts of the country indicated that wards with high parasuicide rates were not especially noted for mobility, and detailed analyses served to exclude population movement as an important cause of ward discrepancies.

TABLE 4.5   Means and variances of the morbidity ratios

Morbidity ratio	Mean	Variance
Crude	107.3	2,628.6
Age-sex standardized	107.5	2,739.7
Multiple standardized	101.0	993.1

The conclusion was therefore drawn that the six factors examined were not sufficient to account for the discrepancy in area rates, though they go some way towards identifying the source of variation between wards.

Discussion

The method of standardization used in this study is well-established. One of its principal features is that allowance is made for the interaction of all variables with each other. A simultaneous standardization procedure of this type has clear advantages over any method in which the effects of variables are considered successively, since no inferences have to be made about the correlations between the variables.

It is important to appreciate just what has and has not been achieved by the procedure adopted. It is now possible to say that about two-thirds of the variance in the ward morbidity rates can be 'accounted for' in the statistical sense that the source of a proportion of total variance has been identified. It is not possible to say that the variables used in the standardization procedure 'cause' parasuicide to a degree reflected in the reduction of inter-ward variation; they can be only indirectly related to 'causal' processes, the precise relationship remaining obscure.

However, the main conclusion must be that residence in different city wards remains an interesting source of difference in the rates of parasuicidal behaviour. It is possible that the inclusion of other census-type variables might have accounted for the residual variation; it should also be remembered that standardization is dependent on the way the variables are subdivided. Observation of people in Social Class V has suggested that there are at least two distinguishable groups subsumed in this category (Askham, 1969). It is probable that many parasuicide patients belong to the lower of the two groups though no account could be taken of such a distinction in the study.

Alternatively, census-type variables, however sensitively classified, may in themselves be inadequate to explain the area differences. A description of high-rate parasuicide areas has been presented in the first section of this chapter; as well as exhibiting signs of poverty and deprivation, they are also noted for various types of law-breaking, including drunkenness and breach of the peace (often involving minor assault). It is tenable that many of the varieties of deviant behaviour found in problem areas have common roots in the attitudes, beliefs and values of the residents in these communities. These values are coloured, but not solely determined, by economic position.

This line of reasoning has been developed in the guise of subcultural theories (e.g. Cohen, 1955; Downes, 1964). Wolfgang and Ferracutti (1967) postulate 'subcultures of violence' where the resort to physical violence is more acceptable, and is considered appropriate to a wider variety of situations than would be the case in society at large. It is probable that parasuicide, also, is more acceptable, as well as more common, in certain subcultural groups. In communities where impulsive behaviour takes precedence over long-term planning and where meaning is often communicated through action rather than by subtle verbal exchanges, parasuicidal behaviour would be expected to accord better with the overall life pattern. This is not to claim that parasuicide is normative in any culture, but it is suggested that for some groups the act represents less of a confrontation with accepted modes of behaviour and will invoke fewer sanctions than in groups where advance planning and verbal communication is of greater importance. Both the salience of parasuicide as a behavioural option and the circumstances by which it may be triggered may be prescribed by the culture.

In addition, high-rate communities will afford their members more chance of personal contact with parasuicide, and therefore of imitative behaviour. How such 'modelling' is related to the cultural background is clearly a complex matter that may repay closer study.

4.3 PARASUICIDE AS COMMUNICATION

Introduction

It was suggested in Chapter 1 that the modern era in the study of parasuicide began with the recognition of the interpersonal significance of the event (Stengel *et al.*, 1958; Rubenstein *et al.*, 1958; Farberow and Schneidman, 1961). By now it has become a clinical commonplace that parasuicide may represent a cry for help, although a variety of other 'messages' may also be 'intended'. These have been commented on by various writers, but apart from the major study by McCulloch (1965) there has been very little systematic description of the social consequences of parasuicide and there appears to be no work in which parasuicide has been formally studied as a signalling process.

Apart from its intrinsic interest there is an additional reason for examining parasuicide as a form of communication. The epidemiological and ecological studies already presented lead to the conclusion that subcultural differences might be important in accounting for variation in rates between the different sections of the city. This hypothesis has not yet been tested directly. It would, however, gain in plausibility if it could be demonstrated that parasuicide does indeed serve a communication function, since a system for conveying information is one of the hallmarks of a culture. Evidence that parasuicide has a 'language' aspect would at the least increase the prima facie relevance of cultural studies.

In order to demonstrate that parasuicide is a vehicle by which the patient conveys information to others in his circle, it is first necessary to have an operational definition of communication. None appears to exist which commands widespread agreement, despite intense theoretical work by linguists, ethologists, and communication scientists (see Hinde, 1975). It has therefore been necessary — despite the acknowledged complexities of many of the key issues — to try and derive a test for the communication hypothesis by considering some of the components of communication, the genesis of the parasuicidal act, and the social context in which it commonly occurs. The reasoning behind the approach to be adopted here can only be indicated in summary form; it runs as follows.

The problem of deciding whether an action or event functions as a signal cannot be resolved by reference to the conscious intent of the actor. A blush may indicate embarrassment, but such 'symptomatic' behaviour may be quite contrary to the wishes of an individual, who may indeed prefer to conceal rather than reveal such information about his inner state. Or a person may use a pejorative term in everyday speech without any awareness that he is revealing his prejudices, in which case information has been conveyed without registering in the actor's consciousness. The transmission of a message can therefore only be established by studying the behaviour of the people who receive the hypothesized signal. Two approaches are possible in theory. The first might be to map out for a recipient the variety of responses which he makes to a number of acts by the transmitter, and to demonstrate that the resulting matrix of stimuli and responses is non-random. This technique was used by early information theorists, but is scarcely feasible for present purposes, if only because it would call for a precise itemization of a range of behaviours and responses in patients and their close associates, and there is little indication of how this could or should be done.

An alternative strategy involves consideration of the frequency of analogous behaviour in the recipients. In general, symmetrical activity in human beings occurs rarely and appears to be confined to more or less ceremonial occasions, such as greetings. At such times two individuals may bow to each other or each produce identical extensions or their arms in order to shake hands. When such occasions arise an observer aware of the infrequency with which such behaviours occur when the individuals are alone or in other social situations, and of their relatively common manifestation when two individuals come together, might well conclude that he is witnessing part of a communication process.[1] If pressed to do so he could spell out the grounds for this intuitive conviction in formal probabilistic statistics.

Much more commonly human interactions are asymmetrical if only because the relationship between two individuals is usually asymmetrical. Thus in a dyad one is usually requesting, explaining, demonstrating, etc., while the other is not, or at least is not doing so at exactly the same time. The point to be made, however, is that the recipient finds himself in the same relationship to the other individual as the 'transmitter' initially held in relation to him — that is to say, should the recipient in turn become an explainer, demonstrator, etc. — then he will adopt recognizably similar behaviours on assuming his new role. Indeed, if he failed to do so, an observer would have no grounds for believing that the two individuals shared the same communicational system.

An analogy might be helpful. A man in a burning house might vigorously wave to his neighbours for help. One would hope that the neighbours would not merely wave back with equal vigour but would fetch rescue apparatus. All the same, if any of those neighbours were themselves caught in a similar predicament, then presumably the type of signals they emitted would be of a similar character to those they were currently witnessing.

Considered alone, such similarity is perhaps too restrictive a criterion, in that a communication pattern may exist even if similarity is not demonstrable; the neighbours in the example may never themselves have a fire. Nevertheless a conservative criterion may be no disadvantage in the early stages of an enquiry. Moreover, as parasuicide is accepted usually to be a response to common psychological stresses, there should be no lack of occasions on which the behaviour could be displayed.

If it can be shown that an act such as parasuicide possesses the formal characteristics of a signal, the next question to arise concerns the content of that signal or, in simpler terms, its meaning. Nothing has been said to demonstrate that the *meaning* of the act is the same irrespective of which particular patient and his entourage are being considered. Such uniformity can scarcely be proved; indeed, clinical experience suggests that it is improbable. But it is relevant to consider that signals occurring in a natural setting are invariably part of an elaborate code or structured pattern of socially shared meanings, other parts of which include such behaviours as weeping, screaming or physical violence, to say nothing of spoken language itself. Such socially shared systems of meaning invariably involve substantial numbers of people, even though detailed variations may be unique to quite small groups: a family quarrel can usually be recognized at once, even if some of the terms of abuse or the historical references are private to the family involved. A reasonable simplifying assumption is to consider the meaning of parasuicide as uniform. A group approach, in fact an epidemiological study, is then in order.

There is also the question of how to define for investigation the group supposed to share an understanding of the meaning of the parasuicide act. It could be that the whole of society is the appropriate unit. Instead the communication hypothesis has been taken to indicate that clusters of individuals exist for whom the act has a well-recognized social meaning, and that an individual in this group need only engage in quasi-institutionalized parasuicidal behaviour in order to convey a preformed message to other members, that is to say, to perform a ritual.

The social unit or units among whom parasuicide has this institutional quality are collectively designated a subculture. That term has attracted much debate and a voluminous literature: here it is used to indicate more than simply a collection of individuals with similar attitudes and beliefs; it also necessitates their being socially interrelated. Thus the unemployed, for example, who have a high rate of parasuicide, would not be considered as a subculture since they do not represent a socially cohesive body. Conversely, gypsies could be considered to be a subculture since they are organized in social networks such as families who share generally similar value and language systems.

In parenthesis it also seems that a 'parasuicide subculture' is likely to be one in which there is a relative lack of emphasis on verbal communication with greater value attached to the immediate discharge of emotion and the use of physical methods to convey meanings. There is also likely to be an emphasis on short-term relief of feelings as against long-term planning, and hence possibly a greater use of violence. There are analogies here with the concept of the 'delinquency subculture'.

In operational terms the representatives of the subculture to be studied were taken as the set (family and intimate friends) of the parasuicidal patient. For reasons already given the homologized group represented by all such friends and kind were studied collectively.

The final hypothesis constructed in consequence of these considerations was that the rate of parasuicide among the patients' sets would be higher than that in comparable groups from the general population. Just what is meant by 'comparable' in this context is not quite as straightforward as may at first appear; the point is taken up again in the Discussion section.

Method

Between 16 January and 31 March 1967 (approximately 10 ten weeks) an attempt was made by Dr Eng-Seong Tan to interview all parasuicides admitted to the centre. One patient who died, and who was therefore categorized as a suicide, was omitted: patients with multiple admissions were interviewed only once. For each patient identifying data were collected and the psychiatric diagnosis noted: in addition each was asked to name certain of his kin and close friends, as detailed below, with their approximate age and current address, and their addresses over the previous 4 years.

For a random sample of 10 per cent of the patients, information was sought in the same way from another family member at visiting times: in no case were discrepancies elicited between the patient's and the informant's account on any important detail such as the identity of family members, address at any relevant time, or age to within 5 years. The method of data collection thus seemed reasonably reliable.

The patients will be termed 'probands' and their relatives and friends 'contacts'. Among the contacts, those admitted to the RPTC during a 4-year survey period (between 1 January 1963 and 31 December 1966) were subsequently identified from the hospital registers. This retrospective design means that the positive contacts, i.e. those admitted for parasuicide, came into hospital prior to the probands' admissions.

The probands

Since the patient turnover is necessarily high at the RPTC many are discharged within a day of admission and it was not possible to interview all patients, especially as the interviewer could not be constantly present. During the study period 181 parasuicides were admitted at least once, and 135 were interviewed: the 46 patients not interviewed included one deaf-mute and one who was too ill, physically, at the close of the study. Table 4.6 relates the proband sample to all patients admitted by duration of stay, and shows that the greatest proportional deficity was among the very rapidly discharged patients, as would be anticipated. A comparison of the probands and total patient group by age and sex showed that each age-sex subgroup was represented in approximately equal proportions.

TABLE 4.6   Characteristics of proband sample by duration of stay

Length of stay in days	No. of patients admitted			No. of patients interviewed			Percentage of patients interviewed
	M	F	Total	M	F	Total	M + F
0 —	5	4	9	3	1	4	44.4
1 —	19	34	53	10	20	30	56.6
2 —	19	37	56	16	27	43	76.8
3 —	11	15	26	11	14	25	96.1
4 +	19	18	37	17	16	33	89.2
Total	73	108	181	57	78	135	74.6

The contacts

Each proband was asked to identify and to give the details already specified about his or her father, mother, spouse, children, siblings' spouses: he was also asked to name two close friends and to indicate if they were blood-kin, e.g. cousins. Only those contacts were considered who were alive and resident in Edinburgh for at least part of the 1963—6 period and who were known to be aged 15 or over. The population considered to be at risk consisted of 578 individuals, with men and

TABLE 4.7   Type of kinship of contact population by sex of proband

Type of kinship	No. for male probands	No. for female probands	Total
Spouse	25	34	59
Father	20	27	47
Mother	30	30	60
Child	9	32	41
Twin	1	0	1
Sibling	93	78	171
Half-sib	0	1	1
Sib's spouse	59	54	113
Friend — unrelated	32	49	81
Friend — related	0	4	4
Total	269	309	578

women represented in approximately equal proportions. Table 4.7 shows the composition of the group by type of kinship.

Calculation of expected numbers

Full details of the statistical method have been reported elsewhere (Kreitman *et al.*, 1969, 1970) and the following account is mainly concerned with the general principles.

Rates relating to 1962—3 had already been established by Kessel (1965a) and McCulloch (1965) who kindly made their data available for further analysis. Other data already existed for rates in the city of Edinburgh over the survey period (1963—6): where definitive information was lacking it was possible to make estimates likely to be reasonably accurate. It could thus be calculated for *each* of the 578 contacts the expectation of being admitted at least once to the RPTC for parasuicide during the survey period, on the assumption that each individual was subject to the admission rates which would apply to an 'equivalent person' randomly sampled from the general population of Edinburgh. In determining the expectation of admission attention was paid to the individual contact's

(1) sex
(2) age at the mid-point of the survey, and
(3) area of residence.

By the use of 'area factors' (similar to standardized morbidity ratios) it was possible to represent concisely the effect of a wide range of variables other than age and sex which are correlated with rates of parasuicide (see section 4.1).

(4) Duration of exposure. For each contact the time spent in each ward during the survey period, or time spent outside the city, was recorded to the nearest month and in the calculations due allowance was made for any change of address. Individuals whose addresses were not known for any part of the 4-year period were assumed to be living in the ward with the highest risk of admission; the small bias so introduced would tend to support the null hypothesis.

Having established for each contact his likelihood of admission it was then possible to determine the total number of individuals expected to be admitted in the whole group of contacts (or any subgroup thereof). This expected number was then compared with the number actually identified.

Results

17 members of the contact population were admitted to the centre at least once during the survey period. This is significantly greater than the expected number of 4.23 obtained from the computations detailed above.($p < .001$).

Further analyses were made according to the characteristics of (1) the probands, (2) the contacts, and (3) proband/positive-contact pairs.

(1) By proband characteristics

Duration of stay It will be recalled that the sample of probands under-represented patients rapidly discharged from the ward during the study. The sample was therefore dichotomized at 2 days (as suggested by Table 4.6) and the number of positive contacts (E) to be expected for each group was calculated. It was not desired, however, to test for an excess in each of the groups individually but rather

TABLE 4.8 Proband characteristics: age and sex, and distribution of positive contacts

Proband characteristic	No. of contacts at risk	Positive contacts		
		No. observed (O)	No. expected (E)	Proportion expected (E^1)
Sex				
male	269	8	2.11	8.48
female	309	9	2.12	8.52
Total	578	17	4.23	17.00
	$x^2 = 0.054$ df = 1 $p < 0.80$			
Age				
−34	299	14	2.27	8.93
35+	279	3	1.96	8.07
Total	578	17	4.23	17.00
	$x^2 = 6.063$ df = 1 $p < 0.02$			
Age and sex				
M−34	135	5	1.17	4.70
35+	134	3	0.94	3.78
F−34	164	9	1.10	4.42
35+	145	0	1.02	4.10
Total	578	17	4.23	17.00
	$x^2 = 9.026$ df = 3 $p < 0.05$			

to determine whether the magnitude of the excess was proportionately the same in both. Therefore in this, and in the following comparisons, the calculated expected numbers in each group have been multiplied by the ratio of the total observed parasuicides (17) to the total expected (4.23). Thus the revised expected numbers (E^1) have been made to total the observed number (17) and the observed and expected distributions between groups have been compared using a χ^2 test. For duration of stay no significant difference was found between the briefly admitted group and the others.

Age and sex   Age and sex were considered in an analogous manner, and the results are given in Table 4.8. There appears to be no difference in the frequency with which men or women have a positive contact, but patients below 35 years of age have a relative excess, and older patients a relative lack of such contacts ($p < .02$). The data also suggest ($p < .05$) that this age effect is principally found among women, though the numbers on which this calculation is based are small.

Mode of suicidal attempt   Distinguishing probands who had taken drug overdoses from those who had used gas or injured themselves, as in Table 4.9, shows that all the positive contacts were among the entourage of the self-poisoners. Mode of attempt is thus significantly associated with the distribution of positive contacts ($p < .05$).

Other variables examined for an effect on the distribution of positive contacts included social class, marital status, previous admissions to the RPTC, the psychiatric diagnosis on admission, personality type, birth order, and size of sibship. None yielded statistically significant findings.

TABLE 4.9   Proband characteristics: mode of attempt and distribution of positive contacts

Mode of attempt	No. of contacts at risk	Positive contacts		Proportion expected
		No. observed	No. expected	
		(O)	(E)	(E^1)
Drugs	476	17	3.34	13.42
Other	102	0	0.89	3.58
Total	578	17	4.23	17.00

$\chi^2 = 4.535$, df = 1, $p < 0.05$.

(2) By contact characteristics

It seemed possible that certain classes of the contact population might be especially likely to have an excess of 'positives' among them. Age and sex were found to be unimportant in this connection, nor could it be shown that any one of seven types of kinship with the proband was specially at risk. Although the number of contacts in each kinship category was sometimes small, it seemed important to consider the possibility that the excess of positive contacts in the population at risk might reflect genetic linkage with the probands. Kinship categories were therefore summarized into those with blood relationships (parents, siblings, children, and related friends) and those without blood ties (spouses, spouses of sibs, and unrelated friends). No significant difference was found.

(3) Patient—contact relationship

Finally the 17 pairs of patients and their positive contacts were examined.

Time interval   The time interval between the admissions of the contacts and the probands can be seen in Table 4.10. Since three contacts had multiple admissions within the survey period, data for the contacts' first and latest admissions are shown separately. Though the numbers are very small it can be seen that most of the contacts' admissions (by either classification) tend to fall in the latter part of the survey period.

TABLE 4.10   Interval between admission of positive contacts and patients in 1967

Year of contacts' admission	Interval between admissions (years*)	No. of positive contacts admitted at stated interval	
		First admission of contact	Last admission of contact
1963	4	4	2
1964	3	2	2
1965	2	4	3
1966	1	7	10

*Represents difference in calendar years of admissions, not actual dates.

Age, sex and kinship   The small number of pairs and the diversity of kinships make the data little more than anecdotal in this context. Table 4.11 illustrates the matching between probands and positive contacts by age, sex, and the kinship of the contact *to* the proband. No female patient over 35 had a positive contact, and no positive contacts were men over 35. Nearly all the positive male contacts were brothers. Within the series there was no statistically significant concordance for age or sex. The averages of the probands on admission and the positive contacts at the mid-point of the survey period were very similar, with respective means and standard errors of 25.5 ± 1.9 and 24.9 ± 3.2.

Diagnosis   There was no significant association within the series of pairs on illness diagnosis using four broad diagnostic categories. The personality diagnosis (see chapter 2) of one positive contact was uncertain; among the remaining 16 pairs, eleven were alike in being classified as normal or abnormal, evidence for the latter being addiction to drugs, alcoholism or markedly psychopathic behaviour. This rather high proportion is of interest but is not great enough to permit rejection of the null hypothesis.

TABLE 4.11   Age, sex, and relationship of positive contact to probands

	Probands			
	Male		Female	
Positive contacts	−34	35+	−34	35+
Male				
−34	Brother Brother Brother	Brother	Brother Brother Boyfriend	
35+				
Female				
−34	Girlfriend Sister-in-law	Wife Step-daughter	Daughter Sister Sister-in-law	
35+			Mother Friend Friend	

Precipitating events   An explanation of the findings might be that the paired parasuicidal episodes might simply reflect common stresses falling on several family members at the same time. This argument is more complex than at first appears and its relevance to the main hypothesis is uncertain, but nevertheless the case records were examined in some detail to determine whether such common stresses could be detected. In two pairs it appeared that the act of one partner could be construed as a consequence of that by the other, but there was no evidence of a common cause. Similarly, there was no evidence in the remaining 15 pairs of any common precipitating events, and there were no examples of suicide pacts. On the other hand, the case notes often testified to the poor organization and social inadequacy of many of the families, an observation in keeping with the subcultural hypothesis rather than against it.

Discussion

The central methodological problem in this study, if its rationale is accepted, has been the estimation of the number of individuals among the contacts who would be expected to have at least one episode of hospital treatment for parasuicide during the survey period. Demonstration of an excess of observed to expected positive contacts in such a population, with expectation derived solely from data on age, sex, and duration of risk, would be inadequate, since such a result could be interpreted to mean little more than that the families and close friends of the probands shared the social stresses which are so widespread among patients attempting suicide. To make allowance for commonality of experience, 'area factors' have been used to supplement demographic data. These factors reflect not only defined variables likely to influence rates of attempted suicide but also further and as yet unidentified variables which at present can only be demonstrated geographically. How far the patients are typical of their areas has been explored elsewhere (Philip and McCulloch, 1966; McCulloch and Philip, 1967b). Here it must be mentioned that characteristics which distinguish the city wards may also distinguish between the patient (and his family) and the rest of the population within his own ward. Thus a level of social disorganization which is typical of a particular ward may under-represent the amount of disorganization to be found among the parasuicides (and their families) within that ward. In so far as this is so, the expected number of positive cases in the contact population will have been under-estimated. Even though compensatory biases have occurred at other stages of the analysis the results must clearly be interpreted with caution.

The most important single finding was the four-fold excess of the observed to expected number of positive contacts. This alone does not establish the 'language' theory of parasuicide but certainly enables the hypothesis to survive a possible refutation.

Significantly more younger than older probands had a positive contact and there was evidence that the age effect might be particularly important for women. Both these findings are in accord with what is known of other forms of 'communicated' psychopathology, such as epidemic hysteria and *folie à deux*. It was also found that positive contacts were significantly more numerous for probands using self-poisoning than for those inflicting self-injury. It is noteworthy that the rapid rise in admission rates for parasuicide in Edinburgh over the last 7 years (chapter 2) has been entirely due to increasing self-poisoning: it is thus possible that the rise is at least partly due to 'contagious' case-to-case spread. However, the present data relate to the existence of a special subculture rather than its possible expansion, while the concept of communication implicit in such terms as epidemic hysteria or contagion is rather different from that developed at the beginning of this section.

Among the contact population, age and sex did not influence the proportional excess of positive individuals. It was also found that those contacts linked genetically with the probands had no significant excess of positive cases when compared with the remainder. Any familial transmission of predisposition to parasuicide is therefore likely to be cultural rather than genetic.

If it is correct that the findings are compatible with the communication hypothesis, then the 'recipients' in the communication process, namely the probands, have been more closely identified than the 'transmitters' or positive contacts. It may well be that only certain classes of individuals behave as members of the parasuicide information system. But clearly further understanding would require close study of pairs of individuals. In this respect the present study has yielded too few examples for adequate analysis, and can only serve as a pointer. The data showed that 17/135 or approximately 12.5 per cent of hospital-treated patients in the series were members of pairs in which both individuals had a recent history of parasuicide. Routine data collection in 1973 and 1974 on all admissions indicates that that proportion is reasonably constant. With a 'yield' of this size further studies should be feasible.

Lastly, it may be mentioned that the test of the signal theory described here is only one of many possible tests. Only 'symmetrical' responses, where the form of communication (the act) is alike in both the positive contact and the proband have been considered, for reasons already explained. But it seems highly likely that other forms of behaviour are more typical antecedents or consequences of suicidal attempts and might provide a less constricted (or stringent) method of testing. Their delineation and the study might contribute not only to a further understanding of parasuicide but of pathological systems of communication in general.

NOTE

1 More precisely, that the two individuals share a code of interpersonal behaviour, and one which they are both activating. Logical distinctions can be drawn between the concepts of (a) information, (b) a signal, and (c) the code of which a given signal is part. These will not be pursued here, but it may be taken that in the human context at least the idea of a signal and of a codified system of meaning are mutually dependent. There can be no signal without a code, and no 'natural' (operative) codes without signals.

5

PSYCHOLOGICAL STUDIES

The general aim of the studies reported in this chapter is to provide some psychological information of a descriptive nature on those citizens of Edinburgh and its environs who were admitted to the RPTC. When these studies were being considered there was already in existence a considerable body of psychiatric and social information on the patients. It was felt that a descriptive psychological approach would complement the information gathered from these earlier studies and would provide pointers to areas worthy of more detailed psychological enquiry. The paucity of psychological test data on parasuicide in Britain and the varied quality of the data available from other parts of the world made it imperative to adopt a broad approach.

The admission policy of the Poisoning Treatment Centre (chapter 1) had led to the population under study being more diverse in its characteristics than groups of parasuicides studied elsewhere. Compared with other centres the Edinburgh population contains fewer psychiatrically ill persons; distress, unhappiness, and impulsiveness are more common than delusions. No 'attempted suicide personality' has been identified by psychiatrists or social workers, although these clinicians have frequently commented on the high frequency of impulsive behaviour, poor interpersonal relationships, and undesirable social conditions in parasuicide.

5.1 THE PSYCHOLOGICAL LITERATURE

Most of the literature emanates from the United States and the majority of persons tested have been psychiatric inpatients in Veterans Administration hospitals. Even when reports on completed suicides are excluded, the studies under review are concerned with very diverse aspects of suicidal behaviour; they deal with persons who have 'attempted suicide', threatened suicide or thought about suicide. These recurring biases in American studies must be kept in mind when assessing the relevance of American studies to British populations.

The tests used fall into three main categories; projective techniques, questionnaires and inventories, and semantic measures. Prominent in the first category have been the Rorschach Inkblots and the Thematic Apperception Test while the Minnesota Multiphasic Personality Inventory has been the most commonly used questionnaire. Semantic measures such as semantic differential techniques and repertory grids have been used less frequently than might have been expected in view of their flexibility.

Projective techniques

The Rorschach has long been the most popular psychological technique in the United States (Sundberg, 1961) despite having been subjected to several scathing

76

reviews, one of the most recent being that by Jensen (1964). Many studies on 'attempted suicide' have used this technique and a variety of strategies have been employed; global assessments, ratios of one scoring category to another, single signs, multiple signs, and content analyses have all been used in the search for the 'suicidal Rorschach'.

Neuringer (1965), in an excellent summary of the work on suicide carried out with the Rorschach, pointed out that contradictory and equivocal results had frequently been due to methodological inadequacies and poor designs. Almost all of the studies surveyed by Neuringer had been retrospective, utilizing protocols culled from files and case records. The time lag between testing and suicide, in the cases where patients had killed themselves, was often one of years rather than months or days. The use of such varied data, especially when coupled with the omnibus definitions of suicidal behaviour used by many researchers, mitigated against the Rorschach producing useful results. Neuringer concluded that there were no specific signs predicting suicide on the Rorschach and that only the check-list devised by Martin (1952) had shown some consistency in identifying suicidal persons over varying conditions.

The Thematic Apperception Test, or TAT, was devised by Murray (1943) to assess the needs and influences, or presses, which determine an individual's behaviour. Since the psychosocial aspects of suicidal behaviour have been widely recognized, it is surprising that the TAT has been used so infrequently. If the Rorschach has been over-popular then certainly the TAT has been neglected.

Shneidman and Farberow (1958) attempted to relate the characteristics of the heroes of TAT stories narrated by patients with the suicidal and non-suicidal behaviour of the latter. They were unable to distinguish suicidal and non-suicidal records at a level better than chance.

Questionnaires and inventories

The MMPI (Hathaway and McKinley, 1943) enjoys a status in the field of self-administered tests comparable with that of the Rorschach among projective techniques. Many American hospitals and clinics administer the MMPI to every patient, a state of affairs which has facilitated retrospective studies.

None of the MMPI scales have been shown to differentiate 'suicidal' from non-suicidal patients with any degree of consistency. A series of studies (Farberow, 1950; Devries and Farberow, 1967; Devries, 1967) showed that more differences on MMPI items between suicidal and non-suicidal respondents occurred when more refined definitions of suicidal behaviour were used and when a variety of demographic variables, such as age, and mental state, were taken into account.

Vinoda (1966) used two inventories, the Hysteroid Obsessoid Questionnaire, or HOQ (Caine and Hope, 1967), and the Hostility and Direction of Hostility Questionnaire, or HDHQ (Caine et al., 1967), in her study which was the first British report on the psychological test characteristics of persons who 'attempt suicide'. The HOQ did not differentiate 'attempted suicides' from her psychiatric or general medical control patients but on the HDHQ the 'attempted suicide' group showed more total hostility than either control group.

Semantic measures

Despite possessing flexibility and the backing of well-elaborated theoretical positions (Osgood et al., 1957; Kelly, 1955), semantic differentials and repertory grids have been used infrequently in studying persons who have behaved in a life-endangering manner. Neuringer (1961, 1967) tested the notion that neurotic-suicidal individuals tended to think in terms of dichotomies. Such thinking, in which there were only blacks and whites, never any greys, trapped the individual in his own system by allowing very few alternatives to be seen in any situation. His study showed that dichotomous evaluative thinking was a characteristic common to many emotionally disturbed persons and was not a form of thinking exclusive to suicidal individuals.

Tatossian and Blumen (1965) compared the semantic differentials of 67 normal French adolescents with those of 27 adolescents who had made a 'suicidal attempt'. The 'attempted suicides' differed from normals only in so far as they used the scales in an all-or-nothing manner reminiscent of Neuringer's subjects. The authors concluded that adolescents who attempted suicide demonstrated in an accentuated fashion traits present in normal adolescence.

Kelly's theory of Personal Constructs (Kelly, 1955) has been popularized in Britain by Bannister (1965). His repertory grid is an idiographic technique and its use in the study of a suicidal individual has been demonstrated by Ryle (1967) who elicited intra-psychic and interpersonal relationships which had value in explaining his patients' suicidal behaviour.

In summary all the major tests in the psychological armamentarium have been used, with varying degrees of sophistication, in the quest for the 'suicidal personality'. Such a quest has been unsuccessful, the results from projective techniques and questionnaire methods alike being equivocal in many instances and contradictory in others. Most of the reports are American and reflect a predeliction towards viewing suicidal threats, suicidal attempts, and completed suicides as phenomena differing in degree rather than in kind. With a few notable exceptions most psychological researchers in this area have displayed a remarkable indifference to the need for adequate definitions of various suicidal behaviours.

In general the methodology of recent papers is better than that of earlier publications but there is plenty of room for improvement. Further, it is doubtful whether men who are inpatients in Veterans Administration psychiatric hospitals and who at some time have threatened or attempted suicide, or who on some subsequent occasion commit suicide, are representative of the threatened suicide, 'attempted suicide', or committed suicide populations of the United States. None the less, such men have formed the majority of persons tested.

These failings in theory and methodology are serious and it must be concluded that the American psychological literature offers little to the researcher investigating the personality characteristics of people who have made a 'suicidal attempt'. The British contribution to this literature, prior to the work to be reported, had been the single study of Vinoda so that the need for a study which presented an overall picture of the personality variables characteristic of parasuicides was very real.

5.2 THE EDINBURGH PSYCHOLOGICAL STUDIES

Two groups of patients were tested psychologically in separate projects which can be conveniently called Study A and Study B. The first group were those seen by McCulloch and Philip (1967b) where the main aim was to ascertain the incidence of certain indicators and where psychological testing played a minor role; the second group (Philip, 1968) were seen with psychological assessment as the main aim. Although the psychological information gained from Study A was limited in range, it allowed comparisons with Vinoda's solitary British study and, in retrospect, helped in the interpretation of results obtained in Study B.

The tests used were chosen because they fulfilled the following criteria: they were objective, standardized instruments which were developed within the framework of formal theories of personality, namely those of Foulds (1965) and Cattell (1965); a substantial body of data relating to normal and psychiatric patients was available for all the instruments, thus facilitating comparisons between parasuicides and other groups, and they had been used extensively in both clinical work and research by the investigator who was in consequence familiar with their administration as well as their strengths and weaknesses.

The Sixteen Personality Factor Questionnaire, or 16PF (Cattell and Eber, 1965), attempts to cover a wide range of personality traits while its derivative, the Neuroticism Scale Questionnaire, or NSQ (Scheier and Cattell, 1961), comprises those personality factors which best differentiate normals from known neurotics. The Symptom Sign Inventory, or SSI (Foulds and Hope, 1968), and the Hostility and Direction of Hostility Questionnaire, or HDHQ (Caine, Foulds, and Hope, 1967), are intended to measure psychiatric symptoms in the case of the former and punitive attitudes in the case of the latter.

The patients tested

Study A was based on 108 patients who had been admitted to the RPTC following an episode of parasuicide. Testing was done as soon as possible after admission. The very fast turnover made it difficult to interview or test every individual passing through the ward. Further, drowsy patients cannot cope with the exacting task of completing personality questionnaires until they are much more alert. By the time they have reached this stage of recovery they are usually ready for discharge and are much less willing to remain. Of the 108 patients, 95 were interviewed (McCulloch and Philip, 1967b) but for a variety of reasons eleven of these patients were not tested; the remaining 84 comprised 32 men and 52 women. Reading difficulties prevented a further four of those tested from completing the NSQ.

A postal follow-up, in which the NSQ and the PI and CD scales of the SSI were sent to each of the 84 patients tested in hospital, was carried out some 5 weeks later. 71 per cent of the women responded to the follow-up and these responders did not differ from non-responders on any major social or clinical variable. Only 47 per cent of the men responded and they contained a significantly disproportionate number of patients who had a history of previous parasuicidal episodes.

In planning Study B it had been intended that every man and every second woman admitted would be tested until 50 patients of each sex had been gathered, but in practice this intention was not fulfilled. Psychological data (SSI, HDHQ, and 16PF) were gathered on 50 men and 50 women over a 5 month period in which time 329 patients (132 men, 197 women) were admitted one or more times for parasuicide. Failure to complete all the tests was due to a number of reasons, the most frequent being lack of understanding due to low intelligence, poor eyesight, illiteracy, impairment of function due to psychiatric state, refusing to complete the test battery, and leaving the ward before all the testing had been completed. The patients who were not interviewed or tested at all fell into two categories: those who stayed in the ward for less than 24 hours and those who were discharged much earlier than expected. It had been foreseen that the former group would prove difficult to run to ground; such patients had proved to be elusive in Study A. Failure to contact the latter group was primarily a function of patient turnover and an irregular pattern of admissions and discharges.

Because of this failure to sample the ward population according to plan it was felt that the patients who completed the test battery might be different in some aspects from those who did not. A check on the medical, social, and demographic data available from the routine data coding sheets was carried out using a random sample of 50 men and 50 women drawn from all the parasuicides admitted during the 5-month period previously mentioned. Data relating to age, civil state, length of stay in the ward, method of suicidal attempt, level of consciousness on admission, psychiatrist's estimate of degree of premeditation, occurrence of suicidal threats, motivating factors, history of previous attempts by the patient or a relative, history of psychiatric or chronic physical illness, abuse of alcohol or drugs, and psychiatric diagnosis were tabulated. The sexes were considered separately. There was only one statistically significant difference between the two groups of women, the random group having been given more diagnoses other than affective disorder or personality disorder. For men four significant differences— all interconnected—emerged: the tested patients were younger, had fewer of their number who stayed 1 day or less in hospital, used aspirin as a method of self-poisoning more often, and had fewer cases of problem drinking. Thus, as anticipated, male patients who stayed only briefly in the ward were under-represented. Although the two groups of women did not differ significantly on this item, they did show a difference in the same direction.

Despite this discrepancy it seems that the patients who were interviewed and completed psychological testing did not differ greatly from the generality of parasuicides in regard to a variety of social and clinical factors, and that with due caution their psychological test results can be generalized to the RPTC population as a whole.

The tests used

The Sympton Sign Inventory

Since both the present author and Vinoda were much influenced by the work of Foulds (1965), the instrument chosen for psychometric classification, both in Edinburgh and in Essex, was the Symptom Sign Inventory, an orally administered test. Its development as a diagnostic measure has been well documented and it is closely bound up with Foulds' theory of personality dysfunction.

Foulds has been concerned to develop measures of traits and attitudes on the one hand, and signs and symptoms on the other, these measures to be independent of each other whenever possible. He considers that traits and attitudes can be distinguished from symptoms and signs in three ways. Traits and attitudes are very common while symptoms and signs are not; the former are essentially egosyntonic while the latter are distressing, either to the patients or his intimates, and lastly traits, and to a lesser extent attitudes, are relatively enduring while symptoms and signs are somewhat transient.

In the present studies two scales of the SSI, i.e. symptom measures, were used. The PD or Personal Disturbance scale (originally called the PI or Personal Illness scale) identifies people who experience difficulty in their personal relationships, this difficulty being so distressing to them or to their intimates that help is sought to alleviate their problems. The second scale, labelled CD or Character Disorder, attempts to identify persons, usually personally disturbed in the sense just defined, who have long-standing neurotic conditions marked by chronic interpersonal difficulties, plaintiveness, and the arousal of antipathy in those who treat them.

Based on the frequency distributions of PD scores for normals and psychiatric patients set out in the SSI *Manual* (Foulds and Hope, 1968) three categories of personal disturbance were set up. Scores of 0 and 1 were considered normal, scores of 2, 3 and 4 considered borderline, while scores of 5 and above reflected personal disturbance. Using these three categories the PD scale would not classify any normals as being personally disturbed, although 10 per cent of a normal group would fall within the borderline category. Only 10 per cent of a psychiatric population would be classed as normal and a further 26 per cent would be in the borderline category.

In using the CD scale with the PD scale the classifications indicated by the former have been given precedence; if an individual is classed as character disordered then his position on the PD scale is not considered. In practice, almost all individuals classed as character disordered would also be classed as personally disturbed.

The Hostility and Direction of Hostility Questionnaire

Foulds's theory of personality lays stress on the need to consider the individual as a person in relation to others. Whereas the ability to enter into mutual personal relations with others denotes the mature individual, egocentricity in thinking and behaving marks out the immature. One feature of egocentricity is the need to apportion blame in any given situation, either on to other people or the self, so that Foulds found punitiveness a useful attitudinal measure of egocentricity. The Hostility and Direction of Hostility Questionnaire, or HDHQ (Caine *et al.*, 1967), was devised to tap various aspects of punitive expression. There is little in the HDHQ which relates to physically expressed behaviour; indeed only six of the 50 test items carry physical connotations of aggressiveness. In consequence an individual scoring high on HDHQ Extrapunitiveness will tend to be cynical, resentful, and easily angered while high scores on Intropunitiveness will be due to frequent expression of self-doubt and self-criticism.

Philip (1969, 1973) has discussed how best to score the HDHQ. Intropunitiveness and Extrapunitiveness are scored separately rather than being combined in a 'Direction of Hostility' score and the extensive normative data presented by Philip (1973) has been used in preference to that contained in the *Manual*.

The 16 Personality Factor Questionnaire

This test, referred to as the 16PF (Cattell and Eber,1965), aims to provide a wide coverage of personality traits. Its theoretical basis lies in the many publications of Cattel, the simplest account of whose position is to be found in *The Scientific Analysis of Personality* (Cattell, 1965). Cattell, more than any other personality theorist, has insisted on the need for the multivariate analysis of personality and the 16PF is the major product of his factor analytic research. His considerable sophistication in the use of factor analysis, combined with an unfortunate predilection for coining neologisms when naming factors, has reduced the impact of his work but recent reviews (Klein, *et al.*, 1967; Goldberg, 1974) have shown a growing appreciation of his contribution to personality assessment.

The 16PF test assesses personality in terms of 16 first-order, obliquely related factors. The *Handbook for the Sixteen Personality Factor Questionnaire* (Cattel *et al.*, 1970) gives a detailed account of the design and rationale of the 16PF in its various forms. Because the first-order factors are intercorrelated to some extent, it is possible to derive from them a lesser number of broad-ranging but less exact secondary dimensions of personality. In the *Handbook* it is claimed that these secondary dimensions are essentially similar across different cultures. Philip (1972) demonstrated that this statement did not hold for all the secondary dimensions. Of the four second-order factors derived from the scores of a group of British normals only one, a dimension of anxiety, was readily identified as similar to the second-order factors listed in the *Handbook:* it can be considered as a measure of general psychological well-being. The second-order factors used were those identified by Philip as being appropriate to a British population.

In addition to the anxiety factor the well-known introversion-extraversion dimension manifests itself in two second-order factors one of which is concerned with social aspects, contrasting the socially shy, submissive person with the person who is outgoing, venturesome, and dominant in social matters, the other tapping more constitutional aspects, identifying at the introverted end of the dimension the person who is habitually aloof and distant from other people. The remaining second-order dimension is a form of tough versus tender-mindedness.

The raw scores of each 16PF scale are usually transformed into standardized scores called 'sten scores'. These scores are used to enable comparison of a person's score on one factor with his score on any other factor, irrespective of the means and variances.

The scores on the NSQ are also expressed in stens. This test was specifically designed to screen out relatively neurotic individuals using those 16PF personality factors, namely tender-mindedness (I+), reticence (F−), submissiveness (E−), and second-order factor anxiety (A+), which best differentiate normals from clinically diagnosed neurotics.

The 16PF, NSQ, and the HDHQ are, in Campbell's (1957) typology, 'voluntary, direct, structured' tests whose purpose is not concealed from the patient or subject. Self-report questionnaires are open to motivated distortion and also to biases due to response sets. Both were carefully considered in the present context, but it was concluded that there was no reason to doubt that the majority of patients are well motivated to be co-operative and truthful in their responses.

Results

Pyschometric measurement of psychiatric disturbance

SSI

The SSI results of women tested in Study A are compared directly in Table 5.1 with the findings of Vinoda (1966). Both groups of parasuicidal women contain

TABLE 5.1   SSI results for Edinburgh Study A and Vinoda's patients

SSI category	Edinburgh Study A		Vinoda's patients (all women)		
	Men %	Women %	Parasuicides %	Psychiatric %	Surgical %
Normal	19	8	8	20	78
Personally ill	31	33	52	56	22
Character disordered	50	59	40	24	0
	$n = 32$	$n = 52$	$n = 50$	$n = 50$	$n = 50$

Character disorder: Edinburgh women/Vinoda's women

$\chi^2 = 3.85$ df = 1 $p < 0.05$

many more character disordered individuals than occur in Vinoda's control groups, but the Edinburgh group has almost 20 per cent more character disorders than Vinoda's patients. (The most likely reason for this difference is that Vinoda's parasuicides were psychiatric inpatients while the RPTC group were unscreened and can be expected to contain a high proportion of character disordered patients who would not be offered or would not accept psychiatric inpatient treatment.) Male parasuicides in Study A yield slightly fewer character disordered individuals than their female counterparts, a difference which disappears if the male cutting point on the CD scale is made at the same place as that for women.

The SSI results for parasuicide tested in Study B are shown in Table 5.2 together with SSI data gathered on a comparison group of patients from the gastro-intestinal ward of a general hospital awaiting some decision regarding treatment, including major surgery, and many of whom emerge as being personally disturbed (Philip and Cay, 1971). While almost half of the parasuicides are seen to be character disordered the incidence of such disorder in the control group is low.

Comparative information on the incidence of SSI-determined character disorder in psychiatric populations is available from Vinoda (1966), McIver and Presly (1974), and an unpublished series gathered by Philip. These three sources are in close agreement, and it can be accepted that an SSI 'diagnosis' of character disorder occurs in about 23 per cent of psychiatric patients.

TABLE 5.2   SSI results for Study B and a control group

SSI category	Study B %	Medical/surgical patients %
Normal	12	27
Borderline	20	29
Personally disturbed	20	35
Character disordered	48	9
	$n = 100$	$n = 79$

Character disorder: $\chi^2 = 29.95$ df = 1 $p < 0.001$

Both Edinburgh studies indicate that about half of any group of parasuicides will produce psychiatric symptomatology indicative of character disorder. This proportion is twice that expected in a psychiatric population and is five times greater than the incidence observed in a group of general hospital patients. A further 20 per cent of the parasuicides in Study B were personally disturbed without being character disordered; this group would manifest marked anxiety and depression. These symptoms would also be exhibited by the borderline disturbed group, but less markedly.

The follow-up from Study A indicates that various changes in SSI symptomatology may occur. Of the 29 patients who were character disordered on initial testing only 14 were still character disordered at retest. Of the 22 initially deemed not to be character disordered six became disordered by the time of follow-up.

These findings raise the general problem of the use of a symptom-based scale to identify an enduring personality trait. McIver (1969) showed that although character disordered psychiatric inpatients showed a reduction in symptomatology when retested, so that most of them were no longer classed as character disordered by the SSI scale, this reduction gave no more than an appearance of improvement in interpersonal relations. At times of crisis, character-disordered individuals over-react with desperate, manipulative behaviour and intense self-pity. This last results in a mass of depressive symptomatology and a high character disorder score. It was only at these peaks of disturbance that character disorders were identified by the SSI scale. Non-symptom indices of character disorder have not yet been perfected. Until then it will remain necessary for clinicians working with parasuicide to look beyond the symptoms of distress to the personal maladjustment which characterizes a high proportion of patients.

Hostility in parasuicide and others

The mean scores obtained by men and women in Study B on the HDHQ are shown in Table 5.3. The values found for Vinoda's 'attempted suicide' group of women are also given. Within the Edinburgh group men are more extrapunitive in the expression of hostile attitudes as measured both by direction of hostility ($t = 3.04$, df = 98, $p < .005$) and extrapunitiveness ($t = 2.00$, df = 98, $p < .05$). Edinburgh women have a higher general hostility mean score than Vinoda's women ($t = 2.48$, df = 98, $p < .025$) but do not differ in the direction of their expression of hostility. (This difference in general hostility, like the difference in the number of

TABLE 5.3   Mean scores for men and women parasuicides on the HDHQ

	Edinburgh Study B				Vinoda's study	
	Men (n = 50)		Women (n = 50)		Women (n = 50)	
	Mean	(sd)	Mean	(sd)	Mean	(sd)
General hostility	26.78	(8.62)	25.08	(9.37)	21.06	(6.44)
Direction of hostility	0.52	(8.19)	5.18	(6.92)	4.38	(6.08)
Extrapunitiveness	16.28	(6.69)	13.66	(6.25)	–	–
Intropunitiveness	10.50	(4.06)	11.42	(4.42)	–	–

TABLE 5.4   Rounded Mean Scores on extrapunitiveness and intropunitiveness

	n	Extrapunitiveness	Intropunitiveness
Men			
Normal subjects (Philip, 1973)	218	10	5
General hospital patients (Philip and Cay, 1971)	40	10	5
Psychiatric inpatients (Philip, unpublished data)			
Neurotics	55	12	10
Personality disorders	84	13	11
Prisoners (Warder, 1969)	48	14	8
Parasuicides (Study B)	50	16	11
Women			
Normal subjects (Philip, 1973)	330	8	7
General hospital patients (Philip and Cay, 1971)	32	8	6
Psychiatric inpatients (Philip, unpublished data)			
Neurotics	102	10	9
Personality disorders	29	12	10
Attempted suicides (Vinoda, 1966)	50	11	10
Parasuicides (Study B)	50	14	11

character disorders in each group, is probably due to Vinoda's 'attempted suicides' being a selected, psychiatric inpatient group, as already mentioned.)

The factorially defined dimensions of extrapunitiveness and intropunitiveness (Philip, 1973) are closer to the original formulations of hostility made by Foulds *et al.* (1960) than the component scores used in the HDHQ *Manual* and it is possible to calculate these factor-based scores for various relevant studies published before Philip's paper. Since in many cases it is possible only to calculate the means and not the standard deviations, Table 5.4 presents only rounded mean scores on extrapunitiveness and intropunitiveness for various clinical groups. Rounded standard deviations for normal men and normal women are ± 4 for extrapunitiveness and ± 3 for intropunitiveness. Parasuicides, both men and women, are the most extrapunitive of all the groups considered and among the highest for intropunitiveness too.

It has been shown (Tables 5.1 and 5.2) that almost half of the parasuicides seen in Edinburgh are character disordered, using the SSI scale. Character disordered and non-character disordered parasuicides differ greatly in their expression of punitive attitudes; male parasuicides who are not character disordered have punitiveness scores similar to those obtained by Warder's violent offenders, while female non-character disordered parasuicides are indistinguishable from psychiatric inpatients. Both male and female character disordered parasuicides are simultaneously extremely extrapunitive and intropunitive, their mean scores being more than two standard deviations above the means for normals on the two scales.

Foulds (1965) has long considered general hostility to be an indicator of poor interpersonal relations. Although the idea of 'general' hostility is not completely logical it is a measure which has empirical value. Individuals who are character disordered were found by Foulds (1967) to have almost unlimited reserves of self-pity, and he suggested that they are highly motivated to evoke the pity of others. Their self-pity is accompanied by more extrapunitive attitudes which tend to evoke not pity but rejection. The simultaneous presentation of anger and resentment with self-pity and the soliciting of the pity of others is comparatively unusual in everyday human discourse and for the character disordered individual proves to be a self-defeating combination.

Factored personality traits in parasuicide and others

The mean scores obtained by the parasuicides of Study B on the factors of the 16PF are shown in Table 5.5 along with the mean scores of Philip's group of normals (Philip, 1972). Parasuicides differ from normals on twelve of the 16 primary factors. It should be remembered that the values in the table are sten scores and that in a standard normal distribution 1 sten is equal to one-half of a standard deviation. Thus a difference of 1 between two mean scores on the 16PF indicates quite a large difference between the groups being compared. The comparison shows that, compared with normals, parasuicides in Cattell's terminology are more outgoing, less intelligent, less stable, less enthusiastic, less conscientious, less venturesome, more suspecting, more self-absorbed, more apprehensive, less radical, more self-sufficient, and more tense.

TABLE 5.5   Sten scores of parasuicides and normals on the primary and second order factors of the 16PF

	Parasuicides (n = 100)		Normals (n = 284)		Levels of significant differences between means using t test
	Mean	(sd)	Mean	(sd)	
Primary factors (high score descriptions)					
A (outgoing)	5.78	(1.77)	5.26	(1.96)	0.05
B (intelligent)	6.41	(1.87)	7.55	(1.63)	0.001
C (stable)	3.64	(2.14)	5.75	(1.86)	0.001
E (dominant)	5.39	(1.78)	5.82	(2.18)	NS
F (enthusiastic)	5.15	(1.89)	5.80	(2.13)	0.01
G (conscientious)	4.21	(1.83)	5.11	(1.82)	0.001
H (venturesome)	4.18	(1.81)	4.95	(1.92)	0.001
I (sensitive)	5.71	(1.79)	5.68	(2.15)	NS
L (suspecting)	6.60	(2.04)	5.23	(2.02)	0.001
M (self-absorbed)	6.24	(1.66)	5.74	(1.90)	0.05
N (sophisticated)	5.16	(2.09)	5.42	(2.17)	NS
O (apprehensive)	7.53	(1.99)	5.77	(1.75)	0.001
Q_1 (radical)	5.29	(1.91)	5.87	(1.85)	0.01
Q_2 (self-sufficient)	6.55	(1.83)	5.81	(2.14)	0.001
Q_3 (self-controlled)	4.61	(2.22)	5.01	(2.08)	NS
Q_4 (tense)	7.08	(2.07)	5.38	(1.95)	0.001
Second-order factors					
Anxiety	7.48	(2.00)	5.42	(1.32)	0.001
Social extraversion	5.52	(1.36)	5.71	(1.74)	NS
Constitutional extraversion	5.44	(1.35)	5.44	(1.46)	NS
Tender-mindedness	6.04	(1.19)	5.61	(1.37)	0.01

These differences are more readily assimilated when the second-order factors are compared; parasuicides score much higher on anxiety and tender-mindedness. Significant differences occur on all save one of the primary factors which contribute to anxiety; parasuicides are more affected by their feelings and more easily upset (C−), feel themselves to be timid and threat-sensitive (H−), are more suspicious and self-opinionated (L+), are more apprehensive, worrying, and self-reproaching (O+), and are more tense and over-wrought (Q_4+). Although they see themselves as being less self-controlled (Q_3−) than normals the difference between the group means is not significant.

Differences in tender-mindedness are due to differences on primary factors F, M, and Q_2, parasuicides being more serious, self-concerned and self-sufficient. The picture presented is one of withdrawal from social contact and social reality rather than tender-mindedness in its more commonly accepted sense.[1]

Table 5.6 compares the mean scores of parasuicides on the 16PF with the mean scores of a large group of psychiatric patients (Philip, unpublished data). In contrast to the host of differences which exist between parasuicides and normals the differences in Table 5.6 concern three primary factors only: parasuicides are more dominant (E+), less conscientious (G−), and less self-controlled (Q_3−) than

TABLE 5.6   Sten scores of parasuicides and psychiatric patients on the primary and second-order factors of the 16PF

	Parasuicides (n = 100)		Psychiatric patients (n = 306)		Level of significant differences between means using t test
	Mean	(sd)	Mean	(sd)	
Primary factors (high score descriptions)					
A (outgoing)	5.78	(1.77)	5.40	(1.86)	NS
B (intelligent)	6.41	(1.87)	6.65	(1.99)	NS
C (stable)	3.64	(2.14)	3.77	(2.06)	NS
E (dominant)	5.39	(1.78)	4.80	(2.20)	0.01
F (enthusiastic)	5.15	(1.89)	4.74	(2.15)	NS
G (conscientious)	4.21	(1.83)	4.91	(2.12)	0.01
H (venturesome)	4.18	(1.81)	4.11	(1.89)	NS
I (sensitive)	5.71	(1.79)	5.68	(2.00)	NS
L (suspecting)	6.60	(2.04)	6.15	(2.01)	NS
M (self-absorbed)	6.24	(1.66)	6.11	(1.98)	NS
N (sophisticated)	5.16	(2.09)	5.12	(2.11)	NS
O (apprehensive)	7.53	(1.99)	7.13	(2.02)	NS
Q_1 (radical)	5.29	(1.91)	5.56	(1.81)	NS
Q_2 (self-sufficient)	6.55	(1.83)	6.56	(1.89)	NS
Q_3 (self-controlled)	4.61	(2.22)	5.22	(2.22)	0.05
Q_4 (tense)	7.08	(2.07)	6.68	(2.08)	NS
Second-order factors					
Anxiety	7.48	(2.00)	7.05	(1.92)	NS
Social extraversion	5.52	(1.36)	4.90	(1.71)	0.001
Constitutional extraversion	5.44	(1.35)	5.18	(1.37)	NS
Tender-mindedness	6.04	(1.19)	6.05	(1.40)	NS

psychiatric inpatients. These differences combine to yield a significant difference between the groups on the second-order factor of social extraversion. Differences on the other second-order factors do not reach statistical significance (although the difference on anxiety, where parasuicides are higher than psychiatric inpatients, is not far short of the 5 per cent level of significance).

The high level of anxiety demonstrated in the parasuicides in both Study A and Study B is a striking finding. Cattell (1964) conceives of anxiety as a disorganizing force or symptom of disorganization rather than a drive or motivation, and such a formulation makes sense of what is known clinically and socially about groups who score high on anxiety. Adcock (1965) has made a good case for the view that Cattell's anxiety factor and Eysenck's neuroticism factor are measuring the same broad area of behaviour which can be called 'emotional upset'. From Cattell's description of the anxious person, showing on the one hand lack of confidence, dependency, and a sense of guilt and worthlessness, and on the other irritability, suspicion of others, and tenseness, it is easy to conclude that the broad term 'emotional upset' can include the behaviour shown by people who score high on general hostility. The correlation between anxiety and general hostility in parasuicides is 0.72, a figure which indicates that the two scales are measuring similar aspects of behaviour without being exactly equivalent.[2]

Reference has previously been made to McIver's (1969) observation that the amount of symptomatology shown by character disorders on the SSI may fluctuate. The follow-up part of Study A showed that some character disordered patients had lost much of their SSI pathology while others had acquired more symptoms. The men who replied to the follow-up request were not representative of the original male sample so Table 5.7 refers to women only. In that table, the initial follow-up NSQ scores are considered by status on the character disorder scale. The two groups who were initially not character disordered did not change on any of the NSQ factors. Those who were originally character disordered but who had lost symptomatology at follow-up became more lively and gay (F+) and less anxious, although their mean retest score on anxiety was still far above average. The The women who were character disordered on both occasions became less tough-minded (I−) and moved to an average point on that scale. But the point to be stressed is that while character disordered women may vary in the amount of psychiatric pathology they display, and may vary in the amount of emotional upset measured by Cattell's anxiety factor, they show a *chronically* high level of such upset.

The most interesting of the 16PF primary factors contributing to the high anxiety level shown by both groups of Edinburgh parasuicides are factors C, O, and

TABLE 5.7   Sten scores for initial NSQs and follow-up NSQs of woman in Study A

SSI category of CD at initial and follow-up test	Initial NSQ					Follow-up NSQ			
	n	I	F	E	Anxiety	I	F	E	Anxiety
not CD, not CD at f.u.	10	4.3	4.1	4.8	7.3	4.8	5.0	4.3	7.00
not CD, CD at f.u.	3	4.7	7.0	5.3	9.3	5.0	6.3	6.0	9.3
CD, not CD at f.u.	12	5.4	5.0	4.7	9.5	4.8	5.8	4.5	8.8
CD, CD at f.u.	9	3.9	5.1	4.6	9.3	5.8	4.4	4.6	9.1

Q_4. Factor C is essentially a trait of emotional integration, gauging the extent to which impulses are controlled and expressed in the pursuit of long-term goals (Cattel, 1957). It is suggested by Cattell that this trait is largely determined by early environmental factors; background variables associated with low scores on factor C include parental disharmony, emotional or over-protective mothering, and histories of truancy or delinquency. Individuals who score low on factor C are dissatisfied, tend to be excessively emotional when frustrated, and constantly complain about ill-health and lack of energy. Coupled with the findings of McCulloch and Philip (see Chapter 4) regarding high rates of various types of social disorder in parasuicides, the results for this trait suggest that some early parent-child relationships are involved in the development of these poorly integrated personalities. Factor O is considered by Cattell to be a dispositional trait, found in most psychiatric groups, which is best characterized by guilt—proneness. High scores on factor Q_4 reflect a high degree of tenseness and inability to relax. Individuals with high Q_4 scores frequently show an incapacity to handle their emotional responses, even in situations where no particular strain or pressure is being applied. Taken together, these three factors portray an individual who is constantly ill at ease, both physically and mentally, and has little control over such states.

Other important 16PF factors on which parasuicides differ from normals are more concerned with how these people interact with those around them. The suspiciousness and feelings of insecurity of factor L, the self-sufficiency and aloneness of factor Q_2, the lack of social spontaneity of factor H, the disregard for conventional morality and unwillingness to accede to cultural demands reflected in factor G, all point not only to a reduction of social contact but also to the asocial nature of whatever contact exists. Some aspects of these factors combine to make parasuicides appear more 'introverted' than normals, but it can be seen that this appearance is due to social aloofness and is quite different to the submissive, depressed kind of introversion shown by psychiatric inpatients.

Summary of psychometric results

Parasuicides present a great deal of psychiatric symptomatology of a neurotic or depressive nature (Kessel, 1965) and the symptomatology is more prevalent immediately after an attempt than at follow-up. The SSI findings are in agreement with this clinical observation but indicate that the pattern of such symptomatology is often such as to bring into prominence the more florid aspects of character disorder rather than to suggest one of the psychiatric illness diagnoses. Half of the parasuicide patients seen in Edinburgh are classed as character disordered on the SSI.[3]

Parasuicides are both more extrapunitive than normals or other kinds of patients tested on the HDHQ. Striking differences in the expression of hostile attitudes occur between character disordered and non-character disordered parasuicides, the former being extremely punitive while the latter are not too far removed from the normal range of such expression.

Parasuicides differ from normals on almost all the factors of the 16PF, especially on those factors contributing to second-order anxiety. On this latter factor parasuicides were more disturbed than pyschiatric patients, with character disordered parasuicides being the most disturbed of all. Anxiety as used in the 16PF and NSQ represents much more than 'butterflies in the stomach'. The parasuicide who has a high anxiety level is in a state of emotional upset which must affect his sense of judgement, his ability to plan adequately, and his reactions to environmental events. Follow-up has shown that this state of upset is not always transient; like the social problems which beset the typical parasuicide, emotional upset may be chronically present, with periods of acute exacerbation.

Emotional upset is the outstanding characteristic of parasuicidal patients, tending to dwarf other features of their personalities. The 16PF results indicate that many parasuicides display a particular form of withdrawal from social life. Their withdrawal from interpersonal contacts is best seen in the light of their lack of social conscience; they are aloof not because they are shy but because they have a disregard for group mores and conventions. This test-finding is consistent with their behaviour; social withdrawal frequently takes the form of leaving home or seeking escape from contact with people through drugs.

In conclusion it must however be stressed that just as clinically there is no 'suicidal personality' so also is there no unique psychological test profile for parasuicides. Impulsiveness and poor interpersonal relationships, high anxiety and hostility are common in parasuicide but they are not ubiquitous nor are such characteristics confined to this particular population.

5.3 RISK TAKING IN PARASUICIDES

Throughout this chapter there has been an emphasis on the *psychometric* psychological study of parasuicide. This does not mean that the present studies are the only source of information about the personalities of parasuicides; in other investigations psychological characteristics have been noted, but these data have been incidental to the main aims. One study (Kennedy *et al.*, 1971) is an exception in so far as it considered 'risk-taking' in parasuicides as a psychological or behavioural variable in its own right.

Cohen (1960) defined risk-taking as 'embarking on a task without being certain of success', and he agreed with Stengel and Cook (1958) that parasuicide is a form of risk-taking because the patient is usually uncertain of the toxicity of the overdose and uncertain whether others will intervene. Later, Stengel (1964) expanded this theoretical view suggesting that parasuicide, gambling and some accidents may all originate from the same need to take risks: he noted that each of these behaviours is associated with drinking alcohol, which Cohen showed had the effect of inducing individuals to take greater risks. At the same time, a concept of the urge to take risks, seen as a relatively stable attribute varying in strength from person to person, was given some validity on the basis of experimental work (Kogan and Wallach, 1964).

Psychoanalysts, including Freud (1904) and Menninger (1936), have often contended that accidents can be unconsciously purposive self-destructive acts. Evidence from accident research supports the assumptions that not all accidents are purely chance events and that individuals differ in their liability to accidents. Greenwood and Woods (1919) showed that the frequency distribution of accidents in munition workers fitted best, mathematically, with the hypothesis of initially unequal liabilities rather than pure chance or a bias in the direction of those who had been involved in at least one accident.

The parallel drawn between suicidal behaviour and gambling has long been evident in such phrases as 'the gamble with death' and 'Russian roulette'. Although in modern society money is the usual item exchanged by gamblers, the ancient Germans risked life, limb, and personal freedom over games of chance (Stekel, 1958), and the ancient Chinese apparently wagered fingers, limbs, and the hair on their heads (Cohen and Hansel, 1956). Moran (1970) investigated the hypothesis that if pathological gamblers are characteristically prone to morbid forms of risk-taking, they are more likely 'to attempt suicide', and among members of Gamblers Anonymous he found eight times the expected rate of parasuicide. It was against this background that Kennedy *et al.* (1971) tested the hypothesis that excessive risk-taking is an enduring habit or life style of parasuicides, who were predicted to have over-indulged in gambling and have more traffic accidents if they drive.

96 consecutive male admissions to the RPTC were compared with 151 consecutive male consulters at general practice surgeries in Edinburgh. The groups were closely similar on social class distribution, age, and civil state (although only the first of these variables was later found to be correlated with gambling).

It was found that significantly *fewer* parasuicides than controls gambled at all, and those who did gamble did so no more frequently, nor did they spend greater proportions of their incomes. Similarly, parasuicides were not more liable to traffic accidents, despite an excess of alcoholics in their number. 40 per cent of both groups were drivers and their accident rates, controlled for age and duration of driving, were no different for either occupational and non-occupational driving.

No correlation was found between gambling and traffic accidents, so that no support was found for the concept of risk-taking as a unitary trait. The pathological gambler's high propensity to parasuicide must have an alternative explanation; perhaps, as Moran himself suggested, it is more likely to be a consequence of social and economic failure. It could be argued of course that if a wider variety of 'risky activities' were studied the risk-taking trait might become manifest in parasuicides. Gambling and traffic accidents are so common, however, that it seemed reasonable to expect the hypothetical risk-taker to show his colours in these activities. Whatever the wider theoretical implications of these results, they indicate that gambling and traffic accidents are not special vices of parasuicides to be added to the long list of their deviant characteristics.

5.4 CONCLUDING COMMENTS

At the beginning of this chapter it was emphasized that the general aim of the two psychometric studies was to provide psychological information of a descriptive nature which would complement other studies and would point to areas worthy of more detailed enquiry. The salient features of the patients studied were the high incidence of psychiatric symptomatology, associated with personality disorder rather than mental illness, and the degree to which 'emotional upset', as measured by Cattell's anxiety factor and by measures of hostile attitudes, is the main characteristic on which parasuicides differ from normals. The poor frustration tolerance, tenseness, and fearfulness shown by parasuicides in their psychological test performances is also evident in their clinical and social histories. The impulsive behaviour commented upon in various psychiatric studies can be subsumed by the psychometric measure of general emotional upset. Although parasuicides as a group differ quite strikingly in some respects from normals, such characteristics are not ubiquitous nor are they confined to the population under study; there is no 'suicidal personality'.

In these studies as in others there is clear evidence that parasuicides have great difficulty in creating and maintaining good interpersonal relationships. The life situations of parasuicides are so disorganized that it is inevitable that new stresses are added to the old. Demographic, social, and personality factors are so interwoven that to search for a 'suicidal personality' is to don a conceptual straight-jacket which restricts the researcher to a very simplistic notion of personality.

Poor interpersonal relations and lack of socialization are common in groups of parasuicides and less common in other groups. This has facilitated the consideration of similarities and differences between various groups. Such comparisons suggest some core personality variables which play an important part in determining an individual's reaction to stress, whether physical, mental or social. The general proposition is that some 'central' aspects of personality, corresponding to Allport's notion of the *proprium* (Allport, 1955), must develop so that a person can function in a competent manner. Given an adequate development of these aspects an individual can cope with most events in his life, though his style of coping will depend on other personality traits. The individual with an above-average development of proprium would, in Foulds's terminology, be able to enter into mutual personal relationships without difficulty. In the event of adversity he would be able to utilize both his own resources and those of other people, having been able previously to relate to them in a mutually satisfying way. The individual with less than average self-development cannot enter easily into mutual personal relationships and so when things go wrong he has to stand alone with his scant resources. As a group, parasuicides have more than their share of the latter sort of person. By relating studies of the *proprium* in this very disturbed group to those of other clinical and non-clinical populations the range and depth of our understanding may be greatly increased.

NOTES

1 Scores for primary factors, E, F, and I, as well as second-order anxiety can be extracted from the NSQ. The parasuicides in Study A emerge as being conspicuously more anxious than normals while their performance on factors E, F, and I parallels that of the Study B parasuicides in that they are less enthusiastic (F−) than normals but do not differ significantly in dominance (E) or sensitivity (I).

2 The links between anxiety, general hostility and the SSI character disorder scales are made more striking when the 16PF scores of character disordered patients. In each case the factor is one which contributes to anxiety which in consequence shows a large difference between the two groups (non-character disorders 6.45 stens, character disorders 8.50 stens).

3 It should be appreciated that the relationship between character disorder and 'illness' as defined by the SSI follows the general model proposed by Foulds (1965). In chapter 3 the more conventional psychiatric approach was used, whereby the presence or absence of both personality disorder and illness are separately assessed.

6

THE REPETITION OF PARASUICIDE AND ITS PREDICTION

Prediction studies have been most prolific in the field of criminology where they date back to the 1920s, when Burgess attempted to identify prisoners suitable for release on parole (cf. Mannheim and Wilkins, 1955). Their aims were essentially practical. Decisions have to be made about the release or imprisonment of offenders and very often such decisions are made on a largely intuitive basis. If it can be shown that certain groups of people are likely to respond in a certain way — for example to violate parole or respond well to certain forms of treatment — then action can be taken on a more rational basis. The *type* of action will not necessarily be evident. The kind of intervention required will be determined by the values of society as much as by the needs of the persons identified. When society's interests can be defined as in conflict with those of the individual — frequently so in criminology — quite different types of action may be indicated depending on whose interest is considered of paramount importance. Predictive scales, however accurate, cannot remove the need for value judgements.

From the earliest days, workers in prediction have been cautious about the claims which should be made for the application of their scales and have commented that although statistical prediction had become feasible, it should not be allowed to obscure the special features of the individual case. More recently, greater emphasis has been given to the danger of labelling people in a derogatory way and, by the very act of labelling, to create a self-fulfilling prophecy. This danger is most evident in prediction studies designed for primary prevention. Scales constructed for the identification of potential delinquents are questionable because they aim to identify a rule-breaker before he himself has adopted any such role, and the labelling may have a harmful effect on both his attitude to himself and on the attitude of others towards him. Scales designed for people whose actions have already resulted in them being termed 'deviant' or 'disturbed' are less open to this criticism since the labelling has already taken place and the question is how to take the most appropriate action.

As has been amply demonstrated, parasuicide is a distress behaviour. A further parasuicide is one indication that the distress has not been resolved and that such intervention measures as have been undertaken have failed. It therefore appears to be in the patients' interest that high-risk parasuicides should be identified, as these are the individuals most likely to be unable to resolve their problems unaided.

6.1 PREDICTIVE SCALES AND THEIR CONSTRUCTION

Excellent reviews of predictive scales in criminology are available (e.g. Mannheim and Wilkins, 1955; Simon, 1971) and they are discussed here only in so far as the methods developed are applicable to other fields of study.

Predictive instruments have certain basic requirements. The scale aims to predict the probability of an individual behaving in a certain way in the future. Firstly, therefore, the criterion behaviour must be clear and objectively definable so that others may be able to replicate the original investigation. Most studies have used a dichotomous criterion: success versus failure. (The term 'failure' has been used to denote an undesirable outcome.) Theoretically, a more differentiated criterion is possible but in practice the correlates of human behaviour have rarely been precise enough for this to be a feasible alternative.

Secondly, the information obtained about the individuals in question must be shown to be correlated with the criterion.

Thirdly, items of information have to be combined, or scored, in such a way as to differentiate the failures and successes. Alternative methods of scoring have been the focus of much attention. Early studies used the 'points' method of constructing a scale. Items such as type of offence or work record were shown to be associated with the criterion and a point allotted for each favourable item. An individual score was obtained by summing the points obtained.

This type of approach has been criticized because it gives equal weight to each item selected; it also fails to take into account interaction between the items. Various methods of weighting items according to the strength of their association with the criterion have been suggested (e.g. Glueck and Glueck, 1950). Since Mannheim and Wilkins's classic study of Borstal boys, multiple regression has become a popular alternative, claiming to provide a weighted score which also takes account of the intercorrelations between the items used. Most data used in criminal (as in psychiatric) studies is, however, qualitative rather than quantitative and thus fails to meet the statistical requirements of multiple regression procedure. The question of the choice of method is discussed more fully below.

Although the central feature of a predictive instrument is the combination of items to predict a criterion, a number of other considerations are relevant either before beginning the construction exercise or in assessing the effectiveness of the scale after completion.

Length of time to which the prediction refers

If the prediction is to have practical application, the behaviour predicted should occur within a reasonably short period. The exact duration of follow-up will depend on many factors but where the aim of the prediction is to indicate who is in need of medical or social intervention and where it may be assumed that such need will be fairly constant, it is likely that 5 years is the maximum period which will be of value. It is improbable that preventive services, medical or social, will be continuously provided for longer than 5 years and will often only be available for much less.

Range of predictive scores

Since resources are always limited, it is often useful to be able to select those individuals who are at particularly high risk of failure. In this case the range of predictive scores is important. It may be valuable to identify even a small group of very high risk individuals; alternatively if there is a large group at very low risk, this may indicate where services may be appropriately restricted.

Overall misclassification

A more general question is the proportion of persons misclassified by the scale as a whole. There are two forms of misclassification: *false positives*, where people are predicted to fail but do not do so; and *false negatives*, where people are predicted to succeed but in fact fail. One or other of these types of misclassification may be regarded as crucial in some studies. Statistical techniques used to describe the overall effectiveness of predictive scales include the phi coefficient and the Mean Cost Rating (see Simon, 1971, for discussion of this topic).

The calculation of the proportion of false positives is sometimes referred to as the 'sensitivity' of the scale; and the proportion of false negatives as its 'specificity' (Goldberg, 1972).

The prediction of rare events (the base rate problem)

Rare events are difficult to predict. Prediction depends on a comparison of groups of 'successes' and 'failures'. When one of these groups is very much smaller than the other the cohort for study has to be excessively large in order to obtain sufficient numbers in the rare group. Moreover even a scale which identifies a high proportion of the small group and a low proportion of the large group is still likely to include too many from the latter for the scale to be effective in practice. Studies of completed suicides have encountered this problem since even in high-risk groups, such as parasuicides or psychiatric patients, the suicide rate is only 1—2 per cent per annum. The optimum base rate for prediction is 50 per cent. Criminological studies have mostly worked with a rate of 25—50 per cent. In parasuicide, the repetition rate is on the low side for predictive purposes—in the region of 16 per cent in the first year of follow-up—but is feasible with large cohorts.

Validation

In constructing a predictive scale, the first stage is to discover which items of information are related to the criterion and combine them into a composite score. The instrument formed in this way merely describes the situation in the construction sample. It is subject to random error and many methods of combining scores capitalize chance associations between variables. Before a scale can be termed 'predictive' it is essential that it be shown to be valid for groups other than that on which it was constructed.

Revalidation

The nature of the group may change over time in various ways. The type of person practising a particular form of behaviour may change or an item previously characteristic of 'failure' may lose its predictive power in response to new social circumstances. 'Poor work history' may, for example, have different connotations in an economic recession than in times of full employment. Revalidation is therefore necessary for a scale in use over several years.

6.2 THE REPETITION OF PARASUICIDE: EDINBURGH STUDIES

The possibility of being able to identify people at high risk of repeating their parasuicidal behaviour was considered important for both practical and theoretical reasons. This question has been approached in two Edinburgh studies and it may be helpful to define the terms used and outline the principal stages in the work before describing the latest predictive scale in greater detail (Study 2).

Definitions

Cohort

A cohort of parasuicides consists of *persons* admitted within a specified period, most commonly a calendar year. When a person is admitted more than once within the period specified, the first admission is regarded as the *key* admission and the later admissions disregarded.

Repeater

In this chapter a repeater denotes someone (a) who was admitted to the RPTC for parasuicide, and (b) who was known to have carried out a further act of self-poisoning or self-injury within a specified time period. Most work defined repeaters as persons readmitted to the RPTC and thus excluded a small proportion admitted to other hospitals as well as any parasuicides treated at home. Further self-harm which resulted in death was included in the definition of repetition, whether or not the patient was admitted to the RPTC.

In the principal prediction study, a repeater was someone who was readmitted to the RPTC for a further parasuicide within 12 months of his key admission or who died by suicide within the same period.

Study 1

Parasuicides admitted to the RPTC between 25 June 1962 and 24 June 1963 were examined by a psychiatrist and a psychiatric social worker and their characteristics reported by Kessel (1965b). These patients were followed up personally and their progress in the 12 months following their discharge has been described by McLulloch (1965). The characteristics of those patients who showed further suicidal behaviour (whether or not this resulted in hospital admission) have been described by Kessel and McCulloch (1966), but no attempt was made at that time to construct a predictive scale. Later, the original cohort was followed up from RPTC records, and persons who had either been readmitted for a further parasuicide attempt or who had committed suicide within *three* years of the cohort admission were identified (Buglass and McCulloch, 1970). Items related to further suicidal behaviour within a 3—year follow-up period were identified and scales constructed to identify those at high risk of repetition. Different items were related to repetition for men and women and separate scales were constructed for each sex. These scales were applied to a new group of patients admitted in 1967 and followed up for one year. The scale for women validated well but the male scale was not predictive at the later date.

The partial success of the first predictive scale resulted in a further attempt to produce a scale which would be satisfactory on validation. It was decided that 12 months following the key admission was a more suitable period than the 3 years accepted in the earlier study. 12 months was long enough for an adequate number of repeaters to be accumulated but also short enough to permit the validation of the scale on a new cohort within a reasonable length of time. Moreover, if the scale were to be used in clinical assessment, or in the design of research projects, anything more than a year's therapy or support would rarely be practicable.

Study 2

The second study focused on two questions. The first was the construction of a new predictive scale (Buglass and Horton, 1974a). The second was to investigate the stability of the characteristics of the parasuicides over time (Buglass and Horton, 1974b).

The 1968 parasuicide intake was used as the construction cohort for the development of the predictive scale. Validation was carried out on the 1969 and 1970 cohorts.

Repetition rates

Despite the increase in parasuicide discussed in earlier chapters, the proportion of RPTC patients who have become repeaters has remained very constant; the repetition rate (readmission to RPTC plus suicides) within a 12—month period ranges from 14 per cent to 17 per cent (Table 6.1).

TABLE 6.1   Repetition of parasuicide within 12 months of admission

Cohort admitted	June 1962– June 1963	July—December 1967	Calendar year 1968	1969	1970
Number of patients	511	416	847	910	1052
% repeaters	16	17	16	17	17

Kessel and McCulloch (1966) found a rate of 19 per cent for repetition within 12 months when the more intensive method of home interviewing was substituted for follow-up from RPTC records. The longer follow-up (from records) of the 1962—3 cohort gave a 3—year repetition rate of 25 per cent. Men have a somewhat higher repetition rate than women in all cohorts studied.

Numerically, completed suicide accounts for few repeaters, although these are clearly an important group in terms of preventive action. The proportion of each cohort dying by suicide within 12 months is around 1 per cent, (Table 6.2). The 3 —year follow-up of the 1962—3 cohort gave a suicide rate of 3.3 per cent.

TABLE 6.2   Completed suicide within 12 months of key admission

	1962–3	1968	1969	1970
Suicides	8	8	7	8
% of total cohort	1.57	0.94	0.77	0.76

The construction of a predictive instrument (Study 2)

The construction of a predictive scale was carried out in a similar manner to that outlined in the discussion of criminological studies. The criterion variable to be predicted was repetition of parasuicide within 12 months of the key admission. Information about individual patients was obtained from their punched card record compiled at the time of the key admission. 24 items were selected from this record; these items described the patient at that time and referred to his social situation, clinical diagnosis and past history.

Two methods of scale construction were used: the 'points' method and predictive attribute analysis.

The 'points' scale

The characteristics of the repeaters and non-repeaters in the 1968 cohort were compared in terms of the 24 items selected from their records. Table 6.3 shows the items on which the comparison was made and whether or not they were significantly associated with repetition. In the first instance the sexes were compared separately. More items distinguish female than male repeaters, perhaps in part because significance is more easily reached with the larger numbers available in the female group. Of the nine items which distinguish male repeaters, eight were also shared by female repeaters. Thus male and female repeaters showed a greater degree of similarity than an Study 1 and it was no longer considered necessary to construct a separate scale for each sex.

Having identified items discriminating repeaters and non-repeaters, the next stage was to combine these in a manner capable of predicting repetition prospectively. Since the data were derived from material recorded routinely on all persons admitted to the RPTC, information on a particular patient was sometimes incomplete. Whereas his past psychiatric history and current clinical state were usually noted, detailed questions about his social circumstances and living conditions were not always asked or recorded. This factor was taken into account in selecting items for inclusion in the scale.

In the first instance a scale was constructed by giving an individual a score of one point for every unfavourable item which (a) discriminated repeaters from non-repeaters at above the 0.001 level of probability, and (b) on which information was available in at least 95 per cent of all cases. This resulted in the selection of six items. Two alternative scales were constructed by reducing the level of probability to 0.01 and, secondly, by scoring all items significant at the 0.001 level, regardless of the proportion of people on whom no information was available. These latter two scales had no greater predictive power than the first (six-point) scale and resulted in the exclusion of more people because of missing information. The six-point scale was therefore preferred. The items included in this scale were: sociopathy, problems in the use of alcohol, previous inpatient psychiatric treatment, previous outpatient psychiatric treatment, previous parasuicide (resulting in hospital admission), and not living with a relative. The distribution of scores by repetition is shown in Table 6.4. People who scored 0 had only a 5 per cent chance of repetition compared with those scoring 5 or 6, of whom 48 per cent were repeaters.

Slightly less than 10 per cent of all cases were excluded from the scale because of missing information on one or more items. These 81 excluded cases were

TABLE 6.3   Comparison of repeaters and non-repeaters 1968
* indicates items associated with repetition at the 0.05 level, ** at the 0.01 level, and *** at the 0.001 level of significance (χ^2 test)

Personal attributes	Male	Female	M + F
Male sex	( )	( )	*
Separated or divorced	—	*	*
Social Class V	**	—	***
Diagnosis of depression	—	—	—
†Diagnosis of sociopathy	**	***	***
†Problem in use of alcohol	***	*	***
Alcohol taken at time of act	—	—	—
Drug dependent	—	*	*
Previous inpatient psychiatric treatment	***	***	***
Previous outpatient psychiatric treatment	**	***	***
Previous parasuicide resulting in hospital admission	***	***	***
Previous parasuicide *not* admitted to hospital	**	***	***
†Separated from mother when under 10 years	—	—	*
†Separated from father when under 10 years	—	—	—
Not living with relatives	*	*	***
†Violence used	**	***	***
†Violence received	—	**	*
Four or more dwelling changes in past 5 years	—	—	**
Less than 1 year at present address	—	—	—
†Overcrowded	—	**	—
Unemployed	—	***	***
†In debt	—	*	—
†Criminal record	—	***	***
Aged 25—44 years	—	**	**

†*Definitions*

Sociopathy: Predominant distress of the patient's situation falls on society.
Problem in use of alcohol: Includes 'excessive drinking' as well as alcohol addiction.
Separation from mother/father: A permanent situation in which parent has ceased to live with patient and includes parental deaths.
Violence used: (1969) Patient known to have used physical force to spouse or other relatives. (1969, 1970) Patient known to have used excessive physical force in past 5 years.
Violence received: (1968) Patient known to have been subjected to physical force from spouse or other relatives (after 1969: 'in past 5 years' added).
Overcrowded: Over 1.5 persons per room.
In debt: Arrears of payment.
Criminal record: Previous court conviction and/or police action currently threatened or in progress.

TABLE 6.4   Six-item scale constructed on 1968 data
(Items scored: (a) sociopathy; (b) problem in the use of alcohol; (c) previous psychiatric
inpatient care; (d) previous psychiatric outpatient care; (e) previous parasuicide admission;
(f) not living with a relative.)

	Score							
	0	1	2	3	4	5	6	Total
Repeaters	14	15	15	30	22	18	4	118
	5%	9%	16%	27%	37%	48%		
Non-repeaters	283	114	79	81	37	16	8	648
	95%	91%	84%	73%	63%	52%		
Total = 100%	297	159	94	111	59	34	12	766

compared with the remainder (766) on whom the scale was constructed. This
comparison indicated that the population on whom the scale was constructed was
not materially different from the total group of RPTC admissions.[1]

Table 6.5 shows the results for validating the six-item scale on the 1969 and
1970 data. Thus, although some shrinkage occurred on validation, the predictive
shrinkage occurred in score groups 3 and 4. In 1970 the main discrepancy was in
the reduced effectiveness of the highest risk groups (5 and 6). The predictive power
of the scale before and after validation was tested by the Mean Cost Rating
(MCR).[2] The MCR of the scale constructed on 1968 data was 0.52; when the scale
was applied to the validation cohorts, the MCR was 0.38 on 1969 data and 0.41 on
1970 data. Thus, although some shrinkage occured on validation, the predictive
power of the scale remained reasonably stable when tested on the two subsequent
cohorts.

A further analysis was made for each sex separately (Table 6.6). In each year the
scale validated for females very satisfactorily. Males showed somewhat more
variation, and, in particular, the decline in the predictive ability of the high-risk

TABLE 6.5   Validation of the six-item scale in 1969, 1970

		Percent repeaters observed in validation cohorts			
		1969		1970	
Score	% repeaters expected	Total n in score group	% rep.	Total n in score group	% rep.
0	5%	299	6%	347	6%
1	9%	205	12%	175	14%
2	16%	120	17%	156	24%
3	27%	114	18%	126	31%
4	37%	63	25%	62	39%
5 6	48%	37	46%	41	29%

TABLE 6.6   Validation of the six-item scale by sex

| | % repeaters in each score group | | | | | |
| | Males | | | Females | | |
Score	1968	1969	1970	1968	1969	1970
0	3%	11%	4%	5%	4%	7%
1	8%	8%	16%	10%	15%	12%
2	16%	16%	24%	16%	17%	24%
3	26%	18%	28%	28%	19%	33%
4	34%	29%	48%	26%	21%	29%
5 6	49%	46%	21%	45%	44%	46%

group in 1970 was entirely accounted for by the men. In 1970, 48 per cent of the men with a score of 4 repeated within the year, but only 21 per cent of those with a score of 5 or 6 were repeaters. It is difficult to establish the importance of this finding. The high-risk group is small — the number of males in 1970 scoring 5 or 6 was only 28 –and is inevitably subject to some fluctuation.

Predictive attribute analysis

Predictive attribute analysis was developed by McNaughton-Smith (1963) as a method of using quantitative data to predict a specific criterion and used to distinguish young offenders with different risks of recidivism (Wilkins and McNaughton-Smith, 1964). It classifies the population under study into groups which have different probabilities of possessing the criterion attribute. It has several advantages. Unlike multiple regression, it does not require continuous data. It does not assume homogeneity in the population studied and permits interaction between attributes to be taken into account in compiling different risk groups. For example, even though age is in itself unrelated to the criterion, young alcoholics and old depressives may both be at high risk, and this type of association can be elicited by predictive attribute analysis.

The procedure is very simple. The criterion to be predicted is selected: in this case, repetition. All items to be used in the analysis are dichotomized to form attributes which can be scored as present or absent for every individual. In this analysis the 24 personal attributes were used. A 2 × 2 chi-squared table is then calculated to relate each attribute to the criterion. The attribute which is most highly related to the criterion, as reflected in the χ^2 value, is selected to subdivide the group. Figure 6.1 illustrates the procedure for 1968 data. The attribute most highly associated with repetition was previous experience of inpatient psychiatric treatment. This attribute was then used to split the original group into two sections: (a) those who had received inpatient psychiatric are and (b) those who had not. This procedure was then repeated for each section, the attribute most highly related to repetition in each section being used to subdivide the group still further. The process of subdivision continues until none of the χ^2 is greater than 3.84. In this way the original group is divided into a number of smaller groups of

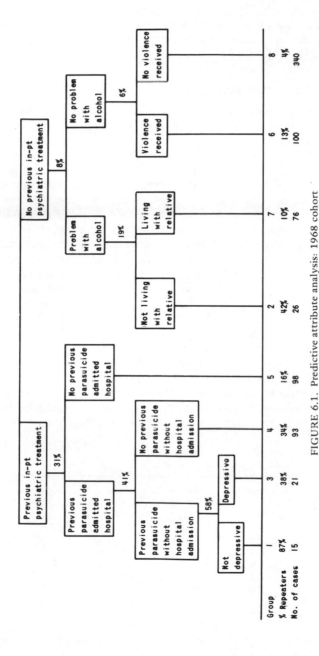

FIGURE 6.1. Predictive attribute analysis: 1968 cohort

people who possess (or lack) a particular constellation of attributes. The proportion in each subgroup who possess the criterion attribute is then calculated.

In the present study, a predictive attribute analysis was carried out on the 1968 cohort. Subgroups with probabilities of repetition varying between 4 per cent and 87 per cent were identified. The 1969 cohort was used to test the validity of these groups as a predictive measure. A new predictive attribute analysis was also carried out on the 1969 cohort.

Results of predictive attribute analysis

Figure 6.1 shows the results of the 1968 analysis. Of those in Group 1, 87 per cent were repeaters. This group was composed of people who had experienced psychiatric inpatient treatment, previous parasuicide resulting in hospital admission as well as parasuicide not resulting in hospital admission, and who were not diagnosed as depressives. At the opposite extreme, a very small proportion (4 per cent) of the patients in Group 8 were repeaters. These were people who had no previous inpatient psychiatric treatment, no problem with alcohol, and were not a recipient of violence. This analysis gave a greater range of predictability than the points scale, and even though Group 1 was very small, the selection of a few individuals at such high risk of further suicidal behaviour was encouraging. To test the validity of the scale, the groups defined by the 1968 analysis were identified in the 1969 cohort and the proportion of repeaters in each calculated. Table 6.7 shows the results of the validation exercise; the high predictive ability of the upper groups disappears when applied in a new sample. Indeed, the group with the second highest proportion of repeaters in 1968 (Group 2) had none at all in 1969.

The failure of the validation exercise indicated that the scale derived from predictive attribute analysis could not be used to identify parasuicides at high risk of repetition. In view of these results, it was of interest to know whether a predictive attribute analysis of 1969 data would give an entirely different structure. Once again the item most highly associated with repetition was previous inpatient care, and the known 'unfavourable' items tended to be associated with poor prognosis. Eleven groups were formed in which the proportion of repeaters ranged

TABLE 6.7   Predictive attribute analysis

	Rep.	1968 Not rep.	Total	1968 % rep.	1969 % rep.
Group 1	13	2	15	87%	48%
Group 2	11	15	26	42%	0%
Group 3	8	13	21	38%	19%
Group 4	32	61	93	34%	29%
Group 5	16	82	98	16%	19%
Group 6	13	87	100	13%	11%
Group 7	8	68	76	10.5%	13%
Group 8	14	325	339	4%	8%
Total	115	653	768		

Percentage of 1968 total excluded because of missing information: 9%.

from 73 per cent to 4 per cent, but none of these groups comprised the same elements as those produced by analysis of 1968 data. It was concluded, therefore, that the inter-item association was too unstable to produce a satisfactory instrument by this means.

The characteristics of the repeaters

In scale construction, attention is inevitably concentrated on finding the most predictive items and on validating the instrument as a whole. Much material relevant to the social and personal situation of the repeater is ignored in this process. This section describes the broader aspects of repetition and considers whether the salient characteristics of repeaters remain constant over a period of time. The question of whether there are different correlates of repetition in men and women is also raised.

The data employed for the comparison of repeaters and non-repeaters were the same as those used in the construction and validation of the predictive scale (Study 2), and consisted of three annual cohorts of patients admitted to the RPTC for parasuicide in 1968, 1969, and 1970. The characteristics compared were derived from the patient's record completed at the time of admission and were all dichotomous items. 24 of the items consisted of the personal attributes already listed in Table 6.3. A further three items referred to illness or suicidal behaviour in the patient's relatives and two to arrangements made for care after discharge from the RPTC.

The results comparing repeaters and non-repeaters in three successive years are shown in Table 6.8. The items which consistently discriminated repeaters from non-repeaters at a highly significant level ($p < .001$) were: a diagnosis of sociopathy, problems in the use of alcohol, previous inpatient psychiatric treatment, previous outpatient psychiatric treatment and previous parasuicide. It may be recalled that these are the items used in the predictive scale, except that 'not living with a relative' did not discriminate between repeaters and non-repeaters in the 1969 cohort. In 1970, the item reached significance, but only at the 0.05 level. This fluctuation illustrates how difficult it is to select items which are consistently predictive and emphasizes the necessity of repeated validation of any scales in regular use.

Items which were consistently associated with repetition above the 5 per cent level of significance were: belonging to Social Class V, dependence on drugs, unemployment, and a history of criminal behaviour. Eight items, including a diagnosis of depression and having taken alcohol at the time of the act, were not related to repetition in any cohort.

The remaining items were associated with repetition in some years but not in others. The greater risk for 1968 patients after referral to social work care is probably explained by the experimental policy in that year of offering high-risk patients special social work support, however slight the likelihood of modifying their subsequent behaviour (Chowdhury et al., 1973). The proportion referred for social work in 1968 was more than twice as high as in subsequent years.

In earlier years the age group 25—44 was over-represented among repeaters. By 1970, the increase in the proportion of repeaters aged under 25 had nullified the association between age and repetition: in 1968 the proportion of repeaters under 25 was 21 per cent; in 1969, 27 per cent, and in 1970, 37 per cent. The

TABLE 6.8 Comparison of repeaters and non-repeaters on 29 items
* indicates items associated with repetition at the 0.05 level, ** at the 0.01 level, and *** at the 0.001 level of significance (χ^2 test)

Personal attributes	1968	1969	1970
Male sex	*	*	—
Separated or divorced	*	—	—
Social Class V	***	**	*
Diagnosis of depression	—	—	—
Diagnosis of sociopathy	***	***	***
Problem in use of alcohol	***	***	***
Alcohol taken at time of act	—	—	—
Drug dependent	*	***	***
Previous inpatient psychiatric treatment	***	***	***
Previous outpatient psychiatric treatment	***	***	***
Previous parasuicide resulting in hospital admission	***	***	***
Previous parasuicide *not* admitted to hospital	***	***	—
Separated from mother when under 10 years	*	**	—
Separated from father when under 10 years	—	—	—
Not living with relatives	***	—	*
Violence used	***	***	—
Violence received	*	—	—
Four or more dwelling changes in past 5 years	**	***	—
Less than 1 year at present address	—	—	—
Overcrowded	—	—	—
Unemployed	***	**	***
In debt	—	—	—
Criminal record	***	***	**
Aged 25–44 years	**	*	—
Family attributes			
Family member received psychiatric treatment	—	—	—
Parasuicide by family member	**	—	*
Suicide by family member	*	—	***
Disposal			
To inpatient psychiatric care	—	—	—
To social work follow-up	**	—	—

non-repeaters did not show this trend, the proportion of under 25s in each of the 3 years being respectively 35 per cent, 35 per cent, and 36 per cent. The proportion of over 45s showed little variation, either by repetition or by year. The effect of this change was that by 1970 the age distribution of the repeaters was much the same as that of the non-repeaters.

Since Study 1 had found different correlates of repetition in men and women, a comparison was made between repeaters and non-repeaters for each sex separately. The general conclusion was that male and female repeaters resembled each other more closely than before. Four of the highly discriminating items already noted — sociopathy, previous inpatient care, previous outpatient care, and previous hospitalized parasuicide — discriminated repeaters and non-repeaters of both sexes in all cohorts ($p < .05$). Drug dependence was significantly associated with repetition in five out of the six (two sexes, 3 years) comparisons. There was a tendency for more items to be associated with repetition in females than in males, perhaps because significance level could be more easily reached with the larger numbers in the female group. In each year the majority of items which distinguished the male repeaters were also predictive for females.[3] (Appendix 6.1 shows the proportion of repeaters and non-repeaters by sex who possessed each of the characteristics investigated.)

The question of the constancy of the characteristics of the parasuicide population was considered in another way. The patients were divided into four groups, male repeaters, male non-repeaters, female repeaters, and female non-repeaters. The 24 personal attributes listed in Table 6.8 were used to describe each group, and the percentage possessing each attribute was noted. These proportions were then ranked and Kendall's coefficient of concordance (Siegel, 1956) for the 3 years was calculated. The coefficients for non-repeaters were very high (males: 0.96; females: 0.97); for repeaters the results were: males 0.92; females 0.77.

The association of family behaviour to repetition can only be touched on briefly here. (A family member was defined as a spouse, parent, sibling, or child.) Table 6.8 indicated that repetition was more common when there was a family history of parasuicide or completed suicide (two out of three cohorts). Examination of the comparisons for each sex showed that the association was stronger for women than for men and that women repeaters are also more likely to have a relative who had received psychiatric treatment. Although information about psychopathology in relatives is likely to be an understimate, the findings nevertheless support the view that repeated parasuicide occurs more readily when there is a family history of self-destructive behaviour. Other aspects of familial clustering are discussed in chapter 4.

Information on the medical seriousness of the act could not be obtained for the first two cohorts. The findings on the 1970 cohort are in line with those of other workers who have shown that the medical seriousness of the act is not related to subsequent suicidal behaviour (Kessel and McCulloch, 1966; Greer and Lee, 1967; Greer and Bagley, 1971; Cohen et al., 1966). 61 per cent of repeaters and 64 per cent of non-repeaters were graded 0 (conscious) on the method of assessment described by Matthew and Lawson (1966). A further 19 per cent and 16 per cent respectively were assessed as grade 1 (drowsy but responds to verbal commands). Only 5 per cent of each group were grade 4 (no response to maximum painful stimulation). There was no association between level of coma and repetition.

Repetition and inpatient treatment

When a parasuicide is admitted to the RPTC the aim of the service is not only to facilitate physical recovery, but also to provide the most appropriate help for his emotional or psychological problems. The repetition rate is some indication of failure to achieve this end. Table 6.8 showed that those admitted to psychiatric inpatient care had the same proportion of repeaters as the remainder. This section explores the determinants of after-care provision a little further.

Patients discharged to a psychiatric hospital were compared with those not so referred for the 24 personal attributes presented above. Table 6.9 shows the items associated with discharge to a psychiatric hospital in each cohort, with repeaters and non-repeaters considered separately. For non-repeaters, the determinants of inpatient care are a diagnosis of depression, having received previous psychiatric treatment and being over 45. In addition the inpatients more commonly have a history of parasuicide, but this association is much less pronounced than that with diagnosis. People not living in a family setting were also more liable to be admitted to hospital. Moreover, the absence of deviant behaviour (no criminal record, no debts, no problem with alcohol) is more commonly found among the inpatients.

Perhaps because of its smaller size. fewer items are related to inpatient care for the repeater group. The significant findings echo those of the non-repeaters — definable psychiatric pathology as evidenced by a diagnosis of depression, and previous treatment in combination with an absence of deviant behaviour (less use of alcohol, less experience of violence, less often a history of criminal behaviour or debts).

Although previous parasuicide and previous psychiatric treatment are shared by repeaters and those referred to inpatient treatment, the other correlates of inpatient care are markedly different from those of repetition. Repeaters are characterized by

TABLE 6.9   Items associated with discharge to inpatient care
* item associated with discharge to inpatient care at 0.05 level, ** at 0.01 level, ***at 0.001 level of significance

	Repeaters			Non-repeaters		
	1968	1969	1970	1968	1969	1970
Female	—	*	—	—	*	*
45 years +	—	**	—	***	***	***
Separated or divorced	—	—	—	—	—	—
Social Class I—IV	—	—	—	—	—	**
Depression	—	***	*	***	***	***
Not sociopath	—	—	—	—	*	*
No problem with alcohol	—	—	**	—	—	*
Not taken alcohol on admission	**	—	**	—	***	***
Drug dependent	—	—	—	—	—	—
Previous inpatient care	—	**	*	***	***	***
Previous outpatient care	—	—	—	***	***	***
Previous parasuicide (hospitalized)	—	—	—	*	*	*
Previous parasuicide (not hospitalized)	—	—	—	—	—	—
Separated from mother when under 10 years	—	—	—	—	—	—
Separated from father when under 10 years	—	—	—	—	—	—
Not living with relative	—	—	—	*	***	***
Violence not used	—	—	—	—	—	—
Violence not received	—	—	**	—	—	—
Four or more dwelling changes in past 5 years	—	—	—	—	—	—
Less than 1 year at present address	—	—	—	—	—	—
Not overcrowded	—	—	*	—	—	—
Unemployed	—	—	—	—	—	—
No debts	—	—	*	—	*	—
No criminal record	—	*	*	—	*	***

conflict with authority, by social problems and by personal inadequacies. The patients selected for inpatient treatment are predominantly older, depressive, and with fewer social problems than parasuicides in general.

Since inpatient care is the most intensive treatment that can be prescribed after parasuicide, it was of interest to consider whether patients of particular diagnostic groups discharged to a psychiatric hospital were less likely to repeat than those given other forms of treatment. Parasuicides were divided into depressives and non-depressives (mostly personality disorders.) For depressives in each of the three cohorts, repetition is unrelated to inpatient treatment on discharge. Non-depressives, on the contrary, are *more* likely to repeat if they are given inpatient care (1968 $p < .01$; 1969: $p < .1$; 1970: $p < .01$).

These results must be interpreted with care. The analysis supports two conclusions. Firstly, the correlates of repetition and of discharge to inpatient care are sufficiently different to suggest that clinicians use criteria other than the probability of repetition in referring patients for inpatient psychiatric treatment. Secondly, patients referred to inpatient care are as likely, or even more likely, to repeat than those not so referred. Too many factors are involved for any causal interpretation to be offered for this latter finding. It is possible that the inpatient regime was not to the patients' advantage; it is more probable that these patients were selected for admission because of the known intransigence of their problems. Without a controlled study it is not possible to make any judgement about the *effect* of inpatient care on the probability of further parasuicide. The after-care study carried out by Chowdhury *et al.* (1973) and described in chapter 8 illustrates the difficulty of preventing repetition in a known high-risk group.

Characteristics of completed suicides

The 23 suicides produced by the three cohorts taken together, each followed up for 1 year, form too small a group for a statistical comparison to be made between them and the remainder of the repeaters. Their scores fell predominantly in the middle of the six-item predictive scale (Table 6.10). As might be expected from studies of completed suicides, they were somewhat older than the parasuicides, half (twelve) being aged 45 or over. Less expectedly, two-thirds of the group were women (eight males; fifteen females). Six had a problem in the use of alcohol, three were diagnosed as sociopaths and eleven had one or more prior parasuicidal episodes resulting in hospital admission. Six were discharged to inpatient care. A diagnosis of depression (with or without attendant personality disorder) was given

TABLE 6.10   Scale score of completed suicides

	Score							
	0	1	2	3	4	5	6	n.k.
1968 cohort	1	4	1	1	–	–	–	1
1969 + 1970 cohorts	–	2	2	8	1	1	–	1
Total	1	6	3	9	1	1	–	2

to 16 (70 per cent) of the suicides at the time of their key admission. Diagnoses made, as is inevitable at the RPTC after only short acquaintances with the patient, are often subject to criticism. Nevertheless, this figure is substantially higher than that for the total group; of patients in the three cohorts combined; 43 per cent had a diagnosis of depression. Whereas 'illness diagnosis' was not predictive of repetition, it may perhaps indicate a greater risk of eventual death by suicide.

Summary and Conclusions

This chapter is devoted to the phenomenon of the repetition of parasuicide. The selection of repetition as a criterion of failure or relapse seems justified in that it is an objective indication that the patient's problems have not been resolved, or have recurred. In no sense is it a complete measure. A person may be very distressed without resorting to parasuicide. Nevertheless, parasuicide is probably one of the least constructive ways of resolving problems and for this reason at least repetition is worth preventing.

Some may question the concentration on repetition rather than on subsequent suicide. There are two reasons for this choice. Firstly, the prevention and understanding of long-term distress seems as important as the prevention and understanding of eventual death by suicide. Secondly, suicide is a rare event, and the difficulties of predicting an uncommon occurrence even in a high-risk population have already been mentioned.

Completed suicide has been included in the definition of a repeater. Although suicides and parasuicides show different group characteristics, Ovenstone (1973a) has demonstrated that suicides who have a history of previous suicidal behaviour share many of the characteristics of the surviving repeaters. Some people have repeat episodes of parasuicide before death by suicide, some acts of parasuicide end in death through 'misadventure' rather than through 'intent' and a distinction of the two is very difficult. It seemed unreasonable, therefore, to treat the suicides as non-repeaters. In any event, the number of suicides in each cohort is very small.

Discussion of the repeaters has concentrated on three aspects: the rate of repetition itself, the characteristics of the repeaters as a group, and the development of the predictive scale to estimate the individual probability of subsequent parasuicide.

Despite the marked increase in parasuicidal behaviour over the last decade, the repetition rate for annual patient cohorts, at least up to 1970, has remained stable at around 16 per cent in the 12 months following the key admission. This is a somewhat conservative estimate as it omits those whose parasuicide or suicide occurred outwith the Edinburgh area and those who were treated at home by their general practitioner.

The characteristics of the repeaters are also reasonably constant. Previous psychiatric treatment, previous parasuicide, sociopathy, problems in the use of alcohol or drugs, unemployment, criminal record, and low social class figured prominently in repetition. The poor prognosis carried by many of these items is supported by the findings of other studies. Kessel and McCulloch (1966), in their 1—year follow-up of the 1962—3 Edinburgh cohort, showed that previous parasuicide, previous psychiatric treatment, and alcohol or drug problems were associated with repetition. Extension of the follow-up of this cohort to 3 years (Buglass and McCulloch, 1970) found that most of these items remained predictive of repetition, in both men and women. Greer and Bagley (1971), in their London study, also found antisocial personality (including alcoholism and drug dependence) and previous suicide attempts to be correlated with repetition. There is, therefore, broad agreement on the psychiatric characteristics which distinguish repeaters from non-repeaters. They are most commonly described as personality disorders who try ro resolve their problems by excessive use of alcohol or drugs, who have already experienced psychiatric attention, and in whose lives parasuicide is a recurrent theme. Contrary to Greer and Bagley's finding, a diagnosis of depression was not associated with a favourable prognosis among Edinburgh parasuicides. Earlier studies in Edinburgh have shown that parasuicides in general are an underprivileged group (e.g. McCulloch and Philip, 1972). The present study demonstrates that the social characteristics of repeaters are those of a group even more markedly under-privileged and in conflict with society. In comparison with non-repeaters they are predominantly of low social class and frequently unemployed. Their past history often includes a criminal conviction; their personal relationships may be marked by violence (this trait, though usually predictive, was not substantiated in 1970 data). It is interesting that non-conflictual hardships as evidenced by overcrowding and debt are not related to repetition. As few studies have included a social description of the repeater group, it is not possible to say whether this picture can be generalized. Bagley and Greer's (1971) finding that repeaters were more commonly drawn from Classes I—III is, however, at odds with experience in Edinburgh.

Some variation in the way an item related to repetition can be expected, if only due to random fluctuation. Nevertheless the increasing proportion of young repeaters is a change which, if continued, may have implications for the character of repetition in general. The Registrar General's Annual Reports shows an increase in completed suicide among the young. Suicide does not, however, mirror parasuicide in other age groups and it is not at present clear how the two phenomena should be viewed: the question is further considered in chapter 9.

An attempt was made to combine the distinctive characteristics of repeaters into a scale which would assign a probability of repetition to a particular individual. Three consecutive cohorts of admissions to the RPTC were used to construct and validate a scale designed to predict repetition within the 12 subsequent months. The scale had the advantage of easy application since it used information routinely collected and was simple to score. One point was allocated for each of six items shown to be highly related to repetition and the total summed. Several questions may be posed. Was it effective? Would more sophisticated methods have produced a better instrument? How should it be used?

In terms of the range of scores, the probability of repetition varied from 5 per cent for people who scored 0, to 48 per cent for people who scored 5 or 6. This range provides considerably more information than the overall or 'base' repetition rate. It does not identify any individual as having more than a one in two chance of becoming a repeater but it does indicate which are the high-risk individuals. Validation on the 1969 cohort gives a similar range (6 per cent to 46 per cent); validation on 1970 data showed the predictive power of the highest risk group to have declined, although the other score groups had much the same predictive ability as in the 2 previous years. Analysis by sex showed that this decline was entirely accounted for by the men. Nevertheless, the fact that the range of predictability is stable in three out of four validation samples — for both sexes in 1969 and for women in 1970 — is encouraging. Using the MCR as an overall measure of predictive power, the results obtained here (0.52 on the construction sample and 0.38 and 0.41 on the validation cohorts) compare satisfactorily with the findings of the Home Office Research Unit's study of the success and failure among young men on probation: for example, using a variety of scale construction methods, MCRs of between 0.11 and 0.31 on validation were found (Simon, 1971).

The disadvantages of the 'points method' have been indicated earlier. Although the six-item scale was considered reasonably satisfactory, it was possible that some other method of combining the data would provide better discrimination. Initially predictive attribute analysis appeared very attractive since it was designed for qualitative data and did not assume homogeneity in the population studied. The results of a predictive attribute analysis did, indeed give a wider range of predictive scores than any earlier construction method. When the 1968 scale was validated on the following cohort, however, it became apparant that the groups identified were not good predictors for 1969. This was despite the fact that the general characteristics of the repeaters have been shown to be similar in the 2 years. The reason for the failure of the predictive attribute analysis appears to be its tendency to capitalize on chance associations. Multiple regression techniques have not been used on the parasuicide data, largely because qualitative data does not satisfy the statistical assumptions required for this procedure. Moreover, multiple regression is as subject to over-fitting as predictive attribute analysis. It provides a good description of the construction sample, but again capitalizes chance associations which are not replicated in the validation. Simon (1971) used seven methods of scale construction in her study of young probationers. She concludes (p. 154):

> In spite of the different theoretical advantages and disadvantages of each type [of method for combining data] it appears that when put to the test on a validation sample, they are likely to come up with predictive instruments of roughly equal power.

In the parasuicide studies the points scale proved more robust than the more sophisticated alternative.

Comparison with studies elsewhere is difficult as little work has been done on the prediction of repetition. Cohen *et al.* (1966) presented a scale which achieved a similar range to that presented here. The follow-up period was very long — 5 to 8 years — and the scale was not validated. Bagley and Greer (1971) carried out a multiple regression on London parasuicides and found that if one of five characteristics was present, the 80 per cent of the repeaters could be identified. They do not, however, give the proportion of non-repeaters these characteristics would identify so no comparison can be made in terms of the two types of misclassification. The multiple regression has not been validated on another cohort. Considerable attention in the United States has been devoted to the identification of completed suicides (cf. Neuringer, 1974). The difference in clinical characteristics as well as the different technical problems associated with this group make comparison unfruitful.

Finally, what are the practical uses of the predictive scale described in this chapter? There is no suggestion that an instrument of this type should replace clinical assessment of an individual patient. In any case, the predictive power is not great enough for therapeutic decisions to be based on it alone. However, it may be of value as an adjunct to clinical assessment. It has been demonstrated that the characteristics of parasuicides discharged to inpatient care are different from those associated with repetition. While there is no evidence that inpatient care as such prevents repetition, the knowledge that a patient is at particularly high risk can be used by the clinician as an additional item of information and may encourage him to pay extra attention to the problems of such patients.

A second function of a predictive scale is to provide a basis for decisions about the allocation of resources. If resources are limited, it may be desirable to concentrate special attention on the group at greatest risk of relapse. For example, in the present study, the largest group of parasuicides consists of those scoring 0, who have a low probability of repetition. If intensive treatment is focused on those scoring 1 or above, the number requiring attention would be reduced by about 40 per cent. The *cost* of such a procedure can be estimated by calculating the amount of misclassification, i.e. the number of repeaters falsely predicted to be non-repeaters and vice versa — and a judgement made on other grounds of the seriousness of such misclassification. An example from the present study is given in Appendix 6.2.

Perhaps the most useful application of a predictive instrument is in designing studies to evaluate treatment innovations. (Chapter 8 contains an illustration of this use.) Since the scale enables patients to be classified according to their level of risk, groups can be structured so that adequate numbers in each risk category are included in the study. In our present ignorance of the effectiveness of specific treatments or after-care programmes, such investigations are badly needed.

NOTES

1 Excluded cases: In general, the excluded cases were less well documented than the others — infomation lacking on one item was associated with the absence of information on other items. For items where missing data was negligible — sex, age, and civil state — the distribution of the excluded cases was indistinguishable from the remainder. A comparison of the two groups on available information for other items produced only two significant differences. The excluded patients were more often categorized as drug-dependent (30 per cent compared with 13 per cent of the remainder) and they were much more likely to be referred to inpatient psychiatric care on discharge from the RPTC. 37 per cent of the excluded, compared with 17 per cent of the remainder, were transferred to hospital. The excess of drug dependents may be explained by the tendency of some of these patients not to co-operate with the ward regime and to take their own discharge before full information has been collected on them. The latter finding is most probably due to clinicians being less concerned to collect complete information on patients whom they know are to be more fully investigated by their psychiatric colleagues in hospital. With regard to repetition, there was a slightly higher, but non-significant, percentage of repeaters among the excluded cases: 18.5 per cent compared with 15.4 per cent in the remainder.

2 The Mean Cost Rating is a measure of predictive power developed by Duncan, Ohlin, Reiss, and Stanton (1953) and discussed by Simon (1971) in the Home Office study of young men on probation. The MCR varies between 0, where there is no differentiation in the 'failure' (in this study 'repetition') rates between groups, to 1, where all groups comprise only repeaters or non-repeaters. It is sensitive to the ordering or ranking of groups and this property is useful in comparing results from one cohort with a validation cohort.

3 The total number of personal attributes which distinguished repeaters, males and females respectively, was: 1968, 9 and 16 with eight items shared; 1969, 9 and 9 — seven shared; 1970, 6 and 11 — six shared.

APPENDIXES

APPENDIX 6.1 Characteristics of repeaters and non-repeaters within 12 months, 1968–70*

	Men						Women					
	% repeaters			% non-repeaters			% repeaters			% non-repeaters		
	1968 $n=64$	1969 $n=60$	1970 $n=75$	1968 $n=273$	1969 $n=292$	1970 $n=311$	1968 $n=69$	1969 $n=67$	1970 $n=108$	1968 $n=441$	1969 $n=491$	1970 $n=558$
Aged 25–44 years	50	47	36	41	41	40	64	55	40	42	41	40
Separated/divorced	22	17	12	18	14	19	22	15	18	11	11	11
Social Class V	57	49	48	36	26	35	29	25	24	17	22	18
Depressed	52	31	45	44	34	35	52	36	48	54	36	49
Sociopath	35	34	35	19	19	22	25	13	20	5	5	9
Problem with alcohol	75	51	44	42	38	41	21	17	27	9	8	11
Alcohol taken at time of act	62	57	57	61	54	54	31	27	30	22	22	24
Drug dependent	16	25	30	15	9	19	26	22	20	13	10	10
Previous inpatient care	63	51	64	30	27	30	61	57	51	23	24	25
Previous outpatient care	52	61	51	31	28	26	56	61	38	28	32	26
Previous parasuicide (hospital)	62	49	55	23	26	27	52	47	51	22	24	21
Previous parasuicide (not hospital)	21	24	19	8	14	15	29	26	19	9	11	14
Separated mother under 10 years	22	12	1	11	4	5	12	11	13	9	5	8

Separated father under 10 years	21	16	10	16	11	10	17	20	19	16	12	13
Not living with relative	46	25	30	28	29	26	28	15	27	15	21	15
Violence used	40	31	26	23	18	19	27	29	10	10	14	10
Violence received	16	17	21	11	9	14	45	36	12	25	26	18
4+ dwelling changes	39	34	26	26	18	15	24	38	14	16	21	12
<1 year at present address	41	40	27	36	29	33	34	40	41	33	30	29
Overcrowded	27	30	22	26	23	26	52	25	14	32	29	25
Unemployed	53	58	56	42	34	39	61	41	48	27	31	32
In debt	24	26	29	25	24	23	32	26	21	17	17	15
Clinical record	52	47	48	41	35	38	24	16	16	5	6	7
Disposal												
Inpatient care	30	19	21	30	21	18	30	40	28	25	30	23
Social care	41	7	35	24	10	32	49	15	36	38	15	30
Relatives experience												
Psychiatric care	18	19	18	19	18	24	36	27	34	22	21	22
Parasuicide	16	11	19	11	8	9	26	12	14	11	9	10
Suicide	7	4	6	3	1	2	8	0	12	2	3	2

*Proportions are calculated from total number of known cases.

114

Appendix 6.2   The use of the six-item scale to define potential repeaters

One use of the scale is to select 'potential repeaters' or high-risk groups. In making this selection, a decision may be made about the degree of misclassification which is acceptable and the size of the group it is possible to treat. Tables I and II below show how the information contained in the scale may be used to estimate the degree of misclassification at any given cut-off point.

TABLE I   Six-item scale, 1968 data. Cut-off point: score 1

	Repeaters	Non-repeaters
Predicted non-repeaters (score 0)	14	283
Predicted repeaters (score 1 or above)	104	365
Total	118	648

Using a score of 1 or above to identify potential repeaters:

88 per cent of repeaters correctly identified (sensitivity);
12 per cent of repeaters falsely predicted as non-repeaters;
44 per cent of non-repeaters correctly identified (specificity);
56 per cent of non-repeaters falsely predicted as repeaters.

Number of patients in 'potential repeater' group, i.e. scoring 1 or more: 469.

TABLE II   Proportions correctly identified at different cut-off levels

	Cut-off point			
	1	2	3	4
Correctly identified as repeaters (sensitivity)	88%	75%	63%	37%
Correctly identified as non-repeaters (specificity)	44%	66%	78%	91%
Number of 'potential repeaters	469	310	216	105

7

THE PRIMARY PREVENTION OF PARASUICIDE

The usual concepts of primary and secondary prevention can readily be applied to parasuicide, the former referring to efforts aimed at preventing a first act of parasuicide and the second to the prevention of repetition. The notion of tertiary prevention does not lend itself easily to an episode of behaviour such as parasuicide, and will not be considered further.

There does not appear to be in the literature any report of a service specifically set up with the aim of prevention of parasuicide, nor have studies of services designed to meet broader needs examined parasuicide as one of the outcome variables. It is therefore necessary to use clinical experience as the starting point from which to proceed in considering the type of service that might be most appropriate.

It is abundantly evident that parasuicidal patients are frequently involved in social crises of many diverse kinds. Assistance at an early stage might prevent a crisis occuring, or if the situation had already become acute, might afford relief. It also appears that parasuicides often come from families which have multiple difficulties, and which are not always already known to agencies. A service to ameliorate some of the stresses would therefore have to embrace a wide range of problems and be available to all, and not simply to individuals already recognized as having a psychiatric disorder or being socially disadvantaged. For evaluation of the service a comparable community not enjoying the benefits of such an organization would be required, with similar monitoring facilities being available in both areas to ascertain changes in the parasuicide rates.

7.1 THE CRAIGMILLAR EXPERIMENT

A 'natural experiment' of just this kind became available when the Craigmillar Health, Welfare and Advice Centre was established in March 1968 to provide to the inhabitants of the Craigmillar ward a wide but integrated range of services supplied by both statutory and voluntary bodies. The essential conception foreshadowed that subsequently embodied in the Social Work (Scotland) Act of 1968, which briefly antedated the corresponding Act in England and Wales. The agencies participating in the work of the centre included the local authority departments responsible for children, probation, welfare, mental health, and health visitors. The voluntary bodies represented included the Royal Scottish Society for the Prevention of Cruelty to Children, the Marriage Guidance Council, Citizen's Advice Bureau, a voluntary organization catering for the disabled, and the Little Sisters of the

Assumption (a religious order). All these organizations were co-ordinated by a specially appointed, experienced and highly energetic social worker, with adequate secretarial and receptionist staff to enable him to function effectively. New referrals were screened by a panel representing each of the participating agencies, together with a psychiatrist and psychiatric social worker. The most appropriate caseworker initially to accept the referral was thus jointly agreed, and close liaison was maintained with other organizations throughout. Most cases were not emergencies in the sense of presenting without a scheduled appointment, but for those who come into this category a special duty officer was constantly available. The majority of clients were self-referred. Contact with the local police and citizens' organizations was excellent, and the centre took an active though limited role in promoting spontaneous community activity such as the organization of play groups by mothers. Morale among the staff was high. Fuller descriptions are available in Ebie (1969), Ebie *et al.* (1970), Ebie (1971).

The population

The city ward in which the centre was established had a population of approximately 26,000. About half were in Social Classes IV and V. The area is well known for its numerous social problems; details can be found in chapter 4, section 4.1, and in Philip and McCulloch (1966). In 1962 and in 1967 the ward ranked second out of the 23 Edinburgh wards for parasuicide (person) rates. There was thus scope for the anticipated effects of this concentrated social work service to make themselves manifest.

No comparable centre existed in any other part of the city. The reorganization of local authority social work services did not come into operation until late in 1969 and its implementaion at the grass roots level was still further delayed. For comparative purposes it might be legitimate to use the rates for 1967–70 for the city as a whole. Another comparison is provided by the rates for Pilton ward, which is demographically very similar to Craigmillar, has almost as many social problems, and had always ranked among the top four wards in the parasuicide hierarchy.

Results

The centre was widely used and accepted 563 new clients in the first year of its operation, representing about 2.5 per cent of all adults in the area.

The essential findings are presented in Table 7.1 for the year before the centre opened in 1968 and for the following 2 years. There was no decline in the Craigmillar rate for 1968; the rate in fact increased in both that year and in 1969, with a slight falling back in 1970. The constancy of the Craigmillar rate was maintained against a background of upward trends in the comparison data, and this might be interpreted as supporting the hypothesis that the centre was having a preventive effect.

However, Pilton and Edinburgh city rates were markedly lower than that of Craigmillar in 1967, the base year for the 'experiment'. Since the 'law of initial values' operates in social no less than in physiological systems, the difference in starting levels may well vitiate all further comparisons (short of a relatively complex analysis, the data for which are not available) and the safest conclusion would appear to be one of 'not proven'.

TABLE 7.1   Craigmillar, Pilton, and Edinburgh city parasuicide
(person) rates per 10,000, 1967–70. Males and females combined,
age 15+

	Year			
	1967*	1968*	1969	1970
Craigmillar	35.5	40.3	43.1	39.8
Pilton	17.2	25.5	30.8	33.6
Edinburgh city	16.3	18.0	22.4	26.3

*The Craigmillar Centre opened in March 1968.
The use of admission rates, and division by sex of both patient and
admission rates, leaves the general pattern unchanged.

A subsidiary question of some interest is whether the centre succeeded in
attracting a clientele broadly similar to that of the patients being admitted to the
Regional Poisoning Treatment Centre. A special study (Ebie, 1969) documented
the characteristics of individuals using the centre during the first 3 months of its
operation. Ebie showed that in relation to the population of the Craigmillar ward,
the users contained proportionately more women, people aged 20–44 years of age,
the married and divorced and Social Class V. A detailed age-sex-marital status
comparison of the clients and the parasuicides seen at the RPTC over the same
period demonstrated that the groups were substantially similar in these respects.
The admittedly limited data thus suggest that an organization such as the centre can
indeed attract people at high risk for parasuicide. This is a potentially valuable
situation, even if no decision can at present be made for the efficacy of the service.

7.2 THE TELEPHONE SAMARITAN ORGANIZATION

The Telephone Samaritan service was established in November 1953 in London by
the Reverend Chad Varah, a priest of the Church of England, as a suicide
prevention service. It has spread rapidly. According to Fox (1975) there were about
150 suicide prevention centres in the United Kingdom by 1974, all offering an
advertised 24-hour service to the distressed and suicidal. New clients contacting
the organization increased from 12,000 in 1964 when records were first kept, to
over 156,000 by 1972.

The service is designed to offer supportive friendship to those who feel alone or
helpless in a crisis which seems insoluble, and to befriend such people until they
regain their confidence or can be put in touch with other helping agencies. It was
hoped that reduction in suicide rates could be achieved. It seems that the initial
emphasis on suicide prevention has to some extent been broadened in more recent
years. However, people in distress over a wide range of problems and without any
particular suicidal intent have always been welcomed as clients and probably have
always represented the majority of the clientele. The initial evangelical connections
of the movement were never conspicuous and in recent years the organization has
become almost entirely secular, even though the clergy continue to play a very
important role. Counselling or 'befriending' is provided by lay volunteers who are
carefully selected and trained for such work. Details of the aims and organization of
the service can be found in Varah (1965).

The efficiency of the Telephone Samaritans as a suicide prevention agency has been much discussed but is not at issue here. Rather the role of the organization in the primary prevention of parasuicide was the focus of study. There was a reasonable prima facie case that it might be effective. The organization is well known and publicized. It is tailored to deal with emergency situations and provides a continuous service by trained staff. The Edinburgh branch was founded in 1959 (the second in the United Kingdom) and by the time of the investigations to be described was well experienced and thoroughly familiar with local problems. It comprised approximately 90 active volunteers. The organization welcomed the approach by the Unit and collaborated actively in a series of joint studies.

Three main investigations were carried out. In brief, the first was concerned to depict the broad epidemiology of Samaritan clients and to compare the pattern with that of parasuicide; the second was to document similarities and differences between Samaritan clients and parasuicides at the level of individual characteristics, and the last, to determine whether an increase in referrals to the Samaritan organization in Edinburgh was reflected by any change in the parasuicide rates.

The general epidemiological characteristics of the clientele of the Telephone Samaritan organization

The aim of the first study was to describe the demographic and social characteristics of the clientele of the Edinburgh branch of the Telephone Samaritans in relation to the general population of the city of Edinburgh, and to describe further selected characteristics of the clientele and their management.

A simple schedule devised for this purpose was completed for each client by the duty Samaritan. Clients' names were omitted from the schedule to preserve their anonymity, and care was taken not to disrupt the normal service provided by the organization; for example, no change was made in the Samaritans' usual method of interviewing. All clients who made contact with the service for the first time between 28 October 1968 and 31 March 1969 (22 weeks) were to be included. During this period there were 364 such clients: schedules were completed for 96 per cent (350) of these. The other 14 were not identified at first; however their records were recovered later and it was found that they were of similar age and sex to the rest of the sample. There were 19 additional first contacts but these were not included in the client category, either because the call was thought to be a hoax or because a third person telephoned on behalf of the troubled individual, who did not himself make contact with the service.

Results

350 people (214 male and 136 female) sought aid for the first time during the study period, but of these only 310 were known to be residents of the city of Edinburgh. Their age distribution is shown in Table 7.2 and the same data used to calculate 5—month first-contact rates are illustrated in Figure 7.1.

It can be seen that at all ages males have higher rates than females. The maximum value of the male curve occurs in the decade 20—29, while the peak for females is a decade later. In both sexes there is a ten-fold difference between the rates for young subjects and the low rates for the elderly.

Further analysis by civel status yielded figures which were sometimes too small

TABLE 7.2   Age of Samaritan clients (Edinburgh
residents only) compared with city population
aged 15 and over

	Clients	
	Males	Females
15–19	12	13
20–29	34	26
30–39	21	26
40–49	14	14
50–59	10	8
60 and over	3	3
Not known	6	8
	n = 189	*n* = 121

to provide reliable rates, so the simpler procedure has been adopted, which at least avoids specious precision, of comparing the percentages in the Samaritan clientele and in the Edinburgh population by age and marital status categories. (See Tables 7.3 and 7.4.)

Single males of all age groups are over-represented among the clients. Married men on the other hand, over-represented among those below 30 are markedly under-represented in the later ages. Widowed and divorced are represented roughly in their proportions among the general population.

Among female clients the pattern is very different. Single women are somewhat under-represented, especially in the younger age groups. Married women are correspondingly over-represented among the younger clients, but among those over 50 they are markedly under-represented. The widowed and divorced are again present in about the expected proportion.

In general terms, the most conspicuous deviations from the general population are in the clients aged over 50, whose under-representation is primarily due to a deficit of the married of both sexes.

The social class distribution of the sample males are shown in Table 7.5. The results must be accepted with considerable caution. For 13 per cent the social class was not recorded, and in a further 17 per cent it was not possible to discover any

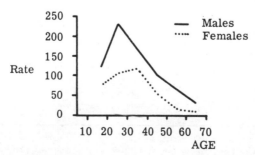

FIGURE 7.1. 5–month inception rates (persons) per 100,000 for males and females

TABLE 7.3   Males: civil status by age; comparison of Samaritan clients (Edinburgh residents only) with city population

	Clients		City population	
	Single %	Married %	Single %	Married %
15–19	28	15	21	9
30–49	9	19	5	28
50 and over	5	6	3	30
All ages	42	40	29	67
All widowed and divorced	6		5	
Cohabiting	4		—	
Not known	7		—	
	$n = 189$		$n = 16070*$	

*Based on 1966 10 per cent Sample Census.
Excluding widowed, divorced, cohabiting, and not known categories, proportion of married, clients $v.$ city C.R. = 5.52, $p < 0.001$.

occupation on which the individual could be classified. It does appear, however, that the upper social classes appear relatively infrequently in comparison with Social Class V which has over six times the rate for Classes I and II. It is possible that by more probing questioning, which was not feasible in the context of the interview, some of these unclassified individuals who are recorded as having no occupation could have been allocated to one of the social class categories. However,

TABLE 7.4   Females: civil status by age; comparison of Samaritan clients (Edinburgh residents only) with city population

	Clients		City population	
	Single %	Married %	Single %	Married %
15–29	15	23	21	10
30–49	3	31	5	24
50 and over	4	7	4	21
All ages	22	61	30	55
All widowed and divorced	11		16	
Cohabiting	3		—	
Not known	3		—	
	$n = 121$		$n = 19756*$	

*Based on 1966 10 per cent Sample Census.
Excluding divorced, widowed, cohabiting, and not known categories, proportion of married, clients $v.$ city C.R. = 2.07, $p < 0.005$.

TABLE 7.5   Social class comparison of Samaritan clients (males) (Edinburgh residents only) with city population

Social Class	Clients %	Rate/1,000*
I and II	6	0.36
III	29	0.73
IV	15	1.20
V	16	2.03
Not classified	17	
Student	3	
Not known	13	
	$n = 189$	$n = 147520*$

*Based on 1966 10 per cent Sample Census.

it is very probable that had they been so allocated they — together with the 13 per cent recorded as 'not known' — would have been classified as Class IV or V, thereby increasing still further the discrepancies shown in Table 7.5.

The living arrangements of the Samaritan clients are of some interest and are compared with those of the city population as far as data on the latter are available in Table 7.6. 19 per cent of the clients lived alone compared with 9 per cent of the city. The proportion of clients living either alone or in lodgings or hostels is significantly higher in males than female clients ($p<.01$).

The problems reported by the clients at their first interview had to be classified rather loosely. Most clients tended to have multiple problems. Consequently those listed in Table 7.7 are by no means mutually exclusive. The items refer to the difficulties as perceived by the client, not as interpreted by the interviewer, which brought him for help at that particular time.

The commonest problem reported by both sexes is financial, affecting over half the men and a third of the women. Of the remaining 'situational problems' the prevalence of alcohol-related difficulties is high in both sexes; drug dependence was mentioned by a fifth of the women, while crime and trouble with the law also

TABLE 7.6   Living arrangements of Samaritan clients compared with city population aged 15 and over (Edinburgh residents only)

	Clients			
	Male %	Female %	All %.	City population %
Living with family or relative	40	70	52 ⎫	91
Living in lodgings	20	11	17 ⎭ 71	
Living alone	25	10	19	9
Not known	15	9	13	—
	$n = 189$	$n = 121$	$n = 310$	$n = 33396*$

*Based on 1966 10 per cent Sample Census.

TABLE 7.7   Presenting problems

	Male %	Female %
Situational		
Accommodation	41	28
Financial	56	35
Work	40	10
Alcohol	19	12
Drugs	1	22
Gambling	5	4
Crime	14	4
Old age	1	2
Personal		
Bereavement	3	7
Loneliness	33	41
Marital	22	43
Pre-marital conflict	9	11
Sexual	11	10
Unwanted pregnancy	3	6

emerged as fairly common. The complaints about gambling sometimes referred to a spouse's behaviour.

Of personal problems the most common was loneliness. This was not unexpected since it had already been noted that 19 per cent of the clients lived alone and a further 17 per cent in lodgings. The relationship between loneliness and living alone was explored in more detail. For men most clients complaining of loneliness were indeed living in an extra-familial situation. For females, however, living by themselves was not a common contributory factor to loneliness, since about 70 per cent of the lonely were living with their families. Fuller details have been presented elsewhere (Chowdhury and Kreitman 1970).

The disposal after the initial contact varied considerably. No formal appointment was made for a client unless requested and usually it was left to the client to make further contact with the Samaritan organization if and when he wished. In only 13 per cent of the male and 17 per cent of the female clients was an appointment arranged at another agency.

In summary men, the young, the lower social classes (males only), and those living alone had the highest rates of first contact with the Edinburgh Samaritans during the study period. Over-representation of certain age-sex-marital status subgroups was also found. A common complaint, at least for women, was of subjective loneliness unrelated to objective living conditions. These characteristics suggest that Samaritan clients differ in many respects from RPTC patients, a suggestion which was investigated directly in the next study.

Comparison of Samaritan clients and parasuicides

For the comparison of the Samaritan clients just described with a corresponding group of parasuicides it was decided that since attention had been limited to Samaritan clients making contact for the first time a similar criterion should be

TABLE 7.8   Percentage distribution of age groups for male and female clients and parasuicides

Age	Males		Females	
	Clients ($n = 189$)	Parasuicides ($n = 93$)	Clients ($n = 121$)	Parasuicides ($n = 132$)
15—19	12	17	13	24
20—24	18	13	11	14
25—29	16	16	16	14
30—39	21	19	26	15
40—49	14	13	14	14
50—59	10	11	8	8
60+	3	11	3	11
Not known	(6	0)	(8	1)

$\chi^2 = 8.564$ df 6   NS $\chi^2 = 13.039$ df 6 $p < 0.05$

applied to parasuicide and only patients presenting with their first-ever episode should be included. Only Edinburgh city cases were studied, and exactly the same 22-week period was used. 222 patients met these criteria, and none was lost from the study.

The first salient finding to emerge was the highly significant difference in the sex ratios of the two groups, 61 per cent of the clients but only 41 per cent of the patients being male. Subsequent comparisons were carried out keeping the sexes separate.

The age distribution, given in Table 7.8, shows that men in both groups had a similar age range but that the client sample contained substantially fewer teenagers and more women in their 30s than was found among the parasuicides.

Figure 7.2(a) illustrates the rates for males. Samaritan clients have higher rates at all ages. In both groups the peak rates occur in the 20—20 age bracket and the relative excess of clients over patient rates is least in the oldest age groups. For females (Figure 7.2 (b)) the curves differ in the first half of life in that the client

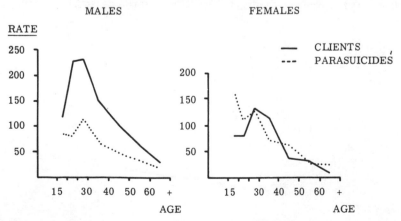

FIGURE 7.2. 5-month inception rates (persons) per 100,000 for clients and parasuicides: males and females

rates are relatively lower in the early years and relatively higher for the 30—39 age group. Beyond that age the curves are very similar and the rates are low.

These findings indicated that both age and sex require to be held constant when examining the distribution of marital state categories. For men no significant differences were found on marital state for any age group or for the series as a whole. For women, however, significant differences emerged: for the women aged below 30, the client group contained only 37 per cent who were single as compared to 69 per cent of the patients. In part this might reflect the rather primitive age standardization which had to be employed, since it will be recalled that the client group contained comparatively fewer adolescents.

Difficulties concerning social class categorization of the clients have already been mentioned. Class V plus 'no usual occupation' together accounted for one—third of the clients as compared to one—quarter of the patients ($p < .01$).

Household composition is illustrated for males in Table 7.9. A smaller proportion of male clients lived in a family setting or with friends than did the parasuicides principally because there were fewer living with their parents. Nearly one-quarter of the clients were living alone. The rather high proportion whose household composition could not be ascertained should caution against emphasis of these discrepancies.

Among females there were no significant differences regarding family as against non-family households, though fewer clients were living with parents — possibly a reflection of the age differences between the groups as previously mentioned — and rather more were in hostels or lodgings.

Rates for each of the 23 wards of the city were calculated for both the clients and parasuicides, for men and women separately. The numerators were often small and the results must be interpreted cautiously. For males the rank order correlation for the two sets of rates across the 23 city wards was moderately high ($r_s = 0.54$). Male clients thus tend to be drawn from the areas of the city which are prominent in their parasuicide rates. For females, however, there was no significant correlation between the two rank orders. Unlike the clear-out clustering of certain wards with high parasuicide rates described in chapter 2, female clients seem to be widely drawn from all over the city.

Other details have been reported elsewhere (Chowdhury and Kreitman, 1971).

TABLE 7.9   Percentage distribution by household composition of male clients and parasuicides

	Clients		Patients	
Spouse	23		26	
Parents	13	} 40	23	} 64
Other relatives or friends	4		15	
Alone	24		15	
Hostel or lodgings	20	} 44	13	} 30
Institution	0		2	
Not known	16		6	
	$n = 189$		$n = 93$	

$\chi^2 = 10.81$ df 1 $p < 0.01$ $\chi^2 = 21.42$ df 5 $p < 0.001$

Discussion

The main findings of both parts of the study can be briefly summarized. The Samaritan clients show a relative excess of men when compared to the parasuicides, but the age distribution of the two groups is similar. The male clients are less likely to be living with their families or friends, though there is no difference in the formal marital status of the groups: there must therefore be an excess of men among the clients who are married but living away from their wives, or if unmarried are living in isolation. More of the clients appear to have no standard occupation and their overall social class position is probably lower than that of the patients. The two groups tend to live in similar parts of the city, notably at the decaying centre or other areas of poor social integration. There is also marginal evidence, which has not been presented, that the client group are less likely to have problems of alcohol or drug dependency.

For women the picture is rather different. They are markedly under-represented among the clients in comparison with the RPTC patients. The female clients were older than the female patients and presumably for this reason are less often unmarried. All the same, the women in the two groups are similar with respect to the proportion living with kin or friends. They differ markedly, however, in their areas of residence, being drawn from widely different parts of the city.

In essence the comparisons show that in both services the majority of cases tended to be young people, who for the most part are individuals in considerable distress. Beyond that, however, the differences between the workload of the two organizations are numerous and complex. If the Samaritan organization is in fact contributing to the primary prevention of parasuicide then it seems to be doing so with respect to a group of individuals who are atypical of parasuicides in general. For this reason it appears that however successful a service of the type currently being operated by the Telephone Samaritans might prove to be, it is unlikely to affect the parasuicide problem very substantially. This does not discount the possibility of a partial contribution: it does mean, however, that no prima facie case exists for a major expansion of Samaritan activities in the hope of markedly reducing the first-ever parasuicide rate. Other functions of the Telephone Samaritan service have not been examined and the conclusions of this section should not of course be taken to imply any kind of evaluation of its broader aims.

The work so far had depicted and compared the broad characteristics of the groups using the two services. The next step appeared to be to gain a clearer understanding of the 'help seeking' represented by consulting the Telephone Samaritans as compared to engaging in a parasuicidal act. The following study was an attempt to open up this question by focusing more on individual attributes and with less attention to demographic and social parameters than previously, although these remained to be confirmed.

7.3 SOME ASPECTS OF DISTRESS BEHAVIOUR

The aim of the next study was to elucidate why some individuals seek relief through support and guidance from an appropriate agency, while others resort to parasuicide. The work noted in previous sections of this chapter suggested that the Samaritans clients and parasuicides were similar with regard to their level of subjective distress and that their problems appeared to cover a broadly similar range. Differences between the groups on a number of demographic and social indices were found, but the investigation to be described was concerned with the most obvious difference of all, namely that the two groups had adopted quite diverse responses, or strategies, in the face of their difficulties. It appeared that the Samaritan clients had taken the apparently rational step of seeking out and utilizing the help offered by an agency which was specially interested 'to help the suicidal and despairing'. However, since many individuals made contact with the Samaritans only fleetingly, even though their problems remained unresolved, it was decided to exclude such transients and to select for detailed study those individuals who continued to work with the Samaritans and maintain contact with them over a period of time; these were referred to as 'persistent help-seekers' as they represented clients making consistent and rational use of the help available to them.

By contrast, the second group, the parasuicides, had had recourse in their distress to the dangerous and relatively ineffective solution presented by self-poisoning or self-injury. For present purposes a subgroup was selected which consisted of those individuals who were clearly capable of making an explicit request for help if they had so wished, or more accurately, were not prevented from doing so by reason of cognitive defect or psychosis. These 'pure' cases of parasuicide represented a group clearly contrasting with the persistent help-seekers in terms of their current distress behaviour.

Sampling procedures

To avoid complexities resulting from an individual's past experience of Samaritan consultation or RPTC treatment of an earlier parasuicide, only individuals making contact with either service for the first time ever were included in the study.

The operational definition of a 'persistent help-seeker' among the Samaritan clients was an individual who made two consecutive contacts with the service for the same problem within a 2-week period, whether or not a formal appointment had been offered. Clients who made their second contact merely to thank the Samaritans or to report that they had continued with a plan to refer them elsewhere were not included, nor were those referred from other organizations. Between February and December 1969, 128 clients were identified as falling within the defined group, of whom 121 or 94 per cent were included in the final study. The remaining seven could not be included, as the Samaritan worker concerned with the case did not feel able to complete the schedule.

Correspondingly, the parasuicides included in the investigation comprised *first-ever* admissions to the RPTC during February and March 1969. Excluded were any patients diagnosed as psychotic or subnormal, those with organic disorder, and any admission from a prison or psychiatric hospital. 97 patients fell within this definition, of whom 93 (96 per cent) were interviewed: the remaining four left the centre before they could be seen.

The use of defined subgroups facilitates their comparison but carries the penalty of raising the further question of how 'persistent help-seekers' are related to Samaritan clients in general, and the parasuicides in the study to all those patients admitted to the RPTC at the same period. These points will be discussed in due course.

Following a pilot investigation, a single schedule was prepared for use with both groups. The Samaritan clients were interviewed by the appropriate Samaritan worker, who usually saw the client on both visits, while all the patients were interviewed by one investigator.

Results

The principal findings concern the comparison between the 'persistent help-seekers' and the first-ever parasuicides. The main points were as follows.

Demographic factors, living group, and employment

Among the persistent help-seekers there was a markedly ($p < .001$) higher proportion of males (64 per cent) than was found among the parasuicides (39 per cent). In view of this difference, in most of the other analyses the sexes have been treated separately. The age distribution shown in Table 7.10 indicates that the male help-seekers were appreciably older than the comparison group, but this was not the case among the females.

For reasons which will be explained in detail below, 22 male Samaritan clients have been excluded from the remainder of the study. They represented a very special subgroup who appeared to be seeking no active help although they fell within the operational definition. Their omission does not affect the interpretation of the age and sex data just referred to.

There was no significant difference in marital status among the male subjects, despite the previously noted differences in age which would have led one to expect relatively fewer single men among the Samaritan clients; actually the reverse was found to be the case. Among the females there was a relative excess of separated, widowed, and divorced women among the Samaritan clients as compared to a preponderance of married subjects among the parasuicides ($p < .01$). It will be recalled that the two groups of women did not differ with respect to age.

There was no difference between the groups for social class distribution either for men or for women.

Among men, nearly half the help-seekers were living alone, a proportion

TABLE 7.10 Age distribution (percentages) and modal age, by sex, of persistent help-seekers and parasuicides

	Male		Female	
	P.h.-seekers	Parasuicides	P.h.-seekers	Parasuicides
Under 20	4	27	7	20
20–29	21	8	30	27
30–39	26	23	28	21
40–49	23	14	18	19
50–59	15	11	9	10
60+	5	17	7	4
Not known	6	–	–	–
	$n = 78$	$n = 36$	$n = 43$	$n = 57$
Modal age	42	36	35	32

$\chi^2 = 19.207$ df 5 $p < 0.01$　　　　$\chi^2 = 6.867$ df 5 n.s.

TABLE 7.11   Household composition of persistent help-seekers and parasuicides: percentage distribution

	Male		Female	
	P.h.-seekers	Parasuicides	P.h.-seekers	Parasuicides
Living with spouse or parents	48	67	49	77
Living with children, sibs, relatives or friends	4	8	23	16
Living alone, in hostels or lodgings	48	25	28	7
	$n = 56$	$n = 36$	$n = 43$	$n = 57$

$\chi^2 (a + b/c) = 4.958$ df 1 $p < 0.05$ $\chi^2 = 5.779$ df 1 $p < 0.02$

significantly greater than that found among the male parasuicides. There were similarly conspicuous differences in their type of living accommodation; the majority of male persistent help-seekers were living in a bedsitter, or in a hostel or similar institution, while the majority of parasuicides lived in a private house, whether their own or that of their parents (Tables 7.11 and 7.12). Among women, too, there was a significant excess of clients living alone and a deficit of those living with their intimate families when compared to the proportions among the parasuicides. Their type of accommodation also reflects these differences.

Only one-third of the men seeking help from the Samaritans were actively employed, a proportion much lower than that among the parasuicides. The difference was made up by the excess of unemployed men rather than by those who were off through sickness (Table 7.13). There were no significant differences among the women.

The subjects in the two groups were asked if they had any friends. The term 'friend' was defined very loosely and was not limited to intimate friendships only. Nevertheless, approximately one-quarter of both sexes in both groups felt that they had no one to whom they could apply this label. Discrepancies in usage of the word

TABLE 7.12   Type of accommodation occupied by the persistent help-seekers and parasuicides: percentage distribution

	Male		Female	
	P.h.-seekers	Parasuicides	P.h.-seekers	Parasuicides
House owned, rented or parental	34	86	53	88
Bedsitter, hostel, other or none	63	14	35	12
Not known	3	—	12	—
	$n = 56$	$n = 36$	$n = 43$	$n = 57$

$\chi^2 = 22.686$ df 1 $p < 0.001$ $\chi^2 = 9.474$ df 1 $p < 0.001$

TABLE 7.13 Employment of persistent help-seekers in
comparison with parasuicides: percentage distribution;
males only

	P.h.-seekers	Parasuicides
Employed	32	58
Unemployed	39	17
Off sick	20	17
Students, retired and permanently disabled	7	8
Not known	2	—
	$n = 56$	$n = 36$

$\chi^2 = 7.339$ df 3 $p < 0.05$
Employed and off sick/unemployed: $\chi^2 = 12.094$ df 2
$p < 0.001$

'friend' by various social classes need not be considered since there were no significant social class differences between the groups.

Among both men and women fewer clients than parasuicides were currently receiving treatment for psychological symptoms from their general practitioner or were attending a psychiatrist: details are given in Table 7.14. For some subjects, however, data were not available. If all the 'not known' cases are assumed to be under care, the difference between the groups disappears for the men but remains statistically significant for the women.

TABLE 7.14 Current psychiatric treatment being received by persistent help-seekers and parasuicides: percentage distributions

	Male		Female	
	P.h.-seekers	Parasuicides	P.h.-seekers	Parasuicides
Yes	21	44	25	61
No	70	56	60	39
Not known	9	0	14	0
	$n = 56$	$n = 36$	$n = 43$	$n = 57$

$\chi^2 = 9.308$ df 1 $p < 0.01$ $\chi^2 = 9.007$ df 1 $p < 0.01$

Source and duration of stress

In Table 7.15 data are presented concerning the nature of the problem reported by the client or patient. These were often multiple for each individual, and the categories used are not mutually exclusive.

For almost all types of problem the proportions are higher in the help-seeker group than in the parasuicides. While it is possible that this is due to a different

130

TABLE 7.15   Percentages of persistent help-seekers and parasuicides reporting specific problems, with rank order of problems

	Male		Female	
	P.h.-seekers	Parasuicides	P.h.-seekers	Parasuicides
Accommodation	32	8	26	5
Finance	49	44	57	32
Debt	30	19	33	25
Employment	42	31	31	18
Physical ill-health	26	25	19	14
Marital	32	22	48	40
Loneliness	46	33	48	40
Bereavement	11	11	7	16
Crime	12	5	10	2
	$n = 56$	$n = 36$	$n = 43$	$n = 57$

$r_s = 0.779$ $p < 0.05$

$r_s = 0.833$ $p < 0.01$

Items are not mutually exclusive

interview setting, it certainly suggests that the help-seekers do not have fewer problems than the patients. When the various problems are listed in rank order of their frequency of report, a high correlation emerges both for male and female subjects. The pattern of difficulties represented by the two groups is thus very similar. Financial problems and loneliness are particularly prominent. An attempt was also made to identify whether the problems reported had been continually present for a considerable period, or were episodic in character or were currently troubling the individual for the first time. Less than half the persistent help-seekers reported continuous stress, though two-thirds of the parasuicides did so, and this held true when comparing like-sex subjects only. The distinction between continuous and recurrent stresses is by no means an absolute one, and perhaps the major point to note is that only a small minority in either group reported that their problems were new or recent. Interestingly, a further proportion denied that they were under any particular stress. Additional details have been reported by Kreitman and Chowdhury (1973a and b).

The relationship of study samples to their parent groups

The persistent help-seekers were compared with the 5-month series of Samaritan clients described in the previous section. For men, the former were significantly older and more often divorced or separated, while for women they were more often single or divorced or separated. Correspondingly, among the present sample of first-ever parasuicides the social class of the men was significantly lower than in the unselected series of parasuicides described in the last section, while among the women fewer were found to be living alone. Table 7.16 summarizes these and other results.

   It is not intended to attempt to interpret these discrepancies in detail. The point to be made is that the samples of persistent help-seekers and of parasuicides as studied in this investigation were not representative of the agency populations from

TABLE 7.16   Differences between present samples and
larger series of Samaritan clients and parasuicides

	Samaritans	Parasuicides
Sex ratio	n.s.	n.s.
Males		
Age	$p < 0.01$	n.s.
Marital status	$p < 0.01$	n.s.
Social class	n.s.	$p < 0.01$
Living group	n.s.	n.s.
Females		
Age	n.s.	n.s.
Marital status	$p < 0.01$	n.s.
Living group	n.s.	$p < 0.05$

which they were drawn. This is not particularly surprising, as they were deliberately selected for a specific purpose, but should caution against generalization.

Discussion

Before reviewing the findings some comment must be made about the 22 men among the Samaritan clients excluded from most of the comparisons. They originally came into the study because they fell within the operational definition of a 'help-seeker', but it transpired that they were vagrants in search (with success) of warmth, rest, and a cup of tea. They usually volunteered no special problems and it often proved difficult to elicit any information from them. Their elimination from the rest of the study does not seriously affect the preponderence of men over women among the Samaritan clients nor, so far as can be ascertained, the observed age distribution among the men.

The difference in the sex ratio between the two groups, with the clients being mostly men and the parasuicides mostly women, was one of the clearest findings. Comparing the males in the two samples, the Samaritan clients were found to be relatively older, though the married amongst them did not represent a larger proportion; in fact there was a tendency for unmarried men to be relatively commoner. The male help-seekers tended to live in lodgings or in institutions rather than with their families and were less likely to be receiving treatment for psychological symptoms. The two male groups did not differ on social class or on the multiplicity or duration of their current problems, nor in the sense of friendlessness. Both groups often reported having no friends, but the clients were significantly more often living in isolation while the parasuicides were living with their families.

The pattern of findings for females was only a little different. The women among the clients were of similar age to the parasuicides but contained a relative excess of separated, widowed, and divorced. Perhaps for this reason they, like the male clients, were more likely to be living alone than were the same-sex parasuicides. Only a minority of clients, as against a majority of parasuicides, were receiving psychiatric treatment from any source. Both groups reported a similar range and chronicity of problems and appeared to be of similar social class and employment status so far as this could be ascertained. Like the men, both groups reported a lack of friends in approximately similar proportions, despite their differences in living group and type of accommodation.

When one attempts to draw these data together and relate them to a choice of help-seeking or parasuicidal behaviour three points emerge. Firstly, the help-seekers of both sexes are comparatively more socially isolated. In both sexes they are less likely to have a spouse to whom they can turn, are more likely to be living apart from their family or friends, and among men at least to have less effective contact through work because of unemployment. In contrast, the parasuicides, who show fewer of these features, are living in an appreciably richer interpersonal environment. They have other people against whom to act and interact, sometimes explosively, and perhaps less need to consult agencies to find others to whom they can relate their difficulties. Their world is already peopled, and seeking new contacts is not a likely resource for them. In a proportion of parasuicides the act may even be best interpreted as a transaction between the patient and his intimate group (see chapter 4).

The second feature is that the apparently rational procedure of help-seeking is found to be resorted to more often among men, and especially for older men, while parasuicidal behaviour is represented preponderantly by women. In part, this sex difference could be explained by the greater social isolation among men than women in our sample. It might, however, also reflect a sex-linked preference for principally 'instrumental' as against principally 'expressive' activity, i.e. a desire to solve an objectifiable problem, in this case by seeking advice and guidance, rather than by emotional appeal or by attempting to intermit an intolerable state of mind. Cooperstock (1971) has proposed a similar view to account for the higher consumption of psychotropic drugs in women.

The hypothesis is advanced with diffidence. The distinction between instrumentality and expressivity in social action has been extensively discussed in sociological writings, but the difference is not always evident when applied to individuals in distress. For example, it is not clear whether a patient in psychotherapy is acting instrumentally to effect symptom reduction and problem resolution, or expressively by ventilating his emotions to a sympathetic listener, or both. Nevertheless, the point seems worth raising.

Thirdly, there is the finding that for both sexes more parasuicides were currently receiving psychiatric treatment, from whatever source, than were Samaritan clients. As it was not possible to assess the psychological health of all subjects at time of contact, it is difficult to interpret this finding clearly. It might reflect a lower rate of psychiatric morbidity among the clients, but could equally represent a greater difficulty on their part in making contact with doctors as with other human beings, as shown for example by their relatively solitary lives.

Hopes for the primary prevention of self-poisoning and self-injury have largely centred on the feasibility of persuading potential patients to consult various emergency services geared to their needs. The model of decision-making implied in such programmes is that a given individual will opt for the more socially desirable course of action if the services are freely provided and if adverse attitudes to their use are overcome. The present results cannot, strictly speaking, either support or refute such a model, since the population sampled was not one of *potential* parasuicides but of those who have proceeded to act. Nevertheless, the findings do indicate that the two groups differ on stable and enduring characteristics. If the variables studied are indeed determinants of behaviour, their effects are unlikely to be easily offset.

On the other hand, it is evident that the findings, though relevant to 'nuclear' groups of Samaritan clients and parasuicides, may not apply to all those falling in either category, and further, that the *subjective* reasons offered by the individual to account for his actions have yet to be considered. These two issues were taken up in the two following studies.

7.4 THE BBC 'BEFRIENDERS' SERIES AND ITS EFFECTS

The series of studies reported in the preceding sections had tended increasingly to underline the disparity between the Telephone Samaritan clientele and the parasuicide cases being seen at the RPTC. They appeared to be individuals with different demographic and social characteristics, and although the levels and type of distress appeared to be not dissimilar, the pattern of help which the individuals were requesting from the two services also appeared to differ markedly. However, the potential impact which the Samaritan organization might make on the parasuicide problem could only be defined more closely through a quasi experimental approach. The opportunity for a 'natural experiment' arose in 1972, and provided the basis of a study by Holding (1974).

If it is hypothesized that the Samaritan organization does prevent parasuicide, then an increase in Samaritan referrals should be associated with a decrease in parasuicide rates, other factors being equal. A BBC programme based on the Samaritans' work afforded an opportunity for testing this hypothesis. The programme in question was an eleven-episode weekly series called 'The Befrienders' screened at peak viewing times on Saturday evenings from 19 February 1972. Each episode portrayed a predicament leading to a suicidal situation; one episode ended with a suicidal death. The opportunity was taken to monitor the effects of this series on new client referrals to the Edinburgh Samaritans and simultaneously on parasuicide admissions to the RPTC.

Method

Three periods were studied in relation to 'The Befrienders' series; the 4 weeks before the series started, the 10 weeks for which it continued and the subsequent 4 weeks. For each period the number of new client referrals to the Edinburgh branch of the Samaritans and the number of parasuicide admissions to the RPTC were compared. Comparisons were also made for both groups with three corresponding periods in 1969, 1970, and 1971. The sexes were combined.

For each of the 4 years and for both groups the average weekly numbers were calculated for the three periods. They are expressed below as percentages, using as a base line for 1972 the average number for the 4 weeks before the series; for earlier years the corresponding weeks of January and February for each year provided the base lines. In addition to monitoring the number of admissions, a random sample of parasuicides during the three periods in 1972 were interviewed and asked whether they had heard of the Samaritans, whether they knew what the Samaritans did, and for those admitted after 'The Befrienders' had started, whether they had watched

134

the series and been influenced by it. 22 admissions were interviewed before the series started, 35 during the series, and 39 over the following 4 weeks.

Results

New client Samaritan referrals

During the 10 weeks of 'The Befrienders' series in 1972, the average weekly new client referrals to the Edinburgh branch of the Samaritans increased by 112 per cent compared with the base line 4 weeks. This contrasts with small decreases over the comparable periods in 1969 and 1971, and a small increase over the comparable period in 1970. For the 4 weeks following the series in 1972, the average weekly increase was 140 per cent compared with increases of 30 per cent, 23 per cent, and 18 per cent in the corresponding periods in the 3 comparison years (Figure 7.3). The numbers of new client Samaritan referrals for the three periods in 1972 and the comparison years is shown in Table 7.17.

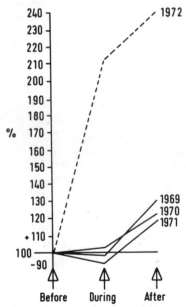

FIGURE 7.3. Average weekly Samaritan new clients

TABLE 7.17   New client Samaritan referrals

Year	4 weeks before 'Befrienders'	10 weeks during 'Befrienders'	4 weeks after 'Befrienders'
1969	80	198	104
1970	88	226	108
1971	110	259	129
1972	100	530	240

Parasuicide admissions to the RPTC

The average weekly parasuicide admissions to the RPTC in 1972 *increased* by 13 per cent during 'The Befrienders' and by 22 per cent during the subsequent 4 weeks. Parasuicide admissions for the corresponding periods in 1969 and 1970 showed similar small increases for the 10-week middle period and rather greater increases for the subsequent 4 weeks. The changes for corresponding periods in 1971 were different and atypical — a 9 per cent decrease for the comparison weeks of the series and a 14 per cent decrease during the subsequent 4 weeks. The numbers involved are shown in Table 7.18, but Figure 7.4 shows the changes more clearly.

TABLE 7.18   Parasuicide admissions to RPTC

Year	4 weeks before 'Befrienders'	10 weeks during 'Befrienders'	4 weeks after 'Befrienders'
1969	82	212	95
1970	90	234	105
1971	152	347	131
1972	129	364	158

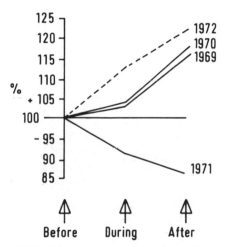

FIGURE 7.4. Average weekly parasuicides

Knowledge of the Samaritans

Amongst the random sample of parasuicides interviewed, 31 per cent during the series had watched one or more episodes compared with 50 per cent in the subsequent 4 weeks. There was no increase, however, in the percentages of parasuicides who said they had heard of the Samaritans as the series progressed — 82 per cent before the series started, 86 per cent during, and 87 per cent after the series. When asked whether they knew what the Samaritans did, 68 per cent before,

63 per cent during, but only 51 per cent after the series were able to describe their role. No parasuicide was influenced by watching an episode during the series, but one admission after the series claimed to have been influenced by what he had viewed; none the less, he completed a parasuicidal act.

Discussion

'The Befrienders' series was, from the viewpoint of the Samaritan organization, evidently a very successful exercise in that it led to a marked increase in the number of new client referrals; the figures cited for Edinburgh were paralled by a similar increase occurring at a national level (Fox, 1971), but the numbers of parasuicides admitted to the RPTC showed no decline and there is no evidence that the series had any preventive effect either during the time it was screened or in the subsequent 4 weeks. Again these findings appear to mirror data obtained at a national level. Thus from the community viewpoint there is no evidence that the Samaritan organization acts as an alternative source of help which leads to a demonstrable reduction in parasuicide.

Such a conclusion fits with the findings documented from the studies described earlier in this chapter, but it may be worth noting that although 'The Befrienders' series had evidently spread awareness of the Samaritans' role among the general population, it had had no effect on the proportions of parasuicides who were familiar with their work. It is thus possible that the parasuicides were not effectively reached by the programme. On the other hand, even before the series began, some 82 per cent of the patients were aware of the existence of the organization and 68 per cent[1] were able to describe its role with reasonable accuracy. These rather impressive figures may suggest there is not much room for further propaganda.

It should also be noted that the TV series was composed on dramas hinging around a potential *suicide*, not parasuicide. It is also possible that the wave of new clients attracted to the organization following the series may in some respects differ from the kinds of individuals who were attending previously; susceptibility to television may have all manner of psychological correlates. Nevertheless, within the limits of the experiment the conclusions remain unequivocal. However valuable the Samaritan organization may be in crisis intervention, the effects of the service do not include a reduction in parasuicide rates.

7.5 ATTITUDES, CHOICE OF ACTION, AND DISTRESS BEHAVIOUR

The next investigation was concerned with patients only, and aimed to ascertain their knowledge of help-giving services, and to elucidate their attitudes towards help-seeking, both in general and in the specific setting of their parasuicidal behaviour. It was based on the same 93 patients described in the Section 7.3.

Information was gathered by a semi-structured interview which took place after the formal psychiatric examination by the service staff had been completed. Most patients appeared relaxed and co-operative. The interview began with a general explanation and an invitation to the patient to assist with the enquiry. Spontaneous discussion was encouraged, direct questioning being employed only if key items of information were not otherwise produced. Each interview lasted about an hour. A reliability check on the classification of some of the attitudinal data was also carried out (see below).

Results

Knowledge of services

Patients were asked whether they knew of anyone in a service role or of any organizations to whom they could have taken their problem had they so wished. Only 15 per cent at the most claimed to be factually unaware of any help-giving agency. The most commonly mentioned source of potential aid was the general practitioner, mentioned by 74 per cent of the patients, followed by a variety of social work agencies (45 per cent). Direct questioning showed that about one-third of the patients knew of the existence and purpose of the Telephone Samaritan organization. Men and women did not differ markedly in their pattern of replies.

Attitudes to help-seeking in general

General attitudes towards seeking help in times of crisis as against remaining self—sufficient were explored in a series of questions, and the replies were categorized as in Table 7.19. About one-fifth of the patients declared that in general terms help-seeking for one's problems from any source was not acceptable behaviour and that one should solve all one's own difficulties oneself. The remainder declared themselves in favour of seeking aid, though some qualified individuals were cited most often, but some patients thought that anyone might serve in times of difficulty. A minority specified that only a relative could, or should, assist.

TABLE 7.19   Attitudes to help-seeking in crises: percentages

	Males ($n = 36$)	Females ($n = 57$)	Total ($n = 93$)
Desirability of help			
Help desirable	53	42	46
Dependent on nature of problem	22	39	32
Help not desirable	25	19	22
From whom help acceptable			
No one	25	19	22
Relative only	14	3	7
Specialized (service) individuals	42	47	45
Anyone available	19	30	26

Attitudes to help-seeking with current problems

Thus the majority of patients knew that help could have been obtained if they had wished, and expressed no disapproval of help-seeking behaviour in times of stress. Nevertheless they had become parasuicides. Discussion then turned to their reasons for resorting to self-poisoning instead of seeking outside aid. For clarity the 14

138

patients who claimed factual ignorance were excluded at this point, even though it is by no means evident that they were unaware of help-giving resources rather than perceiving these as grossly inappropriate to their own needs.

A pilot study on 25 cases, excluded from the main sample, had shown that patients were usually capable of stating explicitly their *main* reasons for not seeking help from 'agencies' and that their statements could be grouped into six classes. These, with illustrative examples, included:

(1) Wanted to die: 'I wanted to die, so I didn't want to tell anyone about my problem or my intention.' 'I thought only death could solve my problem — there was no point in going to see . . .

(2) Too personal: 'It's my marriage — I should try to find the solution myself — I would not discuss it with others.' 'I've got to solve my own personal problems — I can't expect others to do it for me.'

(3) Critical of services: 'I was disappointed and didn't want to go back.' 'He has no time.' 'I cannot talk to him.'

(4) To relieve strain: 'I wanted to have a good sleep, so I would feel better in the morning.' 'I just wanted to calm myself.'

TABLE 7.20   'Reasons' for non-consultation: percentages

	Males	Females	Total
Self-medication to relieve strain	30	31	30
Critical of services	26	13	18
Problem too personal	18	17	18
Wanted to die	22	15	18
To influence others	4	17	13
Help not physically available	0	6	4
Total (n =)	(27)	(52)	(79*)

*Refers only to patients with knowledge of availability of medical and social agencies.

(5) To influence others: 'It was to bring my husband's senses back.' 'To make him [husband] see my point of view.'

(6) Not possible to seek help: 'I'm not allowed to contact my GP without the Matron's permission' (a resident of an old people's home). 'I'm not registered with any GP here.'

These themes also emerged in the main study, and were used as the basis for classification. 12 months after the proformas were completed, the interviewer read over the verbatim notes in the relevant parts of the schedule and blindly classified the statements again. Group (3) was similarly identified in 81 per cent of instances, groups (1) and (4) in 92 per cent, and the remainder on all occasions.

Table 7.20 shows the numbers, by sex, in each group. The 'self-medication to relieve strain' category is the most numerous. Men were more inclined than women to be critical of the agencies available, while women more frequently expressed a desire to influence others, but on the whole the two sexes gave similar responses.

Use of agencies and the role of drugs

The 79 patients who knew of the existence of help-giving agencies were asked whether they had ever discussed their problems with them and whether they had consulted in the 2 weeks before their parasuicide. Only 27 of the group had consulted at *any* time, all but one in the fortnight before admission. Thus a third of the group had sought assistance recently, though doing so had evidently not succeeded in averting their parasuicide. It seemed of interest to tabulate the agency used against the ostensible reason for their self-poisoning or self-injury. This has been done in Table 7.21: of those who allegedly wished to kill themselves over half had recently consulted their general practitioners. It also emerged yet again that general practitioners were the commonest resource and that a disproportionately smaller number of patients had actually used social agencies or the Telephone Samaritans than knew of their existence and purpose.

Patients were also asked about their use of psychotropic drugs, including night sedation. No less than 50 of the 79 were on regular medication. Yet, as the previous table shows, only 20 had ventilated their difficulties with the prescribing doctor. The remaining 30 received repeat prescriptions without actually seeing him or, very exceptionally, without their problems being raised during a consultation; four of the 30 took their difficulties to other agencies. Evidently receiving drugs and assistance with subjective problems are very different things, and many patients received the former without the latter.

Patients who sought advice without their being given pills were very few. There was a clear association between receiving medication and the discussion of difficulties, which is to say that facilities for consultation which did not involve the consumption of drugs were little used.

TABLE 7.21   'Reasons' for parasuicide and recent use of agencies (preceding 2 weeks)

'Reasons'	General practitioner	Social work services	Telephone Samaritans	None	Total
To relieve strain	6	—	—	18	24
Critical of service	4	2	2	6	14
Problem too personal	—	—	—	14	14
Wanted to die	8	1	—	5	14
To influence others	2	1	—	7	10
Help not available	—	—	—	3	3
Total	20	4	2	53	79

Discussion

Comments offered *post facto* by patients about an act for which many could barely account even to themselves must necessarily be viewed with caution. The present study, however, was not concerned with the whole tangle of motivations leading up to the parasuicide, but was confined to the reasons given by patients for their not seeking guidance for their problems instead of resorting to self-poisoning or self-injury. The patient's own expression of these reasons warrants due attention.

The great majority of patients were aware that help could have been offered to them by someone, especially their general practitioner, whose importance as a help-giver has repeatedly emerged. Factual ignorance of any help-giving agency was reported by only a small minority, although there is clearly scope for greater information on the aims and work of the Department of Social Welfare. The same is true for the Telephone Samaritans, the latter being known to only a third of the patients, although this proportion is appreciably higher than the 13 per cent quoted from a London hospital by Bagley (1970). Yet factual information was clearly of little value. A quarter of the group even maintained that seeking help for personal problems was not an acceptable form of behaviour; they believed that personal difficulties were appropriately solved by one's own determination or possibly with some help from an intimate friend.

Such general attitudes may of course have limited relevance for a particular crisis. All patients except the 15 per cent who claimed factual ignorance of a help-giving agency were questioned further about their reasons for not utilizing such services in the present emergency. The findings will be briefly reviewed with particular reference to their implications for preventive action.

The largest group (30 per cent) claimed they were seeking immediate relief from strain and that this could be most rapidly achieved by self-medication in large doses. At least one-third of these patients were currently attending their general practitioner. The 'interruption' (Shneidman, 1964) they sought varied from a few hours sleep to unconsciousness over several days. Whether these patients could have withstood their distress long enough to embark on rational solutions to their problems is at best an open question. Their action was directed entirely towards their current feeling states and not towards the objective or 'instrumental' solution of their problem. As Kessel (1965), Birtchnell and Alarcon (1971) and others have suggested, they could be viewed as individuals with low tolerance to stress living in a drug-oriented culture (although many had in fact consulted with their difficulties at various times in the past). Conceivably, consultation before current events had overwhelmed them might have helped, but this is no more than a speculation. Any such solution would also imply a major extension of services to a scale and degree of enduring success which is scarcely realistic, since the presenting problems reflected a wide range of difficulties often of a long-standing and intractable kind.

The group who thought that various agencies had nothing useful to offer (18 per cent) were often speaking from experience. Most of these patients had been in recent contact with some service, and they represent failures of management. Only improvement in the therapeutic efficiency and management skills of existing agencies, including doctors, seem likely to affect the size of this subgroup.

Those who expressed a wish to die (18 per cent) were in some respects similar to the last mentioned since most of these patients too had been in recent contact with help-givers and represent failures of care (mostly of medical care). Their numbers can only be reduced by better treatment given at an earlier stage.

There were several patients (18 per cent) who considered their problems too personal for ventilation to other people, and none had in fact sought help even from their family doctor. This group may prove exceptionally difficult to reach. These patients had evidently exhausted their own reserves yet had still not sought aid, an attitude which may be viewed as self-sufficiency carried to extremes. In a similar vein, Litman (1971) has commented on the 'god-like self-sufficiency' of certain individuals who proceed to suicide, apparently inevitably. Their attitudes represent perhaps a combination of factors, including both popular concepts of privacy and the actual interest and behaviour of the caring professions. Over the last decade many leaders of psychiatry, for example, have urged a withdrawal of professional interest from 'purely personal' problems. If this view were to be shared by general practitioners, increasing numbers of parasuicides could be the consequence.

The last main group (13 per cent) comprised those patients who clearly stated that their overdose was intended to convey a dramatic message to another person, usually their spouse, and that their purpose could not have been met by any less flamboyant action such as consulting another person about their difficulties. Again it is hard to conceive with realism of any type of service which could have helped them in the manner in which they wished to be helped. It is not possible to say whether at an earlier stage of their difficulties less dramatic means of solution might have appeared appropriate.

That no less than 50 out of 79 patients or 63 per cent (of those who knew of help-giving services) should have been receiving psychotropic drugs is noteworthy, even in the absence of comparative data from non-parasuicides.

That so many parasuicides were already receiving drugs from their doctors (or from psychiatrists) raises the possibility that the availability of drugs may have precipitated the self-poisoning. The possibility remains open for these particular individuals, though it is known that in general only 55 per cent of self-poisoning admissions involve drugs medically prescribed for the patient. The issue of availability of drugs in relation to parasuicide is taken up later in this chapter.

It is also evident that the receipt of drugs is no indicator that the patient is being helped psychologically with his subjective difficulties, since the majority of patients alleged that they had not ventilated their problems with the prescribing doctor. As mentioned, this situation often arose where a patient was given repeat prescriptions without a consultation. It is not known in the remaining cases whether the patient's reticence, the doctor's lack of interest, or both, were responsible for this anomalous situation.

Conclusion

These findings, when considered alongside those reported in earlier sections, suggest certain general conclusions.

(1) Over a quarter of the series were currently in contact with an 'agency' and must be considered as failures of management. This does *not* imply that these agencies are inefficient, since no data have been collected on their successes, but it does indicate that a substantial reduction in parasuicides (especially among those expressing a wish to die) could be achieved if existing methods of management were improved.

(2) There is little hope for reducing the parasuicide rate simply by disseminating factual information about the existence of helping agencies; all but 15 per cent of the patients were already aware of them. On the other hand, an improvement in the efficiency, style and public 'image' of the agencies might induce the many patients — over half the total — who knew of their existence but did not use them, to do so. Most relevant here are those patients who thought their problem too personal or who were critical of the various services.

142

(3) There is evidently a sizeable number of patients who at the time of crisis appear to be outside the reach of any agency; they are those for whom entering a stage of distress and seeking release from it tend to be almost simultaneous, and those attempting to produce a dramatic effect on others. If they are to be helped then intervention must come at a very much earlier stage and before the acute crisis has arisen.

(4) The contribution of the Telephone Samaritan organization has been already reviewed. It is a truism to indicate that the data refer only to the Samaritan organization as it currently functions and not as it might become.

(5) That over half the patients receiving psychotropic drugs reported that they had not discussed their problems with the person prescribing the tablets is a disturbing finding. The reasons for this unsatisfactory situation are not always evident, and it cannot be assumed that the patient's disclosure of his problems would necessarily have averted the parasuicide. Nevertheless, the finding indicates that more listening and perhaps less prescribing by physicians may have a greater role in primary prevention of parasuicide than any other single measure. To achieve it the conditions of general practice and the education of practitioners may have to be reviewed.

7.6. AN OVERVIEW OF THE POSSIBILITIES FOR THE PRIMARY PREVENTION OF PARASUICIDE

The data gained from various studies presented in this chapter provide a framework within which it is possible at least to speculate on where the more important possibilities for primary prevention may be judged to lie. There are five main areas to be considered.

The role of the general practitioner

Since the great majority of patients have been in contact with their general practitioners within the few months preceding their parasuicide (see chapter 3) the possibility of prophylaxis at a primary care level immediately suggests itself. Two main points arise.

Firstly, the increasing prescription over the last decade by general practitioners of psychotropic drugs has frequently elicited the suggestion that the rising numbers of parasuicides is a direct consequence. The inference is drawn that if general practitioners would prescribe less there would be fewer parasuicides.

If this supposition were correct one would expect to find that the number of patients admitted to hospital with self-poisoning from drugs available without prescription should have remained constant over the last decade, and that the increase would be principally due to prescribed drugs, with freely available medication therefore representing a smaller proportion of the total than was formerly the case. The facts contradict this supposition. In 1962 Kessel reported that 15 per cent of admissions were due to overdose with preparations which could be purchased freely at local chemists; these were mostly aspirin or aspirin-containing compounds. In 1973 the proportion of admissions for freely available analgesics was identical. There has been an equal *proportional* increase in the numbers due to both prescribed and non-prescribed drugs. Figure 2.8 (p. 28) illustrates this consistency. Of course the *type* of drug taken reflects what is to hand, and among parasuicides due to drugs the changing pattern of general practice prescribing can be clearly seen.

A second assertion often advanced is that general practitioners should take greater care when issuing prescriptions for large quantities of drugs and should bear in mind the hazards of an overdose. This truism need scarcely be controverted, but it is relevant to recall that only about 55 per cent of parasuicides are carried out with drugs prescribed by the general practitioner *for the patient*. The remainder used tablets issued for another family member, or resorted to non-prescribed preparations. Judicious assessment by the general practitioner could therefore make a useful contribution but could by no means be thought of as eliminating the problem.

The nub of the issue would appear to be not so much whether the general practitioner does or does not prescribe medication, but whether he uses this as a substitute for listening to the patient's problems. Evidence has been presented to show that in a disturbingly high proportion of cases the patient, according to his own report, has not ventilated the difficulty causing his distress: often the overdose follows a visit to the surgery in which the patient has merely collected a repeat prescription. On the other hand, data on the successful prevention of parasuicide by drug therapy or skilled management are not available.

There is clearly a need for more detailed information as to what transpires during the exchange between doctor and patient in a crisis situation, but a prima facie case exists for the better education of general practitioners in basic psychotherapy skills.

Special packaging of drugs

In view of the impulsive nature of a number of parasuicides, the suggestion has been floated that if drugs were prepared in blister packets their ingestion in bulk would be delayed and possibly even prevented. The idea is interesting, but in the absence of any data either way must remain speculative at present.

The use of non-medical services for crisis situations

Not all parasuicides, nor indeed all psychological illness, is explicable in terms of environmental distresses, but the role of adverse interpersonal and social circumstances, at least as a precipitant, need not be belaboured. It is therefore rational to look to services aiming to provide relief to people in distressful situations as possible sources of primary prevention.

Many agencies could have been selected for research into the preventive role that they do or might offer. The one on which attention is focused in this volume was the Telephone Samaritan organization. Previous sections have described the similarities and differences between the people who use the Samaritans as compared to those who resort to overdoses, and have discussed at some length the reasons for concluding that the Samaritan organization does not have an important effect on the prevention of parasuicide. Perhaps the point to be stressed is that it is inaccurate to think that alternative routes to help are viewed by potential patients as largely interchangeable. People appear to go to the Telephone Samaritan organization with quite different aims in mind from those which may prompt an overdose. Once a crisis has developed it is the type of outcome which the individual envisages and his own definition of what help he requires which appear to determine his choice of action. These determinants are no doubt linked in turn to his social, familial, and demographic characteristics.

General advisory services

From what has been said it seems that once a parasuicidal crisis has developed there is no evidence that it can be aborted by the use of crisis-oriented agencies (including general practitioners). If this is so, then it is reasonable to speculate on the possible preventive role of agencies designed to deal with social or other problems before they reach crisis intensity. The very diversity of these problems, however, makes it unlikely that any single-service agency is likely to be particularly useful. The Craigmillar experiment described in an earlier section was, and indeed remains, a strikingly imaginative attempt to bring the resources of the many facets of the Social Work Department, with the assistance of a number of other bodies, to bear upon the needs of a defined area. So far as it has proved possible to evaluate the impact of the centre, the results have been disappointing. It is true that before-and-after comparisons of the kind which have been made are by no means conclusive, and there were many other changes occurring both in Craigmillar and the city as a whole which may well have blurred the outcome. Nevertheless, the most conservative conclusion must be that if the Craigmillar centre did indeed have any effect, it was too small to make any demonstrable impact and that a fully-integrated social work service can only have had a marginal influence on the variance in the parasuicide rate when compared to other factors.

The role of cultural attitudes

The work described in chapter 4 on the ecological and cultural facets of parasuicide, and in particular its role as a communication system in certain subcultures was not carried out with an eye on the possibilities for primary prevention. Parasuicide occurs in all social classes and presumably in any culture, but it is, in Edinburgh at least, a particularly salient feature of social classes IV and V inhabiting specific areas of the city. In general the people in such areas are subject to numerous disadvantages and social pressures which they have not the resources to overcome. The relative lack of an effective 'verbal language' is simply one of their handicaps and it is all too easy to see how in such a social framework parasuicide may play a semi-institutional role. While such communities endure, the prospects for primary prevention do not seem very bright.

On the other hand much requires to be established before any such view can be taken beyond the stage of hypothesis. The 'subculture of deprivation' and the type of language which characterizes it (Bernstein 1971) have existed for a long time, while the escalation of parasuicide is a fairly recent phenomenon. Some additional factor must be operative.

Research for future action

Some possible explanations for the climbing rates were explored in chapter 3 but the limitations of these explanations were also pointed out. A clearer understanding of why the rates have gone up would be a rational (though not an essential) forerunner of efforts to bring them down again, and fundamental research continues to be necessary. The conclusions just listed concerning primary prevention may seem pessimistic though not, it is hoped, nihilistic. Negative conclusions should warn against expensive attempts to expand existing methods and facilities where these have not been proven to be efficacious, but should also act as a spur to more intensive efforts.

Since no single preventive measure is likely to eliminate parasuicide it is necessary to envisage a range of activities. The design of such a programme requires three main steps. The first is to estimate the maximum impact which any component could be expected to have, given completely successful implementation. For example, it has been mentioned in the last section that 63 per cent of a series of first-ever parasuicides were on prescribed medication (usually psychotropic drugs) at the time of their overdose, that is to say, were in contact with doctors. Successful detection and treatment by general practitioners and psychiatrists could thus be expected to have a major impact on the parasuicide problem. Conversely, schizophrenics constitute only a tiny proportion of all parasuicides. A programme which prevented parasuicide among schizophrenics would have a barely discernible impact on the parasuicide rate. For alcoholism or reactive depression, however, such a statement would not be true. The data presented throughout this volume represent a contribution towards estimates of this kind.

Secondly, and much more difficult to assess, is the efficiency of the various agencies and services that might be considered. The point has repeatedly been made that studies based solely on series of parasuicides can only give information about failures. Nothing is known as to how effective psychiatrists or general practitioners are with *potential* parasuicides whose self-damage has been prevented. It is quite possible, if improbable, that the various help-giving resources listed are already functioning at a high level of efficiency. Comprehensive assessment would pose a formidable research problem, but the question is an important one, since in general efforts to improve an already high level of performance by a service are unlikely to be rewarding. A much greater payoff may be obtained by intensifying efforts in services which are functioning at a low level, or by introducing a new approach altogether.

Lastly, there is the question of cost benefit. Until effective preventive measures have been established, discussion under this heading may appear premature, but the issue is raised because it forces attention as to just what 'benefit' is being sought. The prevention of parasuicide is clearly desirable, but the act itself may be merely one facet of a situation of distress, and the real objective should perhaps be the reduction in psychological pain.

NOTE

1 This is an appreciably higher value than was found 3 years earlier in the 1969 study (Section 7.3) though that series comprised only first-ever admissions.

8

THE SECONDARY PREVENTION OF
PARASUICIDE

The problem posed by repetition of parasuicide has already been discussed in earlier chapters. Approximately 20 per cent of patients admitted to the RPTC will repeat their parasuicide within 12 months, and in recent years each annual admission cohort has contained approximately 40 per cent of patients with a previous episode. It also appears that with each episode the risk of a subsequent one increases, although this relationship requires to be precisely documented (see Duffy, 1976). A successful system of management which eliminated repetition would spare the patient the risks associated with self-poisoning or self-injury and would, perhaps equally importantly, indicate that he had either succeeded in avoiding further crises in his life or a deterioration in his psychological state, or had at least found some alternative and less irrational way of dealing with his situation. The relief on medical services would also be very appreciable. The attractiveness of secondary prevention is further enhanced by the patient's being already known to the service and hence identified and accessible. The problem, of course, is to determine whether repetition can indeed be reduced, and if so, which type of care is the most effective.

8.1 THE EFFICACY OF STANDARD SERVICES

The first question which may be adduced is whether the existing type of service offered by general hospitals to their parasuicide patients has any demonstrable effect on their subsequent behaviour. Since much may depend on how the initial sample of patients is defined, it seems logical to begin at the level of general practice. The study by Kennedy (1972b) described in chapter 2 provides the only data of this kind at present available.

In the Edinburgh General Practice Survey it was found that patients admitted to the RPTC after their key episode had a much lower repetition rate during the year than patients who were not admitted to hospital (Table 8.1). Selection rather than treatment could account for this difference, but admitted and non-admitted patients were found to be similar on all the variables which previous hospital studies had shown to relate to repetition, except for a previous history of parasuicide. Table 8.1 also shows that the beneficial effects of admission remain significant after controlling for this variable. The cautious conclusion would seem to be justified that admission to the RPTC prevented repetition in many patients.

If this is so, the question arises as to what aspect of the complex experience of hospitalization might be responsible. The notion that the unpleasantness of

TABLE 8.1   Management after key episode and repetition (percentages)

	Admitted to RPTC	Not admitted
Repeated during survey year	12	38
Did not repeat	88	62
100% (n =)	(142)	(62)

$$\chi^2 = 19.21 \quad \text{df 1} \quad p < 0.001$$

	History of parasuicide in previous years		No history of parasuicide in previous years	
	Admitted RPTC	Not admitted	Admitted RPTC	Not admitted
Repeated	23	47	7	29
Did not repeat	77	53	93	71
100% (n =)	(43)	(30)	(94)	(31)

$$\chi^2 = 4.40 \quad \text{df 1} \quad p < 0.05 \qquad \chi^2 = 16.47 \quad \text{df 1} \quad p < 0.001$$

procedures such as gastric lavage has a deterent effect is not supported by the fact that repetition was equally frequent among admitted patients who did and did not require lavage (Kennedy, 1972a). On the other hand, as Table 8.2 shows, patients who were referred to psychiatric outpatient clinics instead of being sent to the RPTC did no better than those who did not see a psychiatrist at all. This does not necessarily mean that psychiatric intervention has no effect, and that psychiatric service is not an important component in secondary prevention, because non-admitted patients who were referred to psychiatric outpatients were not seen until some days or weeks after their parasuicide: often they had reported the episode to their general practitioner only after a considerable time had elapsed. It could be that the key consideration is that psychiatric intervention is effected at the time of the crisis. Kessel (1965) believed that much could be achieved in one interview at this time because the patient and his relatives were faced with their strong emotions and the realities of their situation. Later, collusion to present an idealized and false

TABLE 8.2   Management of non-admitted patients and repetition (percentages)

	Referred to psychiatric outpatient department	No contact with psychiatrist
Repeated during survey year	38	37
Did not repeat	62	63
100% (n =)	(32)	(30)

$$\chi^2 = 0.01 \quad \text{df} \quad \text{n.s.}$$

picture occurred, making therapeutic change more difficult. Against this, Lawson and Mitchell (1972a) argued that the special psychiatric service in the RPTC was not necessary because the repetition rates among their patients treated in general medical wards without immediate psychiatric cover were much the same as for the RPTC. They quote no figures, and were presumably using further admission to hospital as their criterion of repetition in contrast to Kennedy's use of any episode known to the general practitioner. Their patients were drawn from a predominantly rural area, which further complicates comparison. Nevertheless the possibility must be considered that it is the temporary withdrawal of the patient from a hostile environment and the amplification of his appeal by such a significant event as being admitted to hospital which may in fact be 'therapeutic'. In line with this suggestion is the further finding that continued psychiatric treatment after discharge from the RPTC cannot be shown to lead to a reduced repetition rate, though selection factors may again be operative.

A study reported by Greer and Bagley (1971) and Bagley and Greer (1971) concerned a group of patients seen in the casualty department of a large London hospital after a parasuicidal episode. They compared the rates of (hospital-detected) repetition of parasuicide in two subgroups, namely those who accepted admission and subsequently continued with a planned course of therapy, against those individuals who either declined to be admitted or who at some point broke off their treatment. Since the two groups differed on a number of characteristics, a multiple regression technique was used in an attempt to balance these out, with special attention to those variables which for the group as a whole had a demonstrable relationship to repetition. These authors concluded that the patient who collaborated in planned therapy had a lower repetition rate than those who did not, when due allowance had been made for contaminating factors.[1]

If one provisionally accepts the conclusions drawn by the authors of these three studies and attempts to collate their findings, then the following picture seems to emerge. Among parasuicides known to general practitioners those who are referred at once to a special centre do better than those who are not (Kennedy, 1972b). Of those referred to special centres, those who are admitted or who otherwise co-operate with prescribed treatment do better than those who default (Greer and Bagley, 1971; Bagley and Greer, 1971). Among those who are admitted to hospital there is, however, no difference in outcome whether or not immediate psychiatric attention is given, though the data on which the last statement is based are distinctly inadequate (Lawson and Mitchell, 1972b). In the first two studies at least the authors believed that selection factors were not primarily responsible. However, two points require to be made. The first, which need not be belaboured, is that techniques such as multiple regression or stratification seldom enable firm conclusions to be drawn from manipulation of this sort, and in neither study were matched groups used. Secondly, there is the important consideration that the criterion for repetition has not been uniform but has varied between re-referral to hospital as against detection at the general practice level. At the present state of knowledge any conclusions must therefore remain highly tentative, So far as practical management is concerned, it must also be borne in mind that the prevention of repetition is not the sole justification for the immediate psychiatric management of parasuicides, and that expert psychiatric screening of all such patients can be justified on other clinical grounds.

8.2 A SPECIAL AFTER-CARE SERVICE

Though both ethical and practical difficulties arise in connection with a randomized trial of front-rank care for parasuicide, these problems are much less cogent in the context of after-care. In view of the uncertain state of knowledge it was considered useful and justified to set up (in 1968—9) an experimental after-care programme, the results of which could be compared with those obtained by the standard pattern of service.

Type of service

The first problem was to decide on the form that the new service should take, and here the chief considerations were the more conspicuous difficulties being encountered with the routine pattern of management. At the time of the study about 20—25 per cent of patients were transferred from the RPTC directly to a psychiatric hospital. A roughly similar proportion were referred back to the care of their general practitioners or to a social work agency. The remainder were offered outpatient appointments, but it was known that only about 50 per cent of such appointments were in fact kept; the figure was less if only the repeaters were considered. A number of factors seemed to be responsible for this low contact rate. One was that the actual admission to the RPTC and the emergency psychiatric and social work intervention offered there may have largely resolved the crisis which precipitated the parasuicide. Consequently after an interval of a few days or weeks, the patients may have felt that their difficulties had to a large extent resolved. This may have been true even for patients with recognized psychiatric disorders, since they often tended to define their problems entirely in environmental terms. A second important factor may have been that simply to keep a series of appointments planned some time in advance may have been culturally alien to many patients. They sought help, if at all, only when the situation was critical, at which point it was required instantly, but was not perceived as relevant outside such periods. The inflexibility of the ordinary outpatient system was thus contrary to the patient's own needs and expectations. Thirdly, in line with the tendency to define all problems in environmental terms, patients were sometimes reluctant to accept a definition of themselves as psychiatric cases, as would be implied by their attendance at a psychiatric outpatient clinic. In the existing service when a patient failed to appear for his outpatient visit no further action had been taken, and the onus for continuation left entirely to him.

The new service sought to meet at least some of these problems. Its main features were as follows:

(1) The service was staffed by a psychiatrist and a psychiatric social worker specially designated for the purpose and working full time. They were assisted by two part-time social workers.

(2) These were resonsible for identifying patients for the trial on their admission to the RPTC, for making the clinical and social assessments, and for arranging the details of their after-care.

(3) Three regular outpatient clinics were held each week, two in the centre of Edinburgh and one in a peripheral area of the city characterized by very high parasuicide rates. The patients were offered regular and frequent appointments but

were also seen without appointment at any time both at the clinics and at the RPTC itself.

(4) Because of the known failures to keep formal appointments, especially by repeaters, a home visiting service was an essential component. Any patient who did not keep his appointment was visited at home without delay, usually on the same day.

(5) It was felt necessary to provide an emergency call facility in view of the frequent and acute crisis situations befalling the patients. This emergency system was arranged in collaboration with the Edinburgh Telephone Samaritans, who kindly allowed their telephone number to be used. Prior to discharge from the centre the patient was given the telephone number and instructed how to identify himself should he require to use it. Similarly the Samaritans were given a regularly updated list of the patients in care. On receipt of a call the Samaritan contacted whichever member of the after-care service was on duty by day or night. Telephone requests for help were met by seeing the patient either at the RPTC or in his home, at any hour.

The objectives of the trial were defined as firstly, to provide a form of after-care which would be acceptable to patients and readily utilized by them; secondly, to reduce the frequency of further parasuicide and, thirdly, to improve the patients' psychiatric and social state. It is important to add that the trial was confined to patients who had already at least one prior episode of parasuicide before their current admission, as defined in more detail below. In other words, the entire group might be considered to be at least at moderate risk for further repetition, and the terms high, medium, and low risk used in the following account are relative terms within a group which globally carried a higher likelihood of repetition than would a cohort of first-ever admissions.

The overall design of the trial was as follows.

Method

Following their admission to the centre, all repeaters were interviewed by the psychiatrist of the after-care staff, and their relatives were seen by the psychiatric social workers. A detailed and standardized initial assessment sheet was completed for each patient.

The patients were allocated alternately to a treatment group and a control group. The treatment group was offered the facilities of the after-care service, while the controls were offered routine follow-up from the centre.

Some repeaters were considered to be at such high risk of further parasuicide that allocation to the control group could not be justified on ethical grounds. In order to predict, more accurately than by clinical assessment, which repeaters were at the greatest risk of further parasuicidal acts, use was made of the then-current version of the scales for the prediction of suicidal behaviour (Buglass and McCulloch, 1970). The scales, which differed for the two sexes, are shown in Table 8.3. These predictive scales were intended for use on a heterogenous sample of parasuicides and were not specifically constructed to detect further episodes in a group which already had a postive history. Nevertheless they were the best available at the time and indeed were found to function reasonably effectively.

TABLE 8.3   Repetition risk rating scales

Male	Female
Alcoholism	Previous attempted suicide
Alcohol taken at time of act	Previous psychiatric treatment (inpatient or outpatient)
Violence in key relationship	Psycopathy
	Drug addiction
	Dwelling changes: 4 or more in past 5 years
	Father absent when patient under 10 years
	Mother absent when patient under 10 years

Score 1 point for each factor present

Males:

0 = Low risk
1 or 2 = Medium risk
3 = High risk

Females:

0 or 1 = Low risk
2 or 3 = Medium risk
4, 5, 6 or 7 = High risk

Those patients found to be at high risk were all offered the facilities of the after-care programme but they were excluded from the comparison with the control group. Table 8.4 shows the risk categories of all the patients in the study.

Following his or her discharge, a record was kept of the number of times during the next 6 months that each patient was readmitted to the centre for further acts of deliberate self-poisoning or self-injury. At the end of the 6—month follow-up an assessment was made of the patient's psychiatric state and social situation. These follow-up assessments were performed for about half the patients by the psychiatrist and for the remainder by the psychiatric social worker. In order to test inter—observer variations, 35 patients known to both the staff were assessed separately by each of them. No significant difference in their scores was found. The follow-up assessment was done by personal interview for all but eleven patients who were either in psychiatric hospitals or in prison, or had moved away from Edinburgh. Assessments for the latter were made on information obtained by postal enquiry.

TABLE 8.4   Risk categories

Risk	Treatment	Control	Total
High	42	—	42
Medium	55	68	123
Low	16	16	32
Total	113	84	197

Composition and characteristics of the cohort

197 patients were admitted to the RPTC during 1968 who had had at least one previous admission during the previous 3 years, and therefore qualified for inclusion in the study. 42 of these patients were classified as at high risk of further repetition and were automatically offered the facilities of the after-care programme: they have been excluded from the evaluation as already explained and from the following account: a separate description of their characteristics and outcome is given later. As the high-risk group was taken out after the initial allocation had been made the treatment and control groups were unequal in size.

The remaining patients in the after-care group and the controls did not differ significantly on demographic, social or diagnostic variables. Tables 8.5 to 8.7 give summary data for the combined groups, with the sexes distinguished. The series, being composed entirely of repeaters, differs of course from the more familiar patient cohorts which are dominated by first-ever cases. Table 8.5 shows that the males tended to be most commonly below the age of 30, single, and of Social Class V. The females on the other hand were more often in the 31–49 age bracket, were usually married and drawn from a wider social spectrum.

The psychiatric diagnoses for the experimental and control groups were essentially similarly distributed, and are illustrated in Table 8.6; a depressive illness, most often associated with abnormal personality, was the commonest single diagnosis. A separate classification of personality disorder based solely on clinical assessment showed that only 37 per cent of the series were classified as normal. For this purpose alcoholism and drug addiction were considered as personality variables, and represented 9 per cent and 1 per cent respectively of the total series. Much

TABLE 8.5   Demographic and other characteristics of patients and controls (combined). Percentages (rounded) by sex

	Males	Females	Total
Age			
−30	43	34	38
30–49	37	53	46
50+	21	13	16
Civil state			
Single	35	24	29
Married and with spouse	29	46	39
Married and separated	16	15	15
Widowed or divorced	13	7	10
Cohabiting	6	8	7
Social Class			
I and II	7	8	8
III	22	30	26
IV	15	23	19
V	48	31	39
Other n.k.	7	8	8
(100%) *n* =	68	87	155

TABLE 8.6   Psychiatric diagnosis of treatment and control groups combined, by sex (rounded percentage distribution)

	Males	Females	Total
No formal disorder Acute situational reaction	44	30	36
Depressive illness			
in normal personality	9	18	1 4
in abnormal personality	31	37	35
Organic reaction	1	2	2
Epilepsy	10	6	6
Other	4	8	7
n (100%) =	68	87	155

greater proportions, however, were alcohol or drug abusers short of the classical addition syndromes, and no less than 53 per cent of the total (70 per cent of the men) were considered to have significant problems with alcohol or drugs, or both.

By definition all patients had a history of at least one previous act of parasuicide: 33 per cent of males and 20 per cent of females had a history of two or more such acts. In both males and females over 70 per cent had earlier received psychiatric treatment either as inpatients or outpatients, apart from the period of treatment at the RPTC.

The disruption of interpersonal relationships among the patients was reflected in the high proportion of married but separated individuals, and in the common occurrence of interpersonal physical violence. Table 8.7 shows the use and receipt of violence over the previous 5 years. Both forms were reported by about a third of the subjects.

Difficulties with material aspects of life were even more pronounced than problems of personal relationships. 68 per cent of patients were considered to have serious environmental stresses as the major precipitant of their parasuicidal acts: problems with finance, housing or occupation were found in 57 per cent of males and in 77 per cent of females. 28 per cent were living in overcrowded housing, with

TABLE 8.7   Violence to and from other in past 5 years, by sex (rounded percentage distribution)

	Males	Females	Total
Violence to others			
reported	35	26	32
not reported	65	74	68
Violence received			
reported	46	17	30
not reported	5 4	83	70
N (100%) =	68	87	155

more than 1.5 persons per room. 62 per cent of males were unemployed at the time of their parasuicide.

These then were the characteristics of the patients who entered the study and it can be seen that they were in general both psychologically disturbed and beset with numerous environmental stresses. The only variable on which the treatment and control groups differed was that the former appear to have received violence from others in the previous 5 years to a significantly greater degree; this was true for both sexes. The discrepancy can only have arisen by chance and would tend to militate against a positive outcome for the special service.

As indicated, all patients entering the new service remained under intensive care for a 6—month period. If during that time they required hospital admission this was of course arranged, but the service was again available for them on discharge from hospital for the remainder of the 6 months.

Results

The success of the after-care service was assessed under three headings:

(1) Did it provide effective contact with the patients during their 6 months in care, and was it found acceptable by them?

(2) Did it succeed in reducing the repetition rate of parasuicide?

(3) Did it succeed in improving the patient's psychiatric and social status at the end of the 6—month period?

(1) Acceptability and maintenance of contact

The acceptability of the programme to the patients appeared to be high, as may be assessed with the regularity with which they kept their outpatient appointments. Unfortunately it did not prove practical (for local organizational reasons) to monitor the actual attendance of the control group. It is known, however, that in the year before the study was mounted, i.e. in 1967, only one-third of the repeaters admitted to the RPTC were offered outpatient appointments and that less than 50 per cent of these patients in fact attended the clinics. Of the 113 repeaters in the experimental after-care service (71 in the treatment group and 42 high-risk patients), 81 were offered outpatient appointments, the other 32 being admitted to hospital or returned to inpatient care elsewhere. Of these 81 patients, 65 (80 per cent) kept their outpatient follow-up contacts, 37 per cent regularly and the rest sporadically, mainly at times of crisis. Thus the proportion of repeaters who were in touch with the outpatient service was very much higher during the year than before the service was instituted.

The figures serve as a reminder that a substantial proportion, namely 32 out of 113, or 28 per cent, spent at least the initial part of their 6 months as inpatients. The proportion among the controls was very similar. Thus the effect of the after-care service, which was conceived as essentially supplementary to normal practice, would only be demonstrable among the remaining 72 per cent of the series, but comparisons have been based on total figures as providing a more stringent test.

(2) Further acts of parasuicide

24 per cent of the treatment group and 23 per cent of the control group were admitted with one or more parasuicidal acts during the follow-up period. Table 8.8

TABLE 8.8   Parasuicidal acts during 6—months follow-up treatment
and control groups by sex (percentage distribution)

No. of parasuicidal acts during follow-up	Treatment			Control		
	Male	Female	Total	Male	Female	Total
None	77	76	76	67	88	77
1+	23	24	24	33	12	23

gives the details. There was thus no demonstrable advantage to the experiment group in this respect.

(3) Social and psychiatric status

The initial social assessment recorded the patient's problems with finance, housing, and employment. At the 6—month follow-up period similar ratings were made and the results classified as showing improvement, no change, or depreciation in comparison with the previous assessment. 30 of the treatment group and 43 of the controls were recorded as having one or more such problems at the time of their first 1968 admission. At follow-up, improvement was found in 63 per cent of those with problems in the treatment group, as contrasted with 31 per cent in the control group; the difference is statistically significant ($p < .001$). Further analysis showed that men had benefitted relatively less from the after-care service, 42 per cent of the treated and 26 per cent of the controls being rated as improved, but women had gained much more with corresponding figures of 76 per cent and 36 per cent.

An estimate was also made of alterations in patients' psychiatric state, principally in terms of symptomatology, but also with attention to such factors as violence, excessive drinking, and criminal behaviour. The criteria used to assess change were not as precise as those used to rate social improvement, and accordingly less weight can be given to the findings. With these reservations it was found that there was an improvement in the psychiatric state of 37 per cent of the treated group and 31 per cent of the control group, and in the behaviour (considered alone) of 35 per cent of the treatment group and 25 per cent of the control group. However, though in the direction favouring the service, these differences did not reach statistical significance.

Characteristics of the 'High-Risk' subgroup

There were 42 patients in this class, who had been excluded from the evaluative study for ethical reasons. Ten of the high risk patients had little or no contact with the after-care programme because at the time of their key admission they were either in police custody or were already inpatients in psychiatric hospitals and remained so for most of the 6—month period. Of the remaining 32 patients 18, or 56 per cent, were readmitted with one or more parasuicidal acts. All these readmissions were for patients who were dependent on either alcohol or drugs, the majority on both. Their social personal backgrounds were highly disorganized. Overcrowding was rife, and half were living in hostels, lodgings or institutions; the majority were unemployed, and over 80 per cent admitted having used violence towards their spouse or other key person during preceding 5 years. Further details can be found in Chowdhury, Hicks, and Kreitman (1973).

Discussion

It appears that the experimental after-care service was effective in meeting the first of its three stated aims, namely to reach the patients for whom it was designed and to prove acceptable to them. The costs in terms of manpower and effort should not be underestimated and the two workers involved were kept fully extended by the project, despite the assistance of the established psychiatric services and other agencies such as the Telephone Samaritans. The provision of 24-hour cover, 7 days a week, was particularly demanding.

The second objective, which was to reduce the repetition rate of parasuicide, was not achieved, but before accepting this conclusion fully it is necessary to consider whether, with hindsight, the experiment provided a fair test of the service. It is, for example, possible that although the comparison group was comprised of patients receiving routine after-care, the existence of the experiment might in itself have stimulated the efforts of the regular service staff, as well as considerably lightening their work load. The control group of patients might, therefore, have received more attention than in the preceding years. A parallel situation is reported by Burkhart (1969) concerning an experimental programme for prison parolees. Nevertheless, in the present context, these speculations can scarcely controvert the fact that the service failed to meet its most important objective.

Even allowing for the relatively intractable nature of the patient group selected for the experiment, all of whom had had at least one prior parasuicidal episode and who were therefore automatically at higher risk for repetition, the conclusion can only be disappointing. Other workers have written in a similarly pessimistic vein. Batchelor (1954a, 1954b) was sceptical about the possibility of preventing repetition. He did not consider that admission to a psychiatric hospital was the correct management, and also noted that legal sanctions operative at that time had not acted as a detriment. Robins et al., (1959), dealing with a rather different group, noted that many patients who eventually died by suicide were suffering from manic-depressive psychosis or chronic alcoholism, and concluded that the only way to prevent their death was by closed ward hospitalization. Carstairs (1961) echoed this view, and in some cases of repeated parasuicide he recommended detention under compulsory treatment orders, but he, like Robins et al., was considering death as well as repeated parasuicide when making this proposal.

The most recent and ambitious study of after-care has been reported by Ettlinger (1975) working in Stockholm in an intensive care unit for poisoned patients. She investigated two large groups, each of over 600 patients, treated at the centre before and after the introduction of a special after-care service. The study, unlike the one reported in this chapter, was not confined to repeaters. It was found that the after-care service made no difference to the repetition rate for parasuicide, so far as this could be ascertained (nor, for that matter, to the completed suicide rate).

The third aim of the experimental aftercare service was to reduce the psychiatric morbidity and to improve the social situation of patients entering the service, and in this at least partial success was achieved. The fact that these gains were not reflected in an improvement of the repetition of parasuicide is in itself of considerable interest. If confirmed it would suggest that the causal link assumed to exist between, on the one hand, the patient's psychosocial situation and his mental state, and on the other, his parasuicidal behaviour may be less direct than has been generally assumed, or at least that the introduction of a special service may weaken the correlation in some obscure manner. Alternatively, but equally speculatively, it is possible that reduction in distress due to whatever cause has to reduce intrapsychic tension below a threshold before any effect on parasuicidal behaviour can be demonstrated, and that gains which are too slight to reach this level will not be reflected in repetition rates, however intrinsically desirable. The findings thus serve to open up a series of further problems.

The experiment vividly remained the investigators of the longstanding and often intractable problems which characterize the lives of many of the multiple repeaters. Life-long dependency on alcohol, and/or drugs, unemployment, difficulties with the police, and a chaotic pattern of interpersonal relationships were only too prevalent; they were particularly evident among the high-risk subgroup. Faced with difficulties of this magnitude it would seem reasonable to concentrate on the low— and medium-risk subgroups until more effective techniques are available which might be then applied to the highest-risk patients. But an effective system of management has yet to be devised. It is possible to argue that the after-care experiment provided a service for too short a period, or that it was not sufficiently intensive, or that it called on too little by way of resources, or that only workers specially trained in the sophisticated psychotherapy which is conceivably appropriate for such a patient group might have been expected to produce demonstrable results. Such arguments would be more plausible had some small gain been demonstrated, since undoubtedly the patients did receive care and attention of an intensity well beyond that of any ordinary service organization.

It seems on final reflection that the problem may lie in how to devise a type of care which is radically different from orthodox psychiatric and social work practices. What was implemented was a traditional psychiatric and social work service modified to permit flexibility of time of appointments, where much of the responsibility for maintaining contact was transferred from patients to staff, and which facilitated on-demand crisis intervention. Despite these major modifications, however, the procedures adopted when staff and patients met were based on traditional concepts. Various alternatives might be contemplated but the design, establishment and evaluation of such a service remains a task for the future.

NOTE

1 The benefit in the fully treated group was apparently due entirely to the superior results obtained in first-contact cases. Repeaters failed to show the benefits of sustained care. Similarly, individuals diagnosed as psychopaths showed no gain with continued therapy (Greer, personal communication).

9

PARASUICIDE IN RELATION TO SUICIDE

In the introductory chapter the evolution of awareness that parasuicide was a form of behaviour deserving study in its own right and was not simply a minor variation of completed suicide, was briefly sketched. It was not noted that national traditions have varied somewhat in this respect. Many American writers still regard the distinction as one which may be cheerfully overlooked in practice if not in theory. From France a recent authoritative publication (Ministère de la Santé, 1975) documents 'attempted suicides' and suicides separately, but refers to the former as 'suicidants' and in places discusses parasuicides as 'survivors'.

However, while it is now generally accepted that the two forms of behaviour differ markedly in numerous respects, it is also clear that they have important similarities and that the individuals who engage in the one are also likely to have a higher than average likelihood of engaging in the other. The precise relationship between the two forms of behaviour merits the closest attention.

The problem can be formulated as three distinct questions, even though definitive answers may not be available for all of them. They are:

(1) What are the relative frequencies of the two forms of behaviour, and does the relationship vary in different sections of the community defined demographically, or socially, or both?

(2) What proportion of parasuicides proceed to eventual suicide and how should they be characterized?

(3) What proportion of suicides have an earlier history of parasuicide, and do such individuals differ from suicides whose death had no such precursor?

These questions will be considered in turn.

9.1 THE COMPARATIVE EPIDEMIOLOGY OF PARASUICIDE AND SUICIDE

Completed suicide is one of the most extensively developed areas of social psychiatry. The literature, much of it epidemiological in character, is enormous and no attempt will be made to review it here. A recurrent theme in these writings is how far official statistics on suicide are trustworthy (see, for example, Sainsbury (1973) for a review of the literature). However, all commentators agree that the legal definition is narrower than that which would normally be used by psychiatrists, since the former requires virtually unequivocal evidence that the death was a suicide, while the latter would rely upon the traditional medical practice of gauging the balance of probabilities. The extent of the discrepancy between the figures obtained using the two sets of criteria has been explored by Ovenstone (1972) for Edinburgh, who reported that the Registrar General's figures failed to recognize 32 per cent of deaths judged to be suicides on psychiatric criteria, while McCarthy and Walsh (1966) reported a corresponding figure of 50 per cent in a Dublin series. On the other hand there is little or no misclassification in the opposite direction, in that virtually all legally-defined suicides would be agreed to be such by psychiatrists (Barraclough *et al.*, 1974). Extensive American studies on the same theme lead to a similar conclusion. Both the legal and the psychiatric criterion have certain advantages and disadvantages, and in the work shortly to be described it was decided to employ both.

A similar ambiguity of definition surrounds parasuicide. In particular the identification of cases in terms either of hospital contacts or as being known to their general practitioners without necessarily having a subsequent hospital referral, has already been discussed in chapter 3, where it was shown that rates based on all cases known to general practitioners were approximately 20 per cent higher (for person rates) than those derived from RPTC data alone. (See also Weissman, 1974.)

Finally, there is the difficulty that comparisons between the epidemiology of suicide and parasuicide have hitherto always been based on different populations or studied at different points in time, or both. There does not appear to have been any investigation of a single, closely defined population investigated for both forms of suicidal behaviour over the same period.

The first study to be described in this chapter attempted to remedy these various defects.

Design

Two surveys were conducted in the city of Edinburgh, covering the whole of 1970; one was concerned with suicide, the other with parasuicide.

Suicides were defined and identified in *two* ways. One definition was a legal one, namely all residents of Edinburgh officially recorded as suicides by the Crown Office — the Scottish equivalent of the coroner system in England and Wales or the United States. In Scotland, as elsewhere, such a 'verdict' calls for clear evidence that death was the intended outcome of the act. The second definition subsumed any act of self-damage which on the balance of evidence was considered to be deliberately initiated and which resulted in the individual's death. This is a wider definition than the legal one and the data upon which a decision was reached were more extensive than those routinely available to the legal authorities, including information specially obtained from local psychiatric services, general practitioners, and other sources. The families of the suicides were not approached, in a conformity with the confidentiality requirements of the Crown Office. In ascertaining the number of suicides over the survey year (1970), all suspicious deaths notified to the Crown Office, including all accidents, were reviewed.

Data for parasuicide were obtained from the survey by Kennedy and Kreitman already described in chapter 2. It may be recalled that in this investigation, which also covered 1970, two criteria were used for parasuicide. The first was the standard operational one: a parasuicide was any case of deliberate self-poisoning or self-injury from within the city boundary known to the RPTC. The second source of data was a prospective survey carried out in general practice. A 25 per cent random sample was drawn from the 130 Edinburgh general practices; 94 per cent of doctors in this sample agreed to collaborate. The total population at risk was 82,963 adults, and data on the age, sex, and area of residence composition of this population were obtained from Executive Council records. The general practitioners notified all cases of poisoning and self-injury to the investigators, who

160

subsequently decided if the episode fell within the definition of a non-fatal deliberately initiated act. In calculating the rates, corrections were introduced to allow for inflation error in the local Executive Council records.

Results

During the survey year, 69 suicides were detected in the Crown Office series, using the wider definition of suicide and the ancillary sources of information already mentioned. Of these, 41 or 59 per cent were also officially classified as suicides.[1]

The parasuicide survey detected 278 *episodes* of parasuicide, of which 194 (70 per cent) were treated at the RPTC: 201 persons were involved, of whom 159, or 79 per cent, were seen at the RPTC during the year of study. Parasuicide rates cited below are person rates. Episode rates are not shown, but 19 per cent of parasuicides repeated at least once during the year and the overall episode/person ratio was 1.38/1.

Sex-specific rates

The histogram (Figure 9.1) compares the sex-specific rates for parasuicide and suicide. Using either definition for parasuicide, the rates for women are higher than for men, whereas the converse is true for suicide. The parasuicide rates are, of course, very much higher than those for suicide, and this is particularly so in women.

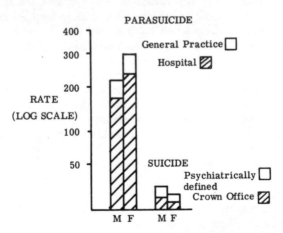

FIGURE 9.1. Person rates per 100,000 by sex

Age-sex specific rates and ratios

Figures 9.2 and 9.3 show that in both sexes the peak rates of parasuicide are among teenagers and young adults, and that the parasuicide rates decline with advancing age. The opposite is true for suicide, where the rates increase with advancing age.

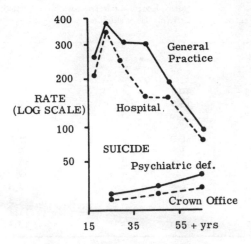

FIGURE 9.2. Male person rates per 100,000 by age

This age gradient in rates of suicide is less obvious from the Crown Office statistics than from those compiled from the special study, and this is particularly so for suicides among women. Table 9.1 shows that whereas parasuicide is almost 40 times more common than suicide among young adults it is only three times more common among the over 55s. Ratios of crude rates which ignore age and sex are thus of little meaning.

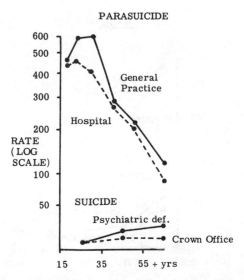

FIGURE 9.3. Female person rates per 100,000 by age

TABLE 9.1   Parasuicide (persons)/suicide ratios

	Factor	Ratio, hospital parasuicides/ Crown Office suicides	Ratio, GP parasuicides/ psychiatrically defined suicides
Sex	M	10.7	8.3
	F	24.5	17.3
Age	15—34	40.2	38.6
	35—54	13.9	10.9
	55+	6.9	3.4
Area	I	30.0	21.1
	II	15.5	9.2
	III	1 41	14.7
Social Class	I + II	9.7	8.0
	III	18.5	13.3
	IV	19.2	11.3
	V	14.0	13.4

Area-specific rates

In calculating area rates the city was divided into three composite areas by clustering the 23 city wards after ranking them according to the 1969 hospital-based parasuicide rates, Area I having the highest rates and Area III the lowest. Figures 9.4 and 9.5 show that the steep gradient in parasuicide rates from Area I to Area III was confirmed in general practice. The suicide rates in males show a similar though less marked trend, but in females there is no such gradient in area rates for suicide.

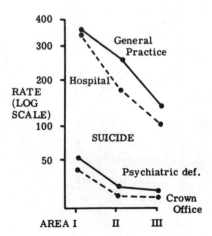

FIGURE 9.4. Male person rates per 100,000 by area of residence

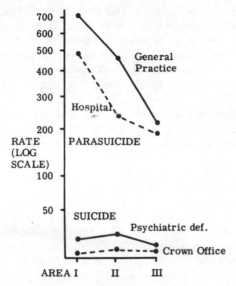

FIGURE 9.5. Female person rates per 100,000 by area of residence

Area I, which has very high rates for parasuicide in both sexes and high rates for suicide in males, is comprised of the central city slums and a large overcrowded tenement housing area developed in the late 1930s to rehouse those living in the worst central districts. Area II, with intermediate rates for parasuicide, is characterized by an inner band of largely working-class suburbs which border on the city docks. Area III with relatively low rates of parasuicide comprised the solid, respectable, predominantly middle-class suburbs on the west side of the city. These ecological aspects are considered in more detail later.

Social-class-specific rates are not available, but some cautious inferences can be made from previous studies and the *parasuicide/suicide* ratios shown in Table 9.1. Hospital studies in Edinburgh have repeatedly shown a steep upward gradient in rates of parasuicide with descending social class, at least for men. The fact that *parasuicide/suicide* ratios varied little with social class suggests that both parasuicide and suicide rates increase in parallel down the social scale.

Overlap between suicide and parasuicide

The overlap between the parasuicide and suicide populations should be noted. Two (1 per cent) of the 201 persons involved in parasuicidal acts in 1970 had committed suicide before the end of the year. 41 per cent of the suicides detected in Edinburgh during 1970 were found to have a history of parasuicide at some time in the past.

Discussion

The more extensive case-finding techniques used in this study showed that hospital data underestimated the frequency of parasuicide by at least 30 per cent for *episodes* and 20 per cent for *persons*, and that Crown Office statistics underestimated the frequency of completed suicide by about 40 per cent. These proportions were certainly large enough to represent potentially serious sources of bias in uncontrolled studies. However, the analysis tended to confirm previous findings that hospital-referred parasuicides and officially recorded suicides are representative, at least with respect to sex, age, and area of residence, of all those ascertained.

The findings confirmed the traditional view that parasuicides and suicides are epidemiologically distinct. Sex and age patterns were quite different, thus supporting the hypothesis that these are different behaviour patterns with different causes.

The rates of parasuicide are obviously very much higher than those for suicide. Moreover, other studies indicate that over time this gap is increasing, as parasuicide rates continue to rise (Aitken *et al.*, 1969, and chapter 2), and suicide rates remain relatively constant or show an overall decline (Kreitman, 1972a). The diverging secular trends also substantiate the view that these two forms of suicidal behaviour are distinct and likely to have different aetiologies (Kreitman, 1972b). This divergence is important, and to be certain of its validity it is necessary to be sure that the rise in the rates of hospital-treated parasuicides in Edinburgh could not be accounted for in terms of more liberal admission policies, and further, that the fall in the number of suicides could not be ascribed simply to more effective medical treatment. The first of these possibilities has already been reviewed and discounted. The second was investigated in some detail, but no supporting evidence was found. It was concluded that there has been a genuine difference in the changes in rates of the two forms of behaviour.

The social class data requires little further comment while the area differences will be discussed more fully later in the chapter. The only other point to be noted in passing is that enquiry from general practitioners turned out to be a very poor case-finding method with respect to completed suicide. In the general practice survey the doctors were asked to report fatal episodes of self-poisoning and self-injury as well as non-fatal ones, but they only identified eight completed suicides in their practices during 1970, whereas scrutiny of the Crown Office records identified 16 suicides from within these practice populations. The omissions occurred because the doctors concerned had received no information from the police or Procurator Fiscal, and had not been involved with the patient around the time of his death.

Although the study confirmed that suicide and parasuicide are different in a number of important respects, so that their causes need to be investigated separately, the findings also illustrated the close relationship between the two. 1 per cent of parasuicides identified during 1970 committed suicide within the calendar year; clearly parasuicides are a very high-risk group for eventual completed suicide, and this has important implications for suicide prevention. It was also found that 41 per cent of completed suicides had a history of parasuicide. In most respects they resembled the suicides more than the parasuicides, but in other characteristics they occupied an intermediate position between the two populations. Ovenstone (1973a) has described this important 'overlap' group in detail. The risk of suicide following parasuicide is taken up in the next section.

9.2 THE RISK OF SUICIDE FOLLOWING PARASUICIDE

Once the similarities, differences and overlap between parasuicide and suicide have been documented, the next question to arise concerns the feasibility of predicting suicide among parasuicidal patients. A WHO (1968) report lists 18 prospective studies of parasuicides in which the proportion of eventual deaths by suicide was ascertained. The report comments that, in general, studies spanning less than 5 years report suicide rates of up to 5 per cent, while where a longer follow-up has been carried out the proportion has been up to 10 per cent.

TABLE 9.2   Suicide following parasuicide

Author and country	Number of patients	Period surveyed Years	Suicide %
Jansson (1962), Sweden	476	1	1.3
Tuckman & Youngman (1968), USA	1112	1	1.4
Kessel & McCulloch (1966), Scotland	511	1	1.6
Schmidt et al. (1954), USA	109	1	1.8
Batchelor & Napier (1954), Scotland	200	1	2.0
Gardner et al. (1964), USA	387	1	2.0
Ettlinger & Flordh (1955), Sweden	500	1	3.6
Ringel (1952), Austria	2897	1—3	0.05
Greer & Bagley (1971), England	204	1½	2.0
McCarthy & Walsh (1965), Eire	159	2—3	3.1
Greer & Lee (1967), England	52	2½	3.8
Hove (1953), Denmark	500	2—3	4.8
Stengel & Cook (1958), England	210	2—5	1.4
Buglass & McCulloch (1970), Scotland	511	3	3.3
Pokorny (1966), USA	250	4	4.4
Ruegsegger (1963), Switzerland	132	2—7	5.3
Motto (1965), USA	193	5—8	8.0
Ekblom & Frisk (1959), Sweden	138	6—8	8.7
Bratfos (1971), Norway	316	8	2.6
Eisenthal et al. (1966), USA	912	8	6.0
Dahlgren (1945), Sweden	230	12	6.1
Ettlinger (1964), Sweden	227	12	13.2
Schneider (1954), Switzerland	372	9—18	8.0

A study by Otto (1971) has not been included as the patients were all children and adolescents.

A more recent survey by Stengel (1972) is summarized in Table 9.2, which has been recast to present the various studies by duration of follow-up in order to illustrate the rising percentage of eventual suicides which such an ordering produces. It is extremely difficult to draw any more specific conclusions from such diverse investigations. Their most striking difference is the nature of the samples. Some refer to psychiatric hospital admission where a high degree of screening has presumably already occurred, others to medical and surgical units where selection is probably largely influenced by the severity of the patient's physical condition; it appears that only two studies, those by Kessel and McCulloch (1966) and Buglass and McCulloch (1970) relate to unselected general hospital *referrals* and can lay claim to any kind of epidemiological basis. Other confounding variables include age (the study by Otto (1971) refers only to children and adolescents, for example), the efficacy of various treatment regimes, the adequacy of the follow-up methods and even the definition of suicide.

Despite their many differences the studies indicate that the risk of suicide following a parasuicide is substantially greater than for a comparable sample of individuals drawn from the general population. In Great Britain the increase in risk is in the order of 100—fold. Further, it appears that the maximum risk is in the period shortly following the parasuicide; thus the long-term studies invariably report maximum annual suicide rates in their cohorts in the early years of follow-up, in line with the relatively high yield obtained by short-term studies. This does not imply that the risk can be assumed ever to become negligible.

But perhaps the question of central importance is what distinguishes within a series of parasuicides the subgroups at maximum risk for eventual death from suicide. There is a large and rapidly expanding literature on this topic. Many investigators are studying diagnostic and psychological characteristics of high-risk patients, and scales of 'lethality' are being developed (Minkoff et al., 1973; Silver et al., 1971) for the prediction of suicide in addition to other uses. Other investigators have taken a rather different approach using characteristics which are essentially demographic. Thus the prediction of suicide among parasuicides was said by Tuckman and Youngman (1963a) to be based on the principle that 'the more closely individuals approximate to complete suicides with respect to sex, race or age, the higher their suicide risk', and in a later study (1963b) they add further variables to the list. The completed suicides to which they refer are of course those derived from the total population.

The latter (or 'demographic') approach has the advantage that the criteria employed are relatively robust, and the disadvantage that the same criteria lead to relatively little by way of theoretical understanding. On balance it seemed a reasonable strategy to use 'demographic' parameters initially in order to identify the high-risk subgroups for clinical purposes and to provide samples which might then be studied at a later stage by means of psychological or other appropriate techniques designed to clarify the *processes* involved. Accordingly an investigation was carried out to test and perhaps refine the Tuckman and Youngman position. Its objectives (among others) were to determine (a) whether age and sex acted in themselves as effective predictors of subsequent suicide, and (b) to compare the suicide rates in age—sex subgroups of parasuicides with rates derived for the population of the city. Ideally a study of this kind should meet three requirements. Firstly, both the parasuicide and suicide data should refer to the same population over the same period of time. This requirement was largely met by using RPTC data, and determining via the General Registrar's Office the occurrence of any suicide in the cohorts investigated. Only individuals resident within the city boundary were included. Secondly, a follow-up study of this kind should seek evidence of life as well as evidence of death, but in the event only evidence of death was obtained. Lastly, it should be recognized that the official GRO criterion for suicide is heavily influenced by legal procedures and hence employs a more restrictive definition than most psychiatrists would feel appropriate. For this reason information was also collected on undetermined deaths (ICD eighth revision E980—989) since these probably represent the largest reservoir of concealed suicidal deaths.

Design

Two 1—year cohorts of patients (persons) admitted to the RPTC in 1968 and 1969 were studied. All deaths from suicide or from 'undetermined causes' occurring in 1968, 1969, or 1970 among the individuals in the 1968 cohort were identified, as were deaths occurring in 1969, 1970, or 1971 in the 1969 cohort. Each cohort thus had a follow-up of 2 to 3 years. To enhance the reliability of the results the data from each cohort were merged, after each had been fully analysed and found to give generally similar results. For this purpose any individuals appearing in the second cohort who had also figured in the first were eliminated from the 1969 series. As in all the other studies reported in the volume, patients who died during their key admission to the RPTC were not counted as parasuicides.

The age divisions used were 15—34, 35—54, and 55 and over, with the sexes being distinguished.

Results

During 1968 and 1969 a total of 1,261 individuals were admitted from an address within the city of Edinburgh; this figure is an unduplicated count of persons over the 2 years. Follow-up identified 24 suicides amongst them, plus a further seven undetermined deaths. Rates for the six age-sex subgroups are indicated in Table 9.3. Although the total series contained a substantial majority of women, men were a little more numerous than women among the suicides. Similarly the older age group contributed disproportionately to the total suicides.

Among the younger people both sexes have low and statistically indistinguishable rates of suicide. In the middle age group the suicide rate among men is dramatically increased in comparison with younger men. It is also much higher than the rates for middle-aged women. There is a further increase in both rates for the older age group, with both sexes showing about twice the rate of the middle group, and men still retaining their lead.

The effect of adding the undertermined deaths to the suicides is illustrated in Figure 9.6. Among males the mortality for the young is unaffected, but the leap in rates for the middle-aged group is more marked than when suicides alone are considered. There is a further rise in the curve to the old age group, although no undetermined deaths were found in this group. Among the females there were no undetermined deaths for the younger group, but the additions to the middle and old group result in a steeply rising curve than when suicides alone are considered.

Summarizing these findings, older males have twice the rate of officially recognized suicide than the middle-aged men, but the latter in turn have over ten times the rate of young men. The period of increased risk for males is thus better considered to begin in the mid-30s than in the 60s. Adding the undetermined deaths supports this contention; the middle group suicide rate then becomes close to that of the older patients. Among women, however, the findings are different. Their rates increase uniformly with age using either criterion of suicide; they are never as high as those for men of similar ages.

Other distinguishing characteristics of the patients who subsequently committed suicide are clearly of great interest, but with the numbers available detailed analysis was not feasible. Among the male suicides personality disorder had been diagnosed at the time of their RPTC admission in almost all. It was usually severe,

TABLE 9.3 Suicide and 'undetermined' deaths (in brackets) among parasuicides: 1968 and 1969 cohorts combined

	Young (age 15–34)			Middle (age 35–54)			Old (age 55+)			Total (age 15+)		
	M	F	Total	M	F	Total	M	F	Total	M	F	Total
Died within calendar year of admission	0	3	3	2	1	3	1	0	1	3	4	7
in following year	1	2	3	2(2)	0	2(2)	1	2	3	4	4	8(2)
in final year	0	0	0	3(2)	2(1)	5(3)	3	1(2)	4(2)	6(2)	3(3)	9(5)
Total	1	5	6	7(4)	3(1)	10(5)	5	3(2)	8(2)	13(4)	11(3)	24(7)
Number at risk	253	480	733	172	200	372	63	93	156	488	773	1,261
% Suicides	0.40	1.04	0.82	4.07	1.50	2.69	7.94	3.22	5.13	2.66	1.42	1.90
S.E.	0.40	0.46	0.35	1.51	0.86	0.84	3.41	1.83	1.77	0.73	0.43	0.38
% Suicides and undetermined deaths	0.40	1.04	0.82	6.40	2.00	4.03	7.94	5.38	6.41	3.48	1.81	2.46
S.E.	0.40	0.46	0.33	1.87	0.99	1.02	3.41	2.34	1.96	0.83	0.50	0.44

Significant critical ratios

	Suicide	Suicide and undetermined deaths
Young: males v. females	—	—
Middle: males v. females	—	2.08*
Old: male v. female	—	—

	Suicide	Suicide and undetermined deaths
Males: young v. middle	2.35*	3.14†
Females: young v. middle	—	—
All: young v. middle	2.07*	2.99†

	Suicide	Suicide and undetermined deaths
Males: middle v. old	—	—
Females: middle v. old	—	—
All: middle v. old	—	—

*p < 0.05
†p < 0.01

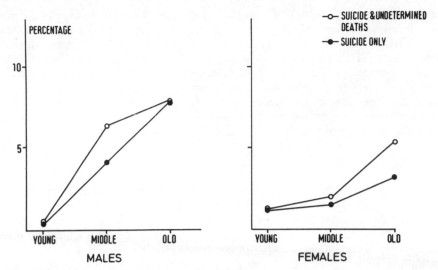

FIGURE 9.6. Suicide and 'suicide plus undetermined' mortality by age and sex

and was associated with alcoholism or drug dependence in about half of them. The specific illness diagnoses included reactive depression, situational reactions, and 'no formal illness': there was also one patient with a manic-depressive disorder. Among the female suicides, personality abnormalities were recognized in only about a third, and none was designated as an alcoholic. The specific illness diagnosis was rather similar to that for males. The importance of personality disorder and, in men, of alcoholism, requires no further elaboration, but a point of interest is the 'no formal illness' group and the allied category of 'acute situational reactions'. The glossary to the eighth edition of the ICD gives little guidance as to how this term is to be applied, and at best the term serves to suggest psychological disturbance which is expected to be transient and does not conform to the pattern of any clearly recognized illness. It is worth noting that in this series of 24 suicides, four patients were considered to be of normal personality and were classified at the time of their episode as either an acute situational reaction or free of all formal disorder. Whatever diagnostic terms may be used, they evidently have little conspicuous pathology, or at least little that was recognized at the time of the overdose, yet they represent one in six of those who subsequently kill themselves. As a subgroup they may require special attention in predictive studies of suicide following parasuicide.

The more precise specification of the high-risk subgroups among parasuicides will evidently have to await the accumulation of larger numbers, but even in the present state of knowledge it is evident that factors which predict suicide are distinct from those which predict repetition of parasuicide. The simple division for age and sex used here distinguishes subgroups with substantial differences in their rates of suicide, but not of repetition of parasuicide, while in the study reported in chapter 6 the patients who subsequently killed themselves fell in the middle, not at the top, of the range of predictive scales for further parasuicide.

To meet the second objective, concerning the Tuckman and Youngman thesis, the average rates for 1968—71 for suicide in the city of Edinburgh were calculated using the same six age—sex subgroups as in the follow-up study just described. The rank order correlation between these general population suicide rates and the risk of death by suicide after parasuicide was $r_s = 0.94$ ($p < .01$ on one-tail test). Adding in the undetermined deaths altered the rank order for both sets of rates but yielded an identical correlation coefficient. The dictum is thus confirmed. It may be worth adding that the curve of age—specific suicide rates for Edinburgh is not exactly like that for the rest of Scotland, nor for England and Wales. It evidently is important to base comparisons of the type just described on populations defined closely.

Discussion

The findings require little elaboration, but it may be mentioned that the possible effects of population mobility have not so far been discussed. In essence it seems that although younger people are in general more mobile, the main effect of differential mobility between the groups is probably to reduce slightly the rates obtained for the middle age group. Correction for migration would tend to enhance the picture already presented. Further details of this aspect and other features of parasuicide in connection with age—sex specific subgroups have been presented elsewhere (Kreitman 1976).

9.3 SUICIDE PRECEDED BY PARASUICIDE

Investigations of the kind described in the last section begin with a group of parasuicides and seek to determine how many individuals subsequently kill themselves and, if the number permits, to establish whether they have any distinguishing characteristics. A complementary but separate question concerns the size and characteristics of a group of suicides who on retrospective enquiry are found to have engaged in some form of parasuicide earlier in their lives.

The number of United Kingdom studies on this topic is not large. The first appears to have been by Sainsbury (1955). He examined a series of 409 suicides ascertained in a London coroner's court between 1936 and 1938, using only the information available in the court records. He found that 9 per cent had a record of an 'attempted suicide', excluding those occurring immediately before the suicide itself, and comments that his figure is probably an underestimate. Stengel and Cook (1958) reported on a series collected in 1953, comprising 117 suicides notified to a London coroner's court: they, too, were restricted to court records for their information. 14 per cent were found to have had an earlier episode of self-damage. These authors, too, suspected that the figure was an underestimate, though they noted that all witnesses at inquests were questioned on the matter.

Over a decade later Seager and Flood (1965) studied the inquests resulting in a suicide verdict in a group of West Country coroners' courts from 1957 to 1961. Any note of hospital referral in the records led to a search for further information from that hospital and they also made some attempt to check all the suicides for a local mental hospital admission. In their series of 325 suicides they found 16 per cent with a history of parasuicide occurring at least 6 months prior to death.

No further studies emerged until the recent work by Barraclough et al. (1974), who investigated 100 suicides occurring in Southern England by collecting comprehensive data not only from the coroner's court and various institutions but by direct interviews with the family of the deceased. They reported that 41 per cent were said by relatives to have had a parasuicidal episode at some stage in their lives. The markedly higher estimate of parasuicides may reflect not only the more intensive case identification techniques, but also the fact that their study relates to a period between 1966 and 1968, which is well after the time when the current fashion for parasuicide became widely established in Britain.

Knowledge of the proportion of suicides with a history of parasuicide is important for two main reasons. Firstly, in individuals with a positive history an opportunity once occurred for intervention and, potentially, the avoidance of the subsequent suicide. In order to plan such prophylactic activities (perhaps as part of a wider suicide prevention programme) it is necessary to know the maximum possible impact a preventive measure may have. Secondly, completed suicide still poses many riddles, and it is possible that these might be clarified by contrasting its varieties, such as suicides with and without a parasuicidal history. Such a comparison had not, apparently, been carried out prior to the study about to be described.

That study in fact began from a rather different point of departure and its initial objective was solely to determine whether it was possible and useful to distinguish different varieties of suicide; it did not, as had all the other investigations in this book, begin with a consideration of parasuicide *per se*. Its background was a dissatisfaction with current concepts of suicide, which have variously adopted either a sociological or clinical system of classification with limited cross reference. There has, of course, been some sharing of these perspectives, enough at least to establish a stereotype of the suicide as that of an elderly, isolated, and depressed individual, with other varieties being considered numerically less important but it was by no means clear that this standard view was correct. It had in fact already been challenged. McCulloch *et al.* (1967) in Edinburgh concluded that *two* groups of suicides could be distinguished, one conforming to the pattern already mentioned, the other being associated with overcrowding, gross disruption of family life, a subculture of violence, and 'attempted suicide'. In Buffalo, Lester (1970) was unable to identify this second group, his results supporting rather the classical pattern described for London in Sainsbury's monograph (1955). However, both the McCulloch and Lester studies were primarily ecological, with very limited or no information on individual cases. Seager and Flood (1965) reviewed a series of suicides in Bristol and commented on a subgroup of about one-third whose death occurred at the end of a long period of psychological disability frequently punctuated by previous 'attempts', while the remainder were evidently more stable individuals whose deaths were associated with a single and specific stress.

The study began with the assumption that suicides were a heterogeneous group and sought to establish two main subtypes or syndromes, empirically derived from both social and clinical data.

Method and results

The law in Scotland requires that all suspicious deaths be notified to the local Procurator Fiscal, who is a legally trained civil servant. The circumstances of the death are investigated by him by private enquiry, and a summary of his findings is then sent to a central office, the Crown Office, presided over by the Crown Counsel, where a decision is reached concerning the mode of death. For the purposes of this study *all* reports reaching the Crown Office on individuals aged 12 years and upwards where the deceased had a resident address in Edinburgh were scrutinized over an 18-month period from October 1969 to March 1971. In this series 106 deaths were regarded as suicides, considering as such all deaths in which the balance of evidence pointed to a deliberate *initiation* of an act of self-damage which resulted in death; overt evidence that the individual intended to kill himself was not considered essential. This definition is, of course, wider than the legal one, and only 66 of these cases were classified as suicides by the legal authorities. However, a detailed comparison of the characteristics of the suicides as recognized by Crown Counsel with those recognized by the investigators revealed that the two groups did not differ substantially; thus very similar findings would have been obtained had attention been confined to the officially-recognized suicides in the series. Details have been presented elsewhere (Ovenstone, 1973b).

For each case a schedule was completed which comprised demographic data together with virtually all the information included in the official records. Supplementary enquiries were then made concerning the deceased's contacts with mental hospital inpatient and outpatient services (both locally and in other areas where relevant), from the general practitioner, the local branch of the Telephone Samaritans, and the RPTC. Local authorities co-operated by supplying details relevant to the deceased's standard of housing and whether there was overcrowding. Additional family, personal, and social information on the background of the deceased was also collected where possible, though no direct approach was made to the families. Thus the evidence reviewed in reaching a decision about the death was usually richer than that available to the Crown Office.

The delineation of subgroups

Two methods were used, quite independently, to identify the subgroups. The first method was essentially descriptive. In addition to data which could be itemized, a variable amount of less structured information was available concerning the personality and life-style of the deceased. On reviewing all the available evidence, it appeared that the series comprised two main varieties of suicide distinguished by the presence or absence of a known earlier 'attempt'. Accordingly, the 106 cases were divided according to whether or not there was a history of parasuicide and the two subgroups were compared on all the variables for which detailed information was present. The details of how this analysis supported the proposed dichotomy are presented below.

The second method was a simple taxonomic exercise, carried out as follows. It was specified in advance that what was required was to delineate two, and only two, subgroups within the total series and to use a monothetic system of classification, that is to say, to use only one variable as the criterion for distinguishing between the two categories. Only variables on which itemized information was available were considered, and the data for each were dichotomized in such a way as to divide the total group as near the median as possible; if no division could be made which yielded at least 10 per cent in the smaller class, that variable was omitted from the analysis, as was any variable which related to events following the death, for example the official verdict. (Both these procedural principles were violated on occasion in the interests of clinical relevance.)

30 variables remained for analysis, one of which was to be selected as the basis of classification. Clearly the most useful was that which would produce the maximum number of significant differences between its subgroups on all the other variables. For example, if the dichotomous variable X produced subgroups which also differed on variables A, B, and C, while Y produced subgroups which differed on no other variables, then X was to be preferred over Y. To identify the best variable, a matrix of χ^2 values showing the association between each pair of variables was prepared. The variable which yielded the maximum *number* of significant associations was then sought. In the event, four emerged as approxi mately equally useful. The procedure was then repeated but using a simple weighting system to reflect the level of statistical significance of the χ^2 values in the matrix, which in the present context could be taken as a reflection of the amount of misclassification incurred. Again, the four most powerful variables were identified. Three of these had also been found using the first method.

Thus, five variables (three emerging by both methods plus one unique to each) were final candidates. Of these, only one correlated with all the others, and this was accordingly selected as the best summary measure. That variable was previous admission to hospital for parasuicide.

This result is, of course, very similar to that derived by the descriptive approach, to which it provides a statistical underpinning, differing only in that hospital admission for parasuicide is specified, as distinct from a history of parasuicide with or without admission. The findings that follow are presented using the division of suicides into those with and without a positive history irrespective of admission. However, the two criteria do not yield absolutely identical findings, and the discrepancies will be touched on later.

9.4 GENERAL CHARACTERISTICS OF THE GROUPS

It may help to intimate at this point that findings are broadly in line with those of Seager and Flood (1965). One subgroup of suicides comprised individuals who had led stable if precariously adjusted lives until some dislocation occurred; they then reacted with a relatively brief depressive episode, sometimes associated with excessive drinking, and soon after killed themselves. The second group were individuals with long-standing and severe personality problems, commonly with chronic alcoholism, who had a history of at least one parasuicidal episode and who eventually committed suicide in a setting of interpersonal chaos rarely associated with events that were independent of their own behaviour. Since the history of parasuicide is the most clearly differentiating feature, the second group will be referred to as the 'parasuicide' or P group, and the former as the 'no parasuicide' or NP group.

The P group numbered 50, or 47 per cent of the series, 24 being males. The date of the most recent parasuicide was known in 47 cases: in 23 it had occurred within 12 months of their death, in 13 between 1 and 3 years previously, and in the remainder at any earlier period. These time intervals did not differ significantly between the sexes. Multiple parasuicides were known to have occurred in 24 cases. Only 31 subjects had been treated at any time at the Edinburgh RPTC, a lower proportion than would be expected from the data quoted elsewhere.

There were 56 cases in the NP group.

Demographic characteristics

Men were rather commoner in the NP group (57 per cent), while the sexes were equally balanced in the P group. The age distribution of the P group tended to peak in the 45 to 54 age bracket and the NP group a decade later, a trend to relative youth seen most clearly among the men. However, these sex and age differences were not statistically significant. Similarly, there were no significant differences in marital status or social class at the time of death.

Life-style and precipitating factors

The NP group appeared to have led reasonably stable lives, even though they were often of limited adaptability and were conspicuously dependent upon some particular person, such as a spouse or parent, for their well-being. The loss by death, or occasionally by divorce or separation, of this 'significant other' occurred as a precipitating factor of the suicide twice as commonly in this group as in the P group. Similarly, the major physical illness was also markedly commoner and likewise appeared to dislocate a previously adequate if precarious adjustment. By contrast, the P group often killed themselves not in response to any unusual external disruption but rather because their chronically ill-organized lives had reached a point of social disintegration. This 'last straw' situation often appeared as a culmination of quarrels with everyone in their circle leaving the individual alienated and alone. Details are given in Table 9.4.

There was also a non-significant tendency for those in the P group to have been off work for longer periods prior to the suicide, and perhaps for this reason debt was significantly commoner amongst them (36 per cent as compared to 14 per cent in the NP group). A history of criminal behaviour was also much more frequent (28 per cent and 5 per cent respectively).

TABLE 9.4   Apparent precipitating stresses: percentage distribution

Main stress	P ($n = 50$)	NP ($n = 56$)
Loss of significant other	18	36
Physical illness	4	18
Other environmental problems*	28	23
No unusual stresses detected	50	23

$\chi^2 = 12.245$ df 3 $p < 0.01$
*Includes conspicuous stresses such as eviction, financial crises, etc.

Psychiatric history and previous personality

About 80 per cent of the parasuicide group had at some time received treatment from a psychiatrist, as compared with 20 per cent in the 'no parasuicide' group. This excess was even more marked of consideration is limited to the 12 months before death (58 per cent of P and 8 per cent of NP group). Many of these contacts were in association with the parasuicidal behaviour. Rather less influenced by the

TABLE 9.5   Personality characteristics: percentage distributions

	P (n = 50)	NP (n = 53)
Alcoholism/drug addiction	46	13
Sociopathy	12	9
'Character disorder'	38	58
Normal	4	19

$\chi^2 = 16.76$ df 3 $p < 0.001$

Positive evidence was required of personality abnormality, and the individuals classified according to the most severe category, with Group 1 having precedence over 2, etc. 'Sociopathy' was coded where there was overt conflict with the law, and character disorder where distress fell primarily on the individual alone.

classifying criterion was the length of time over which there had been medical consultations with any physician for recognized psychiatric disturbance, including personality problems: 84 per cent of the P group compared to 32 per cent of the NP group had had at least sporadic consultations for more than 5 years.

Both groups showed a similar proportion of males who were not working, were unemployed or retired at the time of the act, but in the P group psychiatric morbidity was significantly more common as a reason for not working (15/18) than in the NP group (8/19).

'Previous personality' was not easy to assess in view of the frequency of psychiatric disorder, often long-standing, and also because of limited data in three cases. The major problem, however, was in ascribing a personality description to chronic alcoholics, and for present purposes alcoholism (and other addictions) was grouped with personality deviation. Table 9.5 shows that the P group contains proportionally more of such individuals, and fewer whose personality difficulties caused distress to themselves rather than others, or who were regarded as essentially normal.

The role of alcohol was also illustrated by those individuals who habitually drank in excess of the local (generous) norms, irrespective of their 'personality diagnosis'. About two—thirds of the P group were unusually heavy drinkers, compared with a quarter of the NP series, a highly significant difference.

A family history of either suicide or parasuicide was elicited twice as commonly in the P as in NP group (14 per cent and 7 per cent), but this difference was not statistically significant.

Contact with general practitioners and Telephone Samaritans

All but five of the 106 individuals were known to be registered with a general practitioner. Both groups were stable populations in the sense that they changed their doctors infrequently, although the NP group had been registered slightly longer. The pattern of general practitioner consultation was broadly similar in the two groups if all types of consultation were considered, but when attention was confined to consultation for psychiatric symptoms only, some interesting differences emerged. The number of such contacts was noted for the period of 3 to 6 months before death and also during the last 3 months. At both periods the P group contained significantly more consulters than the NP group, and both groups showed an increase in the number of consulters in the later period (from 69 per cent to 82 per cent in the P, and from 52 per cent to 65 per cent in the NP group). Those who consulted at all did so quite frequently, the average number of visits per consulter in the two 3—month periods being 4.9 and 4.5 for the P group and 3.1 and 4.0 for the NP group.

The different patterns of general practitioner consultation for psychiatric symptoms presumably explain why the P group received significantly more drug prescriptions (90 per cent of all individuals consulting) than the NP group (58 per cent). Similar types of drugs were prescribed to both groups, comprising principally barbiturates plus other psychotropic drugs. 28 per cent in all had regularly received antidepressants.

In the total series, 69 per cent had made contact with their general practitioner (for any reason) within 1 month of their death. These consultations were usually for psychiatric disturbance (93 per cent of the P and 79 per cent of the NP consulters).

Only seven individuals had contacted the Samaritan service. Six of these cases were in the P group. Two had consulted within 1 month of their death, two within the previous 12 months, while in the remaining three cases the last contact had been 3 years previously.

The terminal syndrome

The psychiatric state of the individual shortly before death was not always easy to ascertain, and in two of the NP group no diagnostic opinion could be reached. In the remainder, the chief problem was to categorize a depressive episode occurring in conjunction with chronic alcoholism (in which mood fluctuation is often an expected symptom). Table 9.6 shows a summary classification of the two groups by both 'formal illness' and alcoholism. In both groups, depressive episodes occurred very commonly (86 per cent of the P and 87 per cent of the NP groups), and were present in all but three of the 29 alcoholics. Among the non-alcoholics, mood change occurred in a slightly lower proportion.

TABLE 9.6   Terminal illness and alcoholic status

	No formal illness	Depressive reaction	Other	Total
Parasuicide group				
Alcoholic	2	20	1	23
Not alcoholic	1	23	3	27
Uncertain	—	—	—	—
Total	3	43	4	50
No parasuicide				
Alcoholic	—	6	—	6
Not alcoholic	2	39	5	46
Uncertain	—	2	0	2
Total	2	47	5	54

Two points require to be made. Firstly, the type of depressive illness was predominantly that of a depressive reaction rather than an 'endogenous' illness. Using as criteria of the latter (a) evident biological symptoms such as diurnal variation, weight loss or early morning insomnia, (b) a previous history of mania, (c) a previous episode of depression treated by a psychiatrist and categorized by him as 'endogenous' or 'psychotic', or (d) a bizarre mode of dying such as self-immolation by burning, only 14 per cent of the P group and 16 per cent of the NP group were classified as endogenous depressives. Secondly, many of the depressive reactions occurring in non-alcoholics were associated with heavy drinking, though the drinking pattern was not that of recognizable alcoholism.

Thus the terminal syndrome was in general terms somewhat similar in the two groups. Perhaps the main point to be stressed is that for the NP group it represented a marked departure from their usual state, while for the P group it appeared more as part of a long-standing pattern.

A physical illness of sufficient severity to handicap the individual was identified in 26 per cent of the P group and 38 per cent of the NP group, a non-significant difference. As already noted, illness as a precipitant of suicide figures more commonly among the NP group, in line with the greater importance among them of disruption to their normal pattern of living.

The circumstances and method of the suicide

As Table 9.7 shows, relatively more of the P group intimated their suicidal plans to others beforehand. They more often killed themselves while others were in the vicinity, either in the same room, especially asleep, or in the same house. Drugs and oral poisons were the predominant means of death, while coal gas and self-injury were relatively less often employed. There was no significant difference between

TABLE 9.7   Characteristics of the suicide act in parasuicide (P) and no parasuicide (NP) groups: percentages

	P ($n = 50$)	NP ($n = 56$)	χ^2	df
Prior intimation to others				
Present	40	20	4.28	1
Absent	60	73	$p < .05$	
Uncertain	–	5		
Method				
Drugs/poisons	74	54	18.53	2
Coal gas	10	20	$p < .001$	
Injury, with or without drugs	16	27		
Presence of others				
Alone	52	77	7.14	1
Others in vicinity	48	23	$p < .001$	
Classification of intent				
Definite	54	80	8.42	1
Possible/minimal	46	20	$p < .01$	

the groups in the proportion who took alcohol at the time of the act (44 per cent of the P and 29 per cent of the NP group).

Seriousness of intent to die was assessed in three categories, 'definite intent' being recorded if a suicide note had been left, if a highly lethal method was employed, or if the wish to die had been recently communicated to others. Fewer of the P group were classified as 'definite'.

The criteria for distinguishing the subgroups

All the above findings relate to differences between subjects who did or did not have a history of parasuicide, irrespective of whether or not the episode resulted in hospital admission. The taxonomic method, however, indicated that only when such an episode was followed by admission to hospital was it of importance, while a history of parasuicide without further specification had a relatively weaker discriminatory power. This suggested the possibility that by including in the P group individuals who had not been admitted to hospital the power of the classification was being weakened. It therefore seemed appropiate to examine the P group to determine whether those who were known to the RPTC ($n = 31$) differed from those who were not ($n = 19$),

Significant differences were found in a number of respects. Those admitted were more likely to come from social classes IV and V ($p < .05$); they were more likely to have made multiple previous attempts ($p < .02$); they contained a higher proportion of individuals who abused alcohol ($p < .05$); had more commonly intimated their intent to die to someone in the 3 months before their death ($p < .02$): and had more usually consulted their general practitioner in the last month of their life ($p < .05$).

Putting these characteristics together, it appears that the admitted subgroup were chronic alcohol abusers from the bottom of the social scale, who had made multiple attempts and who admitted their despair to the general practitioner and to others. These characteristics were also found in the non-admitted group but significantly less often. The admitted cases can therefore be considered a nuclear subgroup who show particularly clearly the pattern of chronic disorganization, often with alcoholism, already described.

Nevertheless, it is recommended that the more general characteristic of a history of parasuicide should be used for purposes of 'syndrome delineation', since hospital admission in association with an episode of self-damage must be greatly influenced by local service provisions and similar considerations.

Person scores

Evidence presented so far suggests that there are two clusters of *characteristics* in the series of suicides, but does not indicate whether there are also two groups of *persons*. To investigate this question, a score for each individual was derived by summing over the eight variables already shown to distinguish the 'groups' at the 0.01 level of significance or beyond; for each variable a score of 2 was given if the data were in the direction characterizing the NP group, and 1 if the converse was true. The history of parasuicide itself was added as an additional variable and similarly scored. An individual's score could thus range from 9 to 18.[2]

Figure 9.7 shows the distribution obtained on the total 106 cases. It is

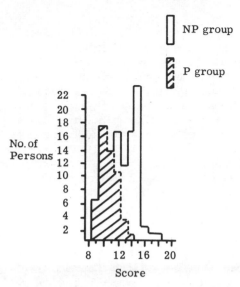

FIGURE 9.7. Distribution of person scores

approximately bi-modal with the two subgroups well distinguished. A cut-off score at 12/13 misclassifies 8 per cent of the P group, and 11 per cent of the NP group, with a total misclassification of 9 per cent.

Other kinds of score were also derived, using additional variables and various weighting schemes, but little additional differentiation was gained. The question of the optimal classifying criteria was not pursued any further; the data have already served to identify the relevant variables, and it would be necessary to use a new sample of cases to demonstrate bi-modality conclusively. It does, however, emerge that the notion of two distinct subgroups remains a tenable hypothesis, which would not have been the case had a normal curve been found.

Discussion

Drawing these findings together, it seems that the P group could have well been termed the 'chronically disorganized' group and the NP group could be referred to as 'the acutely disrupted'.

Among the former, psychological instability and social disruption were conspicuous in a large majority of individuals over at least the 5 years prior to their suicide, and often much longer. Many were sociopaths, drug addicts or alcoholics; relatively often they were not working or were in debt, and had a history of crime. Interpersonal conflicts were prominent, having contributed to the earlier episode of parasuicide and sometimes to the suicide as well. Those whose records did not reveal frank rejection by others, for example after a quarrel, had nevertheless been existing in a marginal state of chronic social failure, inadequately mitigated by recourse to alcohol or drugs. In a few instances, usually female, there was a history of recurrent phases of agitation and depression with parasuicide, such patients often having marked interpersonal difficulties too.

This group was also found to have had relatively frequent contact with psychiatrists, often in consequence of their episodes of parasuicide. They were also in general well known to their general practitioners, at least 80 per cent having consulted for psychological symptoms, often repeatedly, over the last 3 months of their lives. The frequency with which barbiturates were prescribed alone or in combination has been quoted; sometimes addiction followed. Antidepressants were also sometimes used. On clinical grounds, however, it can be seriously doubted if drug therapy alone has a central place in the treatment of such patients whose personality and environmental problems seem to loom so large.

The circumstances of the suicide were also characteristic, the P group more commonly intimating unambiguously their intention to various other people, yet more commonly carrying out the act in the close vicinity of others. They preferred drugs to other methods of killing themselves. If a case were to be argued for 'accidental suicide' as a consequence of deliberate self-poisoning or self-injury, examples would presumably be drawn primarily from this group.

There is little room for complacency regarding the prevention of suicide in the P group. Litman (1971), from his experience of the Los Angeles Suicide Prevention Center, considers that the majority of their clients have chronic situational stresses, and for many suicide appears to be a recurrent problem which crises intervention tends to postpone rather than prevent. Similarly, Wold and Litman (1973) refer to patients who pursue a 'suicidal career'. Over 80 per cent of the suicides in the P group had seen a psychiatrist at some time, mostly within a year of their death. Evidently they benefited little. It is not yet clear whether patients with a *suicidal* outcome, as distinct from a repetition of parasuicide, can be identified at the appropriate time or materially helped.

In other respects the two groups did *not* differ. They were similar with respect to age, sex-ratio, marital status, and social class. These similarities may appear somewhat unexpected in view of the prominence of alcoholism in the P group. Alcoholic suicides are well documented as dying at an earlier age than other diagnostic groups (Murphy and Robins, 1967; Kessel and Grossman, 1961), and also show differences in marital status and social class from other suicides. However, most of the chronically disorganized or P group were not alcoholics, although most of the 29 alcoholics in the total series fell into the P category (Table 9.6). The similarity of the terminal psychiatric syndrome, in which depression and heavy drinking both figure conspicuously, has already been noted.

The characteristics of the acutely disrupted group with no known parasuicide are in general the converse of those already summarized for the P group, though it must be emphasized that the design of the study focuses on *contrasts* between the two categories. For example, the loss of a significant other was considered to have precipitated the suicide in about a fifth of the P group, but twice that proportion in the NP group. Thus loss is important for both categories, but in differentiating *within* a series of suicides it is particularly characteristic of the NP cases.

The comparatively stable lives of the acutely disrupted or NP group have been noted to depend upon a rather fragile basis, such as an exclusive emotional involvement with one particular person. The death or other loss of this key person was a dislocation to which they could not adjust. In others physical disability disrupted the stable life pattern (with the individual apparently maladjusted to the infirmity as judged by frequent and intense complaints, out of proportion to demonstrable pathology, made to the general practitioner). A variety of other crises were apparent precipitants in other instances, but the consequences were similar; either suicide followed quickly, in which case it was deliberately and meticulously executed, or there ensued a period of sleeplessness, anxiety and depression, sometimes with resort to drugs or alcohol, before life was relinquished. The failure to adjust to change has been noted by Bunch *et al.* (1971), who commented that the severity of the bereavement reaction of some suicides could only be fully explained by the individual's personality characteristics. Present data support this view; over half the NP group were classified as having personality disorders, though not commonly of a sociopathic type. The NP group was also well known to the general practitioners, 65 per cent having consulted with recognized psychological morbidity in the 3 months before death, and, as other workers have noted, potential exists here for preventive action. The drug therapy prescribed was not always appropriate, and the psychosocial problems, though often possibly tractable, were not always simple. Yet referral to a psychiatrist in the last year of life was initiated in only 8 per cent. It is tempting to believe that a higher referral rate would have been beneficial — provided that psychiatrists too perceive the necessity for a widely based approach. The suicides of this group certainly appear to offer better preventive prospects than the P group.

The high level of medical consultations contrasts with the low level of contact with the Samaritan service (7 per cent), most of these being in the P group. This finding is similar to the 4 per cent reported by Barraclough and Shea (1970).

The comments on possible preventive action should not be construed as criticism of the efficiency of psychiatrists, general practitioners, or Samaritan organizations. Obviously it is impossible to evaluate the efficacy of any service without data on successes as well as failures. Data from suicides alone can at best merely indicate where further preventive action might be proposed. The same point has already been made in connection with primary and secondary preventive services for parasuicide.

The delineation of the two syndromes presented does not, of course, imply that further varieties may not be identified. A different approach could well have produced a third category, such as the young drug addicts, although their numbers are probably small in the present series. The evidence so far is compatible with the view that the two syndromes refer not only to clusters of characteristics but also to groups of people; however, convincing demonstration of the latter would require a fresh sample. The groups do not appear to differ in demographic characteristics, which limits their applicability for some kinds of epidemiological analysis, but they may nevertheless be important in clarifying comparisons between different areas or populations with respect to suicide. Regional differences in alcohol abuse may be particularly relevant.

9.5 COLLATION OF FINDINGS: THE 'OVERLAP' GROUP

At this point it may be useful to try and draw together the findings of the three studies just described, and to summarize just what has and has not been established, given their particular design features.

The first study was an epidemiological one which indicated the relative magnitude of the rates for suicide and parasuicide. It showed that there were marked discrepancies in the age—sex specific curves, but that despite a difference in magnitude the trends in terms of area of the city and perhaps in social class were parallel.

The second study was a prospective one on a large group of parasuicides and yielded an estimate of the proportion who eventually terminated their lives within 3 years. It also served to identify certain risk factors (by age and sex). It is important to note that as always such comparisons are only sensitive to differences *within* the series, while features common to all parasuicides would not be detected. This may seem a truism but becomes important when one seeks to interpret the results: in very general terms, the importance of characteristic X may change radically according to the presence or absence of characteristic Y, but if Y is ubiquitous or totally absent in the entire group, its presence of absence will not be revealed by a within-group comparison, and the importance of X will not be justly assessed. It is also worth bearing in mind that statistically significant differences between subgroups may be obtained for characteristics which are found only in the minority of each. For these reasons there is much to be said for straightforward descriptive accounts of the individuals who meet the outcome criterion, in this case completed suicide. Unfortunately only 24 cases of confirmed suicide were found, too small a series to inspire confidence. It was noted, however, that virtually all the males who eventually killed themselves suffered from severe personality disorder, or problems related to alcohol, or both. Among the women who eventually died by suicide there were less striking similarities, though it was evident that they often had led ill-organized lives.

A much larger sample of individuals whose parasuicide had been followed at a later date by completed suicide was obtained in the third study, based on a retrospective analysis of a series of suicides. A comparison of those individuals who had and did not have a positive history showed the former to have a disproportionate number with chronic psychiatric instability, chiefly personality disorder, problems with alcohol, and often a protracted existence in socially marginal situations. The results thus fit well with those obtained from the prospective analysis.

This concordance of results increases their persuasiveness, but it is perhaps worth mentioning that the story is not fully rounded off, so to speak. For example, it is not possible in any strict sense to compare suicides with a previous history of parasuicide (obtained from the suicide series) with parasuicides who did not later kill themselves, since the parasuicidal episodes of the former will have occurred at various times in the past and in different parts of the country, so that the construction of an appropriate comparison group is virtually impossible. On the other hand, if a rather less rigorous stance is adopted, it does appear useful to compare this 'overlap' group, i.e. of parasuicides who subsequently die by suicide, with the generality of parasuicides as currently seen. An analysis of just this kind was carried out by Ovenstone (1973a). She found that the overlap group in comparison to parasuicides tended to be older and to be males. They were relatively less often single and more often separated, widowed, or divorced; more often lived alone, and were strikingly more often unemployed. A substantially higher proportion had a criminal record, a history of alcohol abuse, and previous inpatient psychiatric treatment was over three times more common. Virtually none was considered to have had a normal personality. The reader interested in the details of this and other comparisons is referred to the original paper.

These additional characteristics of parasuicides where lives terminate in suicide may be provisionally accepted as additional predictors of risk and as pointers to the need for closer therapeutic attention. They require confirmation and refinement by means of prospective studies. There also remains the need to supplement group descriptions with a clearer understanding of the psychological processes acting in the individual patient.

NOTES

1 This percentage is close to that of 62 per cent described by Ovenstone (1972, 1973b) for a rather larger series which extended beyond the survey year in question. The Registrar General's statistics include a few more suicides than those reported by the Crown Office, but for simplicity of presentation and because the discrepancy is small, only the Crown Office figures are considered here (see references for fuller details).

2 A score of 1 was given if the following nine characteristics were present, and 2 if they were absent or data were incomplete:

A history of parasuicide; intimation of suicidal intent to others, recognized as such, in last 3 months of life; regular and repeated consumption of hypnotics, sedatives, stimulants or antidepressants; chronic alcoholism, alcohol addiction or excessive drinking; a court conviction; previous inpatient psychiatric care; previous outpatient psychiatric care; sociopathy, subnormality, drug addiction or alcoholism; psychiatric instability of more than 5 years.

REFERENCES

Adock, C. J. (1965), 'A comparison of the concepts of Cattell and Eysenck'. *Brit. J. Educ. Psychol.*, 35, 90–97.

Aitken, R. C. B., Buglass, D., and Kreitman, N. (1969), 'The changing pattern of attempted suicide in Edinburgh, 1926–67'. *Brit. J. Prev. Soc. Med.*, 23, 111–15.

Alderson, M. (1974), 'Self-poisoning – what is the future?' *Lancet*, v, 1040–1043.

Allport, G. A. (1955), *Becoming: Basic Considerations for a Psychology of Personality*. Yale University Press, New Haven.

Askham, J. (1969), 'Delineation of the lowest social class', *J. Biolog. Sci.*, 1, 327–335.

'Atkins Report' (1962) Emergency Treatment in Hospital of Cases of Acute Poisoning. Report of Sub-Committee of Standing Medical Advisory Committee of the Central Health Services Council. HMSO, London.

Bagley, C. (1970), 'Causes and prevention of repeated attempted suicide', *Social & Economic Administration*, 4, 322–330.

Bagley, C., and Greer, S. (1971), 'Clinical and social predictors of repeated attempted suicide: a multivariate analysis', *Brit. J. Psychiat.*, 119, 515–21.

Baldwin, J. (1975), 'British areal studies of crime: an assessment', *Brit. J. Criminol.*, 15, 211–227.

Bancroft, J., Skrimshire, A., Reynolds, F., and Simkin, S. (1974), 'Self-poisoning and self-injury in the Oxford area: epidemiological aspects 1969–73'. Paper presented to York Conference on Parasuicide,

Bannister, D. (1965), 'The rationale and clinical relevance of repertory grid technique'. *Brit. J. Psychiat.*, 111, 977–982.

Barraclough, B., Bunch, J., Nelson, B., and Sainsbury, P. (1974), 'A hundred cases of suicide: clinical aspects', *Brit. J. Psychiat.*, 125, 355–373.

Barraclough, B., and Shea, M. (1970), 'Suicide and Samaritan clients', *Lancet*, ii, 868–870.

Batchelor, I. R. C., and Napier, M. B. (1953), 'Attempted suicide in old age', *B. M. J.*, ii, 1186.

Batchelor, I. R. C., and Napier, M. B. (1954a), 'The sequelae and short-term prognosis of attempted suicide', *J. Neurol. Neurosurg. Psychiat.*, 17, 261.

Batchelor, I. R. C. (1954b), 'Repeated suicidal attempts', *Brit. J. Med. Psychol.*, 27, 158.

Beck, R. W., Morris, J. B., and Beck, A. T. (1974), 'Cross-validation of the Suicidal Intent Scale', *Psycholog. Rep.*, 34, 445–446. April 1974.

Bernstein, B. (1971), 'Class codes and control', vol. I. Routledge & Kegan Paul, London.

Beshers, J. M. (1960), 'Statistical inferences from small area data', *Social Forces*, 38, 341–348.

Birtchnell, J., and Alarcon, J. (1971), 'The motivation and emotional state of 91 cases of attempted suicide', *Brit. J. Med. Psychol.*, 44, 45–52.

Bratfos, O. (1971), 'Attempted suicide', *Acta Psychiat. Scand.*, 47, 48.

Bridges, P., and Koller, K. (1966), 'Attempted suicide: a comparative study'. *Comprehensive Psychiatry*, 7, 240–247.

Buglass, D. (1976), 'The relation of social class to the characteristics and treatment of parasuicide', *Soc. Psychiat.*, 11, 107–119.

Buglass, D., Dugard, P., and Kreitman, N. (1970), 'Multiple standardisation of parasuicide ("attempted suicide") rates in Edinburgh', *Brit. J. Prev. Soc. Med.*, 24, 182–186.

Buglass, D., and Horton, J. (1974a), 'A scale for predicting subsequent suicidal behaviour', *Brit. J. Psychiat.*, 124, 573–578.

Buglass, D., and Horton, J. (1974b), 'The repetition of parasuicide: a comparison of three cohorts', *Brit. J. Psychiat.*, 125, 168–174.

Buglass, D., and McCulloch, J. W. (1970), 'Further suicidal behaviour: the development and validation of predictive scales', *Brit. J. Psychiat.*, 116, 483–491.

Bunch, J., Barraclough, B., Nelson, B., and Sainsbury, P. (1971), 'Suicide following bereavement of parents', *Soc. Psychiat.*, **6**, 193—199.
Burkhart, W. R. (1969), 'The parole work unit programme: an evaluation report', Brit. J. Criminol., 9, 2.
Caine, T. M., Foulds, G. A., and Hope, K. (1967), *Manual of the Hostility and Direction of Hostility Questionnaire (HDHQ)*. University of London Press.
Caine, T. M., and Hope, K. (1967), *'Manual of the Hysteroid-obsessoid Questionnaire (HOQ)*. University of London Press.
Campbell, D. T. (1957). 'A typology of tests, projective and otherwise', *J. Consult. Psychol.*, **21**, 207—210.
Carstairs, G. M. (1961), 'Characteristics of the suicide prone', *Proc. Roy. Soc. Med.*, **54**, 262.
Cattell, R. B. (1957), *Personality and Motivation Structure and Measurement*, Harrap, London.
Cattell, R. B. (1964), 'Psychological definition and measurement of anxiety', *J. Neuropsychiat.*, **5**, 396—402.
Cattell, R. B. (1965), *The Scientific Analysis of Personality'*, Penguin Books, Harmondsworth.
Cattell, R. B., and Eber, H. W. (1965), *The 16 Personality Factor Questionnaire*, 3rd ed. I.P.A.T. Champaign, Illinois.
Cattell, R. B., Eber, H. W., and Tatsuoka, M. M. (1970), *The Handbook for the Sixteen Personality Factor Questionnaire (16PF)*. I.P.A.T., Champaign, Illinois.
Cavan, R. (1928), *Suicide*. Reissued by Russell, Russell Inc., New York (1965).
Chowdhury, N. and Kreitman, N. (1970), 'The clientele of the Telephone Samaritan organisation', *App. Soc. Stud.*, **2**, 123—135.
Chowdhury, N., and Kreitman, N. (1971), 'A comparison of parasuicides ("attempted suicide") and the clients of the Telephone Samaritan Service', *App. Soc. Stud.*, **3**, 51—57.
Chowdhury, N., Hicks, R. C., and Kreitman, N. (1973), 'Evaluation of an after-care service for parasuicide ("attempted suicide") patients'. *Soc. Psychiat.*, **8**, 67—81.
Cohen, A. K. (1955), *Delinquent Boys*, The Free Press, New York.
Cohen, E., Motto, J., and Seiden, R. H. (1966), 'An instrument for evaluating suicide potential: a preliminary study', *Am. J. Psychiat.*, **122**, 886—891.
Cohen, J. (1960), *Chance, Skill and luck*, Pelican Books, London.
Cohen, J., and Hansel, M. (1956), *Risk and Gambling: A Study of Subjective Probability*, Philosophical Library, Inc., New York.
Cooperstock, R. (1971), 'Sex differences in the use of mood-modifying drugs: an explanatory model', *J. Hlth. & Soc. Behav.*, **12**, 238—244.
Dahlgren, K. G. (1945), *On Suicide and Attempted Suicide. A psychiatrical and statistical investigation*. A.-B. Ph. Lindstedts Univ.-bokhandel, Lund, Sweden.
Devries, A. G. (1967), 'Control variables in the identification of suicidal behaviour', *Psycholog. Rep.*, **20**, 1131—1135.
Devries, A. G., and Farberow, N. L. (1967), 'A multivariate profile analysis of MMPI's of suicidal and non-suicidal neuropsychiatric hospital patients', *J. Projective Techniques & Personality Assessment*, **31**, 81—84.
Downes, D. M. (1966), *The delinquent solution: a study in Sub-Cultural Theory*, Routledge & Kegan Paul, London.
Duffy, J. C., (1977), 'Frequency distribution of hospital-referred parasuicidal episodes in Edinburgh', *Brit. J. Prev. Soc. Med.*, **31**, (in press).
Duncan, O. D., Ohlin, L. E., Reiss, A. J., and Stanton, H. R. (1953), 'Formal devices for making selection decisions', *Am. J. Soc.*, **58**, 573—584.
Ebie, J. C. (1969), 'A study of the Craigmillar Health, Welfare and Advice Centre with a method of family linkage', M. Sc. Thesis, University of Edinburgh.
Ebie, J. C. (1971), 'Features of psychiatric relevance at an experimental multi-disciplinary social casework centre in Edinburgh', *Soc. Psychiat.*, **6**, 122—128.
Ebie, J. C., Hicks, R. C., Lythe, G. J., and Short, R. (1970), 'An integrated approach to a community's health and social problems', *Health Bulletin*, **XXVIII**, no. 2, 35—41.
Eisenthal, S., Farberow, N. L., and Shneidman, E. S. (1966), 'Follow-up of neuropsychiatric patients in suicide observation status', *Publ. Hlth Rep.*, (Washington), **81**, 977.
Ekblom, B., and Frisk, M. (1959), 'Den vid suicidförsök omedelbart angivna subjektiva orsakens relation till recidivfrekvensen (The relation of the subjective cause stated immediately in attempted suicides to their frequency of recurrence)', *Nord. Med.*, **62**, 1176.
Ettlinger, R. W. (1964), 'Suicides in a group of patients who had previously attempted suicide', *Acta Psychiat. Scand.*, **40**, 363.

186

Ettlinger, R. (1972), *Somatic Sequelae in Suicide and Attempted Suicide*, Nordiska Cokhandelnsforlag, Stockholm.

Ettlinger, R. (1975), 'Evaluation of suicide prevention after attempted suicide', *Acta Psychiat. Scand.*, Supplement 260.

Ettlinger, R. W., and Flordh, P. (1955), 'Attempted suicide: experience of five hundred cases at a general hospital', *Acta. Psychiat. Scand.*, Suppl. 103.

Evans, G. (1967), 'Deliberate self-poisoning in the Oxford area', *Brit. J. Prev. Soc. Med.*, **21**, 97—107.

Fahy, R. J., Brocklebank, J. T., and Ashby, D. W. (1970), 'Syndromes of self-poisoning', *I. J. Med. Sc.*, 8th series, **3**, no. 11, 497—503.

Farberow, N. L. (1950), 'Personality patterns of suicidal mental hospital patients', *Genetic Psychology Monographs*, **42**, 3—79.

Farberow, N. L., and Schneidman, E. (1961), *The Cry for Help*, McGraw-Hill, London.

Flynn, N., Flynn, P., and Mellor, N. (1972), 'Social malaise research: a study in Liverpool', in *Social Trends*, HMSO. London.

Foulds, G. A. (1965), *Personality and Personal Illness*, Tavistock, London.

Foulds, G. A. (1967), 'Some differences between neurotics and character disorders', *Brit. J. Soc. Clin. Psychol.*, **6**, 52—59.

Foulds, G. A., Caine, T. M., and Creasy, M. A. (1960), 'Aspects of extra and intro-punitive expression in mental illness', *J. Ment. Sci.*, **106**, 599—610.

Foulds, G. A., and Hope, K. (1968), *Manual of the Symptom Sign Inventory*, University of London Press.

Fox, R. (1971), 'The Samaritan contribution to suicide prevention', Proc, 6th Int. Congress on Suicide Prevention, Mexico.

Fox, R. (1975), 'The suicide drop — why?' *Roy. Soc. Health J.*, **95**, 9—14.

Freud, S. (1904), *Psychopathology of Everyday Life* Translated into English by A. A. Brill, Macmillan, New York, 1930.

Gardner, E. A., Bahn, A. K., and Mack, M. (1964), 'Suicide and psychiatric care in the ageing', *Arch, gen Psychiat.*, **10**, 547.

Glueck, S., and Glueck, E., (1950) *Unravelling Juvenile Delinquency*, Harvard University Press, Massachusetts.

Goldberg, D. P. (1972), *The Detection of Psychiatric Illness by Questionnaire*, Oxford University Press.

Goldberg, L. R. (1974), 'Objective diagnostic tests and measures', in *Annual Review of Psychology*, ed. P. R. Farnsworth, Annual Reviews Inc., Palo Alto.

Graham, J. D. P., and Hitchins, R. A. N. (1967), 'Acute poisoning and its prevention', *Brit. J. Prev. Soc. Med.*, **21**, 108—114.

Gray, P., and Cartwright, A. (1953), 'Choosing and changing doctors', *Lancet*, ii, 1308,

Greenwood, M., and Woods, H. M. (1919), 'The incidence of industrial accidents with special reference to multiple accidents', Medical Research Committee, Industrial Fatigue Research Report No. 4, HMSO, London.

Greer, S., and Bagley, C. (1971), 'Effect of psychiatric intervention in attempted suicide', B. M. J., **1**, 310—312.

Greer, S., Gunn, J., and Koller, K. (1966), 'Aetiological factors in attempted suicide', *B. M. J.*, **2**, 1352—1355.

Greer, S., and Lee, H. A. (1967), 'Subsequent progress of potentially lethal attempted suicides', *Acta Psychiat. Scand.*, **43**, 361—371.

Hathaway, S. R., and McKinley, J. C. (1943), *The Minnesota Multiphasic Personality Inventory*, University of Minnesota Press, Minneapolis.

Henderson, S., Eastwood, M., and Montgomery, I. (1972), 'Self-poisoning in Edinburgh and Hobart', *Soc. Psychiat.*, **7**, 30—35.

Hershon, H. I. (1968), 'Attempted suicide in a largely rural area during an eight year period', *Brit. J. Psychiat.*, **114**, 279.

'Hill Report' (1968) Hospital Treatment of Acute Poisoning. Report of Sub-Committee of Standing Medical Advisory Committee of the Central Health Services Council. HMSO, London (1968).

Hinde, R. A. (ed.) (1972), *Non-Verbal Communication*, Cambridge University Press.

Hinde, R. A. (ed.) (1975), *Non-Verbal Communication*, (new ed.), Cambridge University Press.

Holding, T. (1974), 'The B.B.C. "Befrienders" series and its effects', *Brit. J. Psychiat.*, **124**, 470—472.

Holding, T. A., Buglass, D., Duffy, J. C., Kreitman, N. (in press), 'Parasuicide in Edinburgh — a seven year review 1968—1974. *Brit. J. Psychiat.*

Hove, H. (1953), 'Reddede selvmordspatienters skaebne', *Ugeskr. Laeg.*, **115**, 645.

Hoyt, H. (1939), *The Structure and Growth of Residential Neighborhoods*, Federal Housing Aministration, Washington, D.C.

Jansson, B. (1962), 'A catamnestic study of 476 attempted suicides, with special regard to the prognosis for cases of drug automation', *Acta Psychiat. Scand.*, **38**, 183.

Jensen,, A. R. (1964), 'The Rorschach technique: a re-evaluation', *Acta Psychologica* **22**, 60—77.

Katschnig, H., and Sint, P. (1973), 'Are there different types of attempted suicides? A cluster analytic approach', Proc. 7th Int. Congress on Suicide Prevention, Amsterdam.

Kelly, G. A. (1955), *The Psychology of Personal Constructs*, Norton & Co., New York.

Kennedy, P. F. (1972a), 'Poisoning treatment centres', *B. M. J.*, **4**, 670 (corresp.).

Kennedy, P. F. (1972b), 'An epidemiological survey of attempted suicide in general practice in Edinburgh', M.D. Thesis, University of Leeds.

Kennedy, P. F., and Kreitman, N. (1973), 'An epidemiological survey of parasuicide ("attempted suicide") in general practice', *Brit. J. Psychiat.*, **123**, 23.

Kennedy, P. F., Kreitman, N., and Ovenstone, I. M. K. (1974), 'The prevalence of suicide and parasuicide ("attempted suicide") in Edinburgh', *Brit. J. Psychiat.*, **124**, 36—41.

Kennedy, P. F., Phanjoo, A. L., and Shekim, W. O. (1971), 'Risk-taking in the lives of parasuicides (attempted suicides)', *Brit. J. Psychiat.*, **119**, 281—286.

Kessel, N. (1965a), Milroy Lectures, Roy. Coll. Phys. London, 1 and 3 February 1965.

Kessel, N. (1965b), 'Self-poisoning', *B. M. J.*, **2**, 1265, 1336—1340.

Kessel, N., and Grossman, G. (1961), 'Suicide in alcoholics', *B. M. J.*, **2**, 1671—1672.

Kessel, N., and McCulloch, W. (1966), 'Repeated acts of self-poisoning and self-injury', Proc. Roy. Soc. Med.. **59**, 2, 89—92.

Kessel, N., McCulloch, J. W., Hendry, J., Leslie, D., Wallace, I., and Webster, R. (1964), 'Hospital Management of attempted suicide in Edinburgh', *Scot. Med. J.*, **9**, 333.

Kessel, N., McCulloch, W., and Simpson, E. (1963), 'Psychiatric service in a centre for the treatment of poisoning', *B. M. J.*, **2**, 985.

Klein, G. S., Barr, H. L., and Wolitzky, D. L. (1967), 'Personality', in *Annual Review of Psychology*, (ed. P. R. Farnsworth), Annual Reviews Inc., Palo Alto.

Kogan, N., and Wallach, M. A. (1964), *Risk-taking: A Study in Cognition and Personality*, Holt, Rinehart & Winston, New York.

Kreitman, N. (1972a), 'Suicide in Scotland in comparison with England and Wales', *Brit. J. Psychiat.*, **121**, 83—87.

Kreitman, N. (1972b), 'Aspects of the epidemiology of suicide and "attempted suicide" (parasuicide)', in *Suicide and Attempted Suicide*, 45—52, Skandia International Symposium, 29—30 September 1971. (Eds. J. Waldenström, T. Larsson and N. Ljungstedt), Esselte Trycke, Stockholm.

Kreitman, N. (1976), 'Age and parasuicide ("attempted suicide")', *Psycholog. Med.*, **6**, 113—121.

Kreitman, N., and Chowdhury, N. (1973a), 'Distress behaviour: a study of selected samaritan clients and parasuicides ("attempted suicide" patients)', Part I: 'General aspects', *Brit. J. Psychiat.*, **123**, 1—8.

Kreitman, N., and Chowdhury, N. (1973b), 'Distress behaviour: a study of selected samaritan clients and parasuicides ("attempted suicide" patients)', Part II: 'Attitudes and choice of action', *Brit. J. Psychiat.*, **123**, 9—14.

Kreitman, N., and Philip, A. E. (1969), 'Parasuicide'. *Brit. J. Psychiat.*, **115**, 746—747.

Kreitman, N., Smith, P., and Tan, E. (1969) 'Attempted suicide in social networks', *Brit. J. Prev. Soc. Med.*, **23**, 116—123.

Kreitman, N., Smith, P., and Tan, E. (1970), 'Attempted suicide as Language: an empirical study', *Brit. J. Psychiat.*, **116**, 465—473.

Lawson, A. A. H., and Mitchell, I. (1972a), 'Poisoning treatment centres', *B. M. J.*, **4**, 799 (corres.).

Lawson, A. A. H., and Mitchell I. (1972b), 'Patients with acute poisoning in a general medical unit', *B. M. J.*, **4**, 153—156.

Lester, D. (1970), 'Social Disorganisation and completed suicide', *Soc. Psychiat.*, **5**, 175–176.

Litman, R. (1972), 'Experience in a suicide prevention centre', in *Suicide and Attempted Suicide*, 217–230, Skandia International Symposium, 29–30 September 1971. (Eds. J. Waldenström, T. Larsson and N. Ljungstedt), Esselte Trycke, Stockholm.

Lukianowicz, M. (1972), 'Suicidal Behaviour: an attempt to modify the environment', *Brit. J. Psychiat.*, **121**, 387–390.

Lyons, H., and Sharma, S. (1972), 'Attempted suicide by self-poisoning', J. Irish Med. Assoc., **65**, 435–438.

McCarthy, P. D., and Walsh, D. (1965), 'Attempted suicide in Dublin', *J. Irish med. Ass.*, **57**, 8.

McCarthy, P. D., and Walsh, D. (1966), 'Suicide in Dublin', *B. M. J.*, **1**, 1393–1396.

McCulloch, J. W. (1965), 'The social consequences of acts of deliberate self–poisoning or self-injury', M.Sc. Dissertation (unpublished), Edinburgh.

McCulloch, J. W., and Philip, A. E. (1967a), 'Social factors associated with attempted suicide: a review of the literature', *Brit. J. Psychiat. Soc. Work*, **9**, 30–36.

McCulloch, J. W., and Philip, A. E. (1967b), 'Social variables in attempted suicide', *Acta Psychiat. Scand.*, **43**, 341.

McCulloch, J. W., and Philip, A. E. (1972), *Suicidal Behaviour*, Pergamon Press, Oxford.

McCulloch, J. W., Philip, A. E., and Carstairs, G. M. (1967), 'The Ecology of Suicidal Behaviour', *Brit. J. Psychiat.*, **113**, 313–319.

McIver, D. (1969), 'Changes in psychological state in character disordered and neurotic patients', M.Sc. Dissertation (unpublished), University of Edinburgh.

McIver, D., and Presly, A. S. (1974), 'Towards the investigation of personality deviance', *Brit. J. Soc. Clin. Psychol.*, **13**, 397–404.

McNaughton-Smith, P. (1963), 'The classification of individuals by the Possession of attributes associated with a criterion', *Biometrics*, **19**, (2), 364–366.

McQuitty, L. L. (1957), 'Elementary linkage analysis for isolating orthogonal and oblique types and typal relevancies', *Educ. & Psychol. Measurement*, **17**, 207–229.

Mannheim, K., and Wilkins, L. (1955), *Prediction Methods in Relation to Borstal Training*, HMSO, London.

Martin, H. (1952), 'A Rorschach study of suicide'. Unpublished Doctoral Dissertation, University of Kentucky.

Matthew, H., and Lawson, A. A. H. (1966), 'Acute Barbiturate Poisoning – a review of the two years experience', *Quart. J. Med.*, **35**, 539–552.

Mayfield, E., and Montgomery, D. (1972), 'Alcoholism, alcohol intoxication and suicide attempts', *Arch. Gen. Psychiat.*, **27**, 349–353.

Menninger, K. A. (1936), 'Purposive accidents as an expression of self-destructive tendencies', *Int. J. Psychoanal.*, **17**, 6–16.

Ministère de la Santé (1975), *Morbidité et mortalité par suicide*, Inserm, Paris.

Minkoff, K., Bergman, E., Beck A. T., and Beck, R. (1973), 'Hopelessness, depression and attempted suicide', *Am. J. Psychiat.*, **130**, 455–459.

Mintz, R. S. (1970), 'Prevalence of persons in the city of Los Angeles who have attempted suicide', *Bulletin of Suicidology*, **7**, 9.

Moran, E. (1970), 'Pathological gambling', *Brit. J. Hosp. Med.*, **4**, 59–70.

Morgan, H. G., Pocock, H., and Pottle, S. (1975), 'The urban distribution of non-fatal deliberate self-harm', *Brit. J. Psychiat.*, **126**, 319.

Motto, J. A. (1965), 'Suicide attempts: a longitudinal view', *Arch. gen. Psychiat.*, **13**, 516.

Murphy, G., and Robins, E. (1967), 'Social factors in suicide', *J. Amer. Med. Assoc.*, **199**, 303–308.

Murray, H. A. (1943), *Thematic Apperception Test Manual*, Harvard University Press, Cambridge, Mass.

Neuringer, C. (1961), 'Dichotomous evaluations in suicidal individuals', *J. Consult. Psychol.*, **25**, 445–449.

Neuringer, C. (1965), 'The Rorschach test as a research device for the identification, prediction and understanding of suicidal ideation and behaviour', *J. Projective Techniques & Personality assessment*, **29**, 71–82.

Neuringer, C. (1967), 'The cognitive organisation of meaning in suicidal individuals', *J. Gen. Psychol.*, **76**, 91–100.

Neuringer, C, (ed.)(1974), *Psychological Assessment of Suicidal Risk*, C. C. Thomas, Springfield, Illinois.

O'Neill, P., Robins, E., and Schmidt, E. (1965), 'A psychiatric study of attempted suicide in persons over sixty years of age', *Arch. Neurol. Psychiat.*, **75**, 275–284.

Osgood, C. E., Suci, G. J., and Tannenbaum, P. H. (1957), *The Measurement of Meaning*, University of Illinois Press, Urbana.

Otto, U. (1971), *Barns och Ungdomars självmordshandlingar* Distr. Seelig & Co., Stockholm, Sweden.

Ovenstone, I. M. K. (1972), 'An epidemiological study of suicidal behaviours in Edinburgh', M.D. Thesis, University of Dundee.

Ovenstone, I. M. K. (1973a) 'Spectrum of Suicidal Behaviours in Edinburgh', *Brit. J. Prev. Soc. Med.*, **27**, 27–35.

Ovenstone, I. M. K. (1973b), 'A psychiatric approach to the diagnosis of suicide and its effect upon the Edinburgh statistics', *Brit. J. Psychiat.*, **123**, 15–21.

Ovenstone, I. M. K., and Kreitman, N. (1974), 'Two syndromes of suicide', *Brit. J. Psychiat.*, **124**, 336–345.

Park, R. E., Burgess, E. W. (eds.)(1925). *The City Chicago*, University of Chicago Press.

Parkin, D., and Stengel, E. (1965), 'Incidence of Suicidal attempts in an urban community', *B. M. J.*, **2**, 133.

Philip, A. E. (1968), 'Personality Factors involved in suicidal behaviour', Ph. D. Thesis (unpublished), University of Edinburgh.

Philip, A. E. (1969), 'The development and use of the Hostility and Direction of Hostility Questionnaire', *J. Psychosom. Res.*, **13**, 283–287.

Philip, A. E. (1970), 'Traits, attitudes and symptoms in a group of attempted suicides', *Brit. J. Psychiat.*, **116**, 475–482.

Philip, A. E. (1972), 'Cross-cultural stability of second-order factors in the 16 PF', *Brit. J. Soc. Clin. Psychol.*, **11**, 276–283.

Philip, A. E. (1973) 'Assessing punitiveness with the Hostility and Direction of Hostility Questionnaire (HDHQ)', *Brit. J. Psychiat.*, **123**, 435–439.

Philip, A. E., and Cay, E. L. (1971), 'The reliability and utility of a clinical rating of personality', *Brit. J. Med. Psychol.*, **44** 85–89.

Philip. A. E., and McCulloch, J. W. (1966), 'Use of social indices in psychiatric epidemiology', *Brit. J. Prev. Soc. Med.*, **20**, 122–126.

Pokorny, A. (1966), 'A follow-up study of 618 suicidal patients', *Amer. J. Psychiat.*, **122**, 1095.

Retterstol, N. (1970), *Long Term Prognosis after Attempting Suicide*, C. C. Thomas, Springfield. Illinois.

Ringel, E. (1952), *Der Selbstmord*, Maudrich, Vienna.

Roberts, F., and Hooper, D. (1969), 'The natural history of attempted suicide in Bristol', *Brit. J. Med. Psychol.*, **42**, 303–312.

Robins, E., Murphy, G. E., Wilkinson, R. H., Grassner, S., and Kayes, J. (1959), 'Some clinical considerations in the prevention of suicide based on a study of 134 successful suicides', *Amer. J. Pub. Health*, **49**, 888.

Robinson, W. S. (1950), 'Ecological correlations and the Behaviour of Individuals', *American Sociological Review*, **15**, 351–357.

Rubenstein, R., Moses, R., and Lidz, T. (1958), 'On attempted suicide', *A. M. A. Arch. Neurol. & Psychiat.*, **79**, 103.

Ruegsegger, P. (1963), 'Selbstmordversuche. Klinische statistische und katamnestische Untersuchungen an 132 Suizidversuchspatienten', *Psychiat. et Neurol.* (Basel), **146**, 81.

Ryle, A. (1967), 'A repertory grid study of the meaning and consequences of a suicidal act', *Brit. J. Psychiat.*, **113**, 1393–1403.

Sainsbury, P. (1955), *Suicide in London*, Chapman and Hall, London.

Sainsbury, P. (1973), 'Suicide: opinions and facts', *Proc. Roy. Soc. Med.*, **66**, 9–17.

Scheier, I. H., and Cattell, R. B. (1961), *Handbook for the Neuroticism Scale Questionnaire*, I.P.A.T., Champaign, Illinois.

Schmidt, C., and van Arsol, D. (1955), 'Complete and attempted suicide: a comparative analysis', *Amer. Sociol. Rev.*, **20**, 273–283.

Schmidt, E. H., O'Neal, P. and Robins, E. (1954), 'Evaluation of suicide attempts as guide to therapy', *J. Amer. med. Ass.*, **155**, 549.

Schneider. P. B. (1954), *La Tentative Suicide* Delachaux & Niestlé, Neuchatel and Paris.

Sclare, A. B., and Hamilton, C. (1963), 'Attempted suicide in Glasgow', *Brit. J. Psychiat.*, **109**, 609–615.

190

Seager, C., and Flood, R. (1965), 'Suicide in Bristol', *Brit. J. Psychiat.*, 111, 919—932.

Shneidman, E. S. (1964), 'Suicide, sleep and death: some possible inter-relations among cessation, interruption and continuation phenomena'. *J. Consult. Psychol.*, 28, 95—106.

Shneidman, E. S., and Farberow, N. L. (1958), 'TAT heroes of suicidal and non-suicidal subjects', *J. Projective Techniques*, 22, 211—228.

Siegel, S. (1956), *Nonparametric Statistics*, McGraw-Hill, New York.

Silver, M. A., Bohnert, M., Beck, A. T., and Marcus, D. (1971), 'Relation of depression of attempted suicide and seriousness of intent', *Arch. Gen. Psychiat.*, 25, 573.

Simon, F. H. (1971), *Prediction Methods in Criminology*, HMSO, London.

Smith, A. J., 1972 'Self-poisoning with drugs: a worsening situation', *B M J*, 4, 157—159.

Smith, J. S., and Davison, K. (1971), 'Changes in the pattern of admissions for attempted suicide in Newcastle-upon-Tyne during the 1960's'. *BMJ.*, 4, 412—415.

Stanley, W. (1969), 'Attempted suicide and suicidal gestures', *Brit. J. Prev. Soc. Med.*, 23, 190—195.

Stekel, W. (1958), 'Gamblin', in *Peculiarities of Human Behaviour*, trans. and ed. J. S. von Teslaar, vol. 2, Liveright Publishing Corp., New York.

Stengel, E. (1952), 'Experience into attempted suicide', *Proc. Roy. Soc. Med.*, 45, 613—620.

Stengel, E. (1958), *Attempted suicide: Its Social Significance and Effects*, Chapman & Hall, London.

Stengel, E. (1964), *Suicide and Attempted Suicide*, Penguin Books, Harmondsworth.

Stengel, E. (1970), 'Attempted suicide', *Brit. J. Psychiat.*, 116, 237—238.

Stengel, E. (1972), 'A survey of follow-up examinations of attempted suicides', in *Suicide and Attempted Suicide*, 250—257 Skandia International Symposium, 28—30 September 1971. (Eds. J. Waldenström, T. Larsson and N. Liungstedt), Esselte Trycke, Stockholm.

Stengel, E., and Cook, N. (1958), *Attempted Suicide*, Oxford University Press, London.

Stengel, E., Cook, N., and Kreeger, R. I., (1958) 'Attempted suicide', Maudsley Monograph No. 4, Chapman & Hall, London.

Sundberg, N. D. (1961), 'The practice of psychological testing in clinical services in the United States', *American Psychologist*, 16, 79—83.

Tatossian, A., and Blumen, G. (1965), 'Essai d'application du differentiateur semantique d'Osgood a la comprehension de la tentative de suicide du sujet jeune', *Cahiers de Psychologie*, 8, 189—198.

Tuckman, J., and Youngman, W. (1963a), 'Suicide risk among persons attempting suicide', *Pub. Health Reports*, 78, 585—587.

Tuckman, J., and Youngman, W. (1963b), 'Identifying suicide risk groups among attempted suicides', *Pub. Health Reports*, 78, 763—766.

Tuckman, J., and Youngman, W. F. (1968), 'Assessment of suicide risk in attempted suicide', In *Suicidal Behaviors*, p. 119 (Ed. H. L. P. Resnik), Little Brown & Co., Boston.

Varah, C. (ed.) (1965), *The Samaritans*, Constable, London.

Vinoda, K. S. (1966), 'Personality characteristics of attempted suicide', *Brit. J. Psychiat.*, 112, 1143—1150.

Warder, J. (1969), 'Two studies of violent offenders', *Brit. J. Criminol.*, 9, 389—393.

Weissman, M. M. (1974), 'Epidemiology of suicide attempts 1960/71', *Arch. Gen. Psychiat.*, 30, 737—746.

Whitlock, F., and Schapiro, K. (1967), 'Attempted suicide in Newcastle-upon-Tyne', *Brit. J. Psychiat.*, 113, 423—434.

Wilkins, L. T., and McNaughton-Smith, P. (1964), 'New prediction and classification methods in criminology', *Journal of Research in Crime and Delinquency*, 1, 19—32.

Wold, C. I., and Litman, R. E. (1973), 'Suicide after contact with a suicide prevention center', *Arch. Gen. Psychiat.*, 28, 735—739.

Wolfgang, M. E., and Ferracuti, F. (1967), *The Subculture of Violence*, Tavistock Publications, London.

World Health Organization (1968), 'Prevention of suicide', Annexe 2 et seq. Public Health Paper 35.

INDEX